MW00324795

# Working Capital Management

Founded in 1807, John Wiley & Sons is the oldest independent publishing company in the United States. With offices in North America, Europe, Asia, and Australia, Wiley is globally committed to developing and marketing print and electronic products and services for our customers' professional and personal knowledge and understanding.

The Wiley Corporate F&A series provides information, tools, and insights to corporate professionals responsible for issues affecting the profitability of their company, from accounting and finance to internal controls and performance management.

# Working Capital Management

## Applications and Cases

JAMES S. SAGNER

WILEY

*Library of Congress Cataloging-in-Publication Data:*

Sagner, James S.
    Working capital management : applications and cases / James S. Sagner.
        p. cm. — (Wiley corporate f&a series)
    Includes bibliographical references and index.
    ISBN 978-1-118-93383-1 (cloth); ISBN 978-1-118-93384-8 (epub); 978-1-118-93385-5 (epdf)
1. Working capital. 2. Corporations—Finance. 3. Cash management. 4. Working capital—Case studies. 5. Corporations—Finance—Case studies. 6. Cash management—Case studies. I. Title.
    HG4028.W65S243 2014
    658.15′224—dc23

                                                                          2014012277

*This book is for my colleagues and friends in banking, in the corporate world, and in the universities with which I have been associated. As any author can attest, I have learned far more from them than they have from me.*

# Contents

# Preface

THIS BOOK IS ONE OF a series of textbooks developed by John Wiley and Sons. As the publisher observed the near-chaotic conditions in the credit markets beginning in 2008, it became apparent that there was a need for an explanation of business processes and specific ideas on changes to company structures and procedures.

Working capital management is the art—and increasingly the science—of organizing a company's short-term resources to sustain ongoing activities, mobilize funds, and optimize liquidity. The most important elements are:

- The efficient utilization of current assets and current liabilities of a firm throughout each phase of the business operating cycle.
- The planning, monitoring, and management of the company's collections, disbursements, and bank account balances.
- The management of receivables, inventories, payables, and international transactions to minimize the investment in idle resources.
- The gathering and management of information to effectively use available funds and identify risk.

The liquidity crisis that was experienced in the United States has been the subject of numerous articles, congressional hearings, and general debate. Available data indicate that adjustments have been ongoing and may eventually lead to the opportunity for future business expansion now that this period is coming to an end. Despite some bankruptcies, companies have adjusted remarkably well to the contraction of credit and liquidity and to weakened economic conditions. Our discussion focuses on how businesspeople can continue to be successful in difficult financial times, particularly in the context of limited access to bank credit and other sources of short-term funds.

##  CONCEPT OF THE BOOK

In developing this approach, several components have been included to assist the reader.

- Chapters are of convenient length, approximately 5,000 words. Each chapter begins with a series of learning objectives and ends with a brief summary of material covered.
- Examples and real-world situations are included to provide context for principles and calculations used in working capital management.
- As a banker and consultant, the author has actually worked with more than 250 major U.S. and global corporations and not-for-profits, and has analyzed and helped implement the ideas discussed in the book.
- A concluding chapter contains an explanation of our approach to case analysis and then presents a case (Widget Manufacturing) with solutions.
- Six cases that emphasize various working capital concerns are included in the second part of the book.
- Other useful material is contained in Appendices I and II and the Glossary to supplement the coverage in the main part of the text.

In planning the content, the author and publisher had in mind the needs of several types of readers:

- New working capital managers, including students and recent appointees to any of the functions of working capital.
- Current managers who need a succinct, well-written reference.
- Members of allied professions, including accountants, information technology specialists, marketing and production managers, and others who want to expand their knowledge base.
- Readers outside of the United States who either plan to do business here or are observing their economy as evolving into a U.S.-type of capitalism.

# Acknowledgments

THE AUTHOR IS INDEBTED TO Michele Allman-Ward, who provided assistance in Chapter 9, and with whom he authored an earlier book in the Wiley Essentials series. Michele is a distinguished consultant, lecturer, and author, and has encyclopedic knowledge of global treasury management practices.

Chapter 10, "Information and Working Capital," was coauthored with Arthur C. McAdams, associate dean in the School of Business at the University of Bridgeport (Connecticut). He was senior vice president and director of information systems at People's Bank (Connecticut) leading the implementation of several strategic initiatives, and has many years of experience in systems development and project and process management.

Acknowledgment is also extended to Sheck Cho, Helen Cho, and Judy Howarth, my Wiley editors; and to my former colleagues and clients at First National Bank of Chicago (now JPMorgan Chase) and the team at Sagner/Marks.

You may have questions about the ideas presented in this book. If so, e-mail the author at jsagner@optimum.net with your inquiries. However, a good place to start is to ask your bankers for ideas; they are often on the leading edge of current practice and have access to helpful product information.

# CHAPTER ONE

# Concepts in Working Capital Management

This chapter covers these topics:

- Explanation of the basic concepts of working capital.
- Appreciation for the problems in assigning management responsibility for working capital.
- Consideration of traditional and modern ideas of working capital management.
- Understanding the essential focus of cost in working capital management.
- Applying working capital concepts to a successful company (Best Buy).

WORKING CAPITAL is the arithmetic difference between two balance sheet aggregated accounts: current assets and current liabilities. This calculation is done in a currency, such as U.S. dollars, which is the convention we will be using in this book.

**WORKING CAPITAL CONCEPTS**

Both current assets and current liabilities are composed of several ledger accounts, as shown *in italics* in the Exhibit 1.1 balance sheet. For the company presented in this balance sheet—we'll call it the Rengas Company—the amount of working capital in 2013 was $42.5 million, calculated as current assets ($65 million) less current liabilities ($22.5 million).

### Description of Working Capital Accounts

The accounts noted in italics in Exhibit 1.1 are briefly explained next, with chapters of this book devoted to appropriate management procedures.

- **Cash accounts and short-term investments.** These account categories include cash on hand and in bank accounts, and any short-term investments that are expected to be turned into cash within one year. We'll review the management of cash in Chapters 3 and 4, and of short-term investments in Chapter 5.
- **Accounts receivable.** This category of current assets includes all credit sales where the customer is expected to pay by a future date specified on an invoice. Most companies have small amounts of uncollectible credit sales, and an account called "allowance for doubtful accounts" may be deducted from accounts receivable to reflect this experience. We'll examine receivables in Chapter 6.
- **Inventory.** Most companies hold some combination of raw materials, work-in-process (that is, partially manufactured and assembled), and finished goods. There are various accounting practices for valuing inventory and management concepts regarding inventory, which will be discussed in Chapter 7.
- **Payables.** The accounts payable account represents the amounts owed to creditors for purchases. Payroll is the other significant component of payables. Issues regarding payables will be reviewed in Chapter 8.
- **Other working capital accounts.** Prepaid expenses and accrued expenses often appear on balance sheets. **Prepaid expenses** are assets paid in advance of expenses as incurred; an example is insurance paid in advance of the incurrence of the expense. **Accrued expenses** are costs that have been incurred as of the date of a balance sheet but not paid; an example is payroll for employees whose expense has been incurred but not yet paid. These balance sheet accounts are not specifically discussed in subsequent chapters.

**EXHIBIT 1.1**   Rengas Company Balance Sheet as of December 31, 2012, and 2013

### 2012

| Assets | | Liabilities and Owners' Equity | |
|---|---|---|---|
| Current assets | $ 59,200,000 | Current liabilities | $ 16,500,000 |
| Cash | 4,700,000 | Accounts payable | 11,500,000 |
| Short-term investments | 15,000,000 | Notes payable | 4,000,000 |
| Accounts receivable | 25,500,000 | Accrued expenses | 1,000,000 |
| Inventory | 12,000,000 | | |
| Prepaid expenses | 2,000,000 | Long-term liabilities | 36,500,000 |
| | | Bonds payable | 20,000,000 |
| Fixed assets | 50,000,000 | Mortgage payable | 16,500,000 |
| Plant & equipment | | | |
| (at cost) | 85,000,000 | | |
| Less: Accumulated | | | |
| depreciation | 35,000,000 | Owners' equity | 56,200,000 |
| | | Common stock (50,000 | |
| | | shares) | 10,000,000 |
| | | Retained earnings | 46,200,000 |
| | | Total Liabilities & Net | |
| Total Assets | $109,200,000 | Worth | $109,200,000 |

### 2013

| Assets | | Liabilities and Owners' Equity | |
|---|---|---|---|
| Current assets | $ 65,000,000 | Current liabilities | $ 22,500,000 |
| Cash | 5,000,000 | Accounts payable | 15,000,000 |
| Short-term investments | 15,000,000 | Notes payable | 6,000,000 |
| Accounts receivable | 27,500,000 | Accrued expenses | 1,500,000 |
| Inventory | 15,000,000 | | |
| Prepaid expenses | 2,500,000 | Long-term liabilities | 40,000,000 |
| | | Bonds payable | 20,000,000 |
| Fixed assets | 60,000,000 | Mortgage payable | 20,000,000 |
| Plant & equipment | | | |
| (at cost) | 100,000,000 | | |
| Less: Accumulated | | | |
| depreciation | –40,000,000 | Owners' equity | 62,500,000 |
| | | Common stock (50,000 | |
| | | shares) | 10,000,000 |
| | | Retained earnings | 52,500,000 |
| | | Total Liabilities & Net | |
| Total Assets | $125,000,000 | Worth | $125,000,000 |

■ **The infrastructure of working capital.** Infrastructure involves those activities that are essential for managers to proceed. These include international working capital (Chapter 9), information and working capital (Chapter 10), and management of the working capital cycle (Chapter 11). Chapter 11 also provides a quick recommendations summary. Chapter 12 introduces the working capital cases that follow.

There are numerous considerations in the optimal management of working capital. For example, what are appropriate procedures for managing cash? For reducing accounts receivable? For improving the performance of accounts payable? We will examine these and many other issues throughout this book.

## Ideas Basic to Working Capital

Various concepts and conventions are used to explain and illustrate ideas on working capital management:

■ **The term *bank* refers to commercial banks, although other financial services companies and some vendors provide many of the services described.** Vendors are noted when the relevant topic is discussed; for example, payroll services are provided by four leading firms that are noted in Chapter 8. Freight invoice auditing firms are also discussed in that chapter, but there are so many companies in that business that we have not attempted to list them.

■ **Float is critical to an understanding of working capital.** The concept of **float** refers to funds in the process of collection or disbursement. While the complete elimination of float is impossible, the calculation of the amount of float is critical in considering alternative processes. For example, in Chapter 3 we examine the bank product of lockboxing.[1] In deciding on the use of this service, we need to know the potential to save collection float as compared to the current system.

■ **Concepts basic to finance but not defined as working capital are reviewed in Appendix I.** These include fixed assets, long-term liabilities and owners' equity on the balance sheet, and relevant income statement accounts. In addition, we demonstrate the calculation of the **cost of capital** (weighted average cost of capital, or WACC), which is used to value float. The WACC is the weighted average of a firm's cost of debt (after tax) and cost of equity (common stock and retained earnings), and is expressed as a percentage. For the purposes of our book examples, we use 10 percent as the cost of capital.

■ **Reviews should be conducted by relevant functions to analyze each element of working capital.** For example, in payables, managers would examine the percent of payments made by check, the cost of those transactions, the extent of cash discounts offered and taken, the results of account reconciliation, the incidence of fraud, and other issues. As an essential part of this process, it is useful to document the delays and organizational units involved in the movement of forms, files, and other records, including computer systems.

 ## IMPROVING WORKING CAPITAL MANAGEMENT

The traditional functional scheme of corporate management—such as sales, manufacturing, finance, and technology—prevents any one manager from having direct responsibility for working capital. Most often, the only common "manager" is the chief executive officer (CEO) or chief operating officer, who seldom has knowledge of or interest in the specific functioning of those activities.

### The Missing Working Capital Manager

Since few organizations (if any) have a functional position for "working capital manager," consideration of these issues has not typically been a major focus for management. For this reason, companies that are focusing on this concern default responsibility to finance, where cash and various forms of capital reside. As a result, the initiative for a working capital program often begins in the office of the chief financial officer (CFO) or the treasurer.

However, this presents a dilemma for any manager attempting to improve working capital: The issue of violating someone else's turf, or area of responsibility, may prevent the appropriate action or the necessary cooperation from occurring. The author well remembers encountering hostile reactions when asking a payables manager how his/her department functioned or when asking a plant manager about what appeared to be stale raw materials and parts. Suggestions are provided later in this section for overcoming these objections—but it is a delicate job of diplomacy!

### Payment Stream Matrix: First Draft

The recommended initial step is to prepare a draft **payment stream matrix,** listing working capital flows by name, dollar volume, and manager. The matrix becomes a kind of road map to understanding and improving the business by

**EXHIBIT 1.2**    Illustrative Payment Stream Matrix

| Name of Cash Flow, Mechanism, and Type* | Managed Where? | Manager | Supervisor | Annual $ Volume |
|---|---|---|---|---|
| 1  Product W, Lockbox Receipts, C | Home Ops, Anytown | Rebecca Rhea | Sandy Sparrow | $500 million |
| 2  Product X, Office Receipts, C | Division A, Anytown | Betty Bear | Charles Capybara | $250 million |
| 3  Product Y, Wire Transfers In/Out, C | Division B, Anytown | Tony Tiger | Ursula Unicorn | $1.2 billion |
| 4  Product Z, ACH Collections, C | Big Dept, Sometown | Wendy Walrus | Yetta Yak | $100 million |
| 5  Accounts Payable, Check Disbursements, D | Large Dept, Sometown | Zachary Zebra | Anthony Alligator | $30 million |
| 6  Accounts Payable, ACH Disbursements, D | Vivi Section, Yourtown | Denise Dolphin | Erik Eagle | $25 million |
| 7  Payroll, Direct Deposit, D | Inter Section, Mytown | Frances Flounder | George Gopher | $80 million |
| 8  Payroll, Check Disbursement, D | Grope Group, Ourtown | Harry Halibut | Ira Ibex | $75 million |

*C = collection; D = disbursement

indicating those major activities that drive short- and intermediate-term successes and failures. A **working capital flow** is an activity of the organization that generates a cash inflow or outflow (see Exhibit 1.2):

- Inflows, or collection flows, usually result from the sale of products or services, although collections can occur from interest income, the sale of fixed assets, and other sources.
- Outflows, or disbursement flows, are accounts payable (to vendors for purchases), payroll, payments on fixed debt, and other uses of cash.

## Payment Steam Matrix: Final Version

The draft matrix is used to bring other functions within an organization into the working capital review. It is usually necessary to involve managers in all of the disciplines of the business, including sales, operations, and finance. Input from customers and vendors can be helpful in understanding their perspective of how a transaction occurs and to make the process more efficient and effective for all parties. Obviously, revisions to the matrix are expected and will improve the quality of the information that is developed.

The typical process for this activity involves one to three meetings of an ad hoc task force or committee of company managers. Often the president will request that his direct reports send a fairly senior person(s) who has (have) in-depth knowledge of that organizational activity. The collaboration of this group will result in a fair representation of significant working capital flows.

Efforts should be devoted to the major flows—usually those more than $1 million per month in activity—to allow the development of improvements through the application of technology, redesign of existing processes, and consideration of outsourcing to banks and vendors. A single product-line company may only have 12 to 15 major flows; a global firm with numerous business units could have 100 flows. It is necessary to prioritize the working capital effort in this manner to realize significant results and motivate manager participation.

## Overcoming Resistance to Change

Bringing change to companies is often an extremely difficult task regardless of the logic of an innovation or the demonstrable savings that may result. Here are some ideas on meeting internal resistance:

- Solicit the support of senior management. Promote the program through presentations to middle managers and educational events to explain where opportunities can be found.
- Reward employees who work outside of finance for each idea suggested and accepted, and again when it is successfully implemented. These incentives draw company employees into the change process and foster an environment that controls naysayers. Rewards do not have to be cash, although that is certainly a strong incentive. Any recognition or award can promote cooperation, the submission of useful ideas, and an organizational spirit.
- Use any available marketing devices to publicize the effort, including articles in the company newspaper, announcements at company meetings, e-mail messages, and promotions through cafeteria or lunchroom events. If a company can sell a product or service, it can sell working capital efficiency!

##  THE SIGNIFICANCE OF WORKING CAPITAL

Why is working capital management important? In truth, businesses have not paid sufficient attention to working capital in past years, and have focused instead on such concerns as raising and using debt and equity capital, choosing information and manufacturing technology to run operations, and attempting to develop domestic and global marketing strategies to sell product. However, recent economic problems—specifically, the Great Recession that began in 2008—have forced companies to consider ways to improve profitability, to cut costs, and to make business processes efficient. These are not just necessary actions—they are required for survival!

### Working Capital: The Traditional View

Working capital has traditionally been considered as a positive component of the balance sheet. The Rengas Company, with $65 million of current assets and $22.5 million of current liabilities, has a current ratio of 2.9:1 (calculated as $65 million ÷ $22.5 million, to be discussed in Chapter 2). Good performance has been considered as this type of result for the working capital relationship, with the higher the result, the better. Similar results hold for other ratios.

This thinking has been driven by the attitude of lenders and financial analysts that working capital constitutes a store of value to repay such debts as borrowings. Bankers are trained to look at financial ratios and demand numbers that exceed preset standards. In the past, this demand was to enable the bank to force a company to borrow to put more cash on the balance sheet, thereby growing the bank's loan portfolio.

### Working Capital: The Modern View

The newer view is that working capital is undesirable in that it constitutes a drag on financial performance. Current assets that do not contribute to return on equity (ROE) hinder the performance of the company, and may hide obsolete inventory that may not be salable and receivables that may not be collectible. The emphasis now is on reducing current asset accounts to the point that current liabilities can be funded from the ongoing operations of the business. That is, cash collected from sales is used to pay for payables and payroll, with the minimum in idle current asset accounts.

The concept of working capital as a hindrance to financial performance is a complete change in attitude from earlier conventional wisdom. However, working capital has never actually contributed to a company's profits or losses;

instead, it just sits on the balance sheet awaiting disposition. No returns are directly generated by cash or accounts receivable, and inventories provide returns only when sold at prices above cost. In fact, there is a significant cost in carrying working capital, which can be calculated using the cost of capital.

If the financial manager attempts to drive working capital down to nearly zero, he or she must actively manage each asset and liability category. Today the discipline of working capital management is a growing field of practice, involving financial managers, marketing managers, accounts receivable and payable managers, order-entry and invoicing supervisors, and other staff.

 ## COST AS *THE* WORKING CAPITAL ISSUE

The modern view of working capital changes the focus to cost efficiencies from the management of and accounting for assets and liabilities. This change started in the 1970s with the focus of banks on cash management, using such products as lockbox and electronic funds transfer. We will review the current status of cash and liquidity in Chapters 3 and 4. The objectives of these efforts include the following:

- Managing the entire timeline of a business process in order to achieve major cost savings.
- Optimizing cost efficiency by using a scenario methodology that determines the costs of the various operational processes for handling a business process.
- Seeking additional methods to capture working capital cost efficiencies.

### Working Capital Timeline

Exhibit 1.3 provides a working capital timeline for the full range of transactions that take place for the business process of collections (above the timeline) and disbursements (below the timeline). The essence of cost management is the efficient design of an entire business process, not a single step or action within that process. The basic methodology advocated is a multiphase approach:

- Develop a baseline for the all-in costs for the full timeline of an existing business process, such as the collection process.
- Analyze and cost multiple alternate scenarios for handling that process.
- Specify nonquantifiable factors.
- Select the most appropriate scenario.

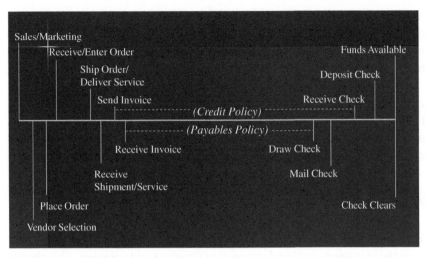

**EXHIBIT 1.3**  Working Capital Timeline

A change to only one element along the timeline is flawed for three reasons:

1. **The unseen solution.** It is impossible to examine all possible alternative procedures in optimizing the timeline.
2. **Objective evaluation.** All the elements within each alternative may not be properly analyzed.
3. **Timeline element interactions.** The impact of one timeline element on another may not be considered.

The interrelations among elements on the timeline are difficult to analyze, making it difficult to find the optimal solution for the full business process. Unfortunately, companies tend to perpetuate past practices, leading to embedded costs and inefficient practices.

## Working Capital Cost Elements

The two most critical cost elements to analyze are float and processing expenses.

### Float

Float involves funds in the process of collection or disbursement. These activities have inherent delays, which are costly for a company. Although float cannot be eliminated, every step of the cash-flow timeline can be examined to search for savings opportunities.

Consider an example in which a large electronics manufacturing company allowed customers to delay payments while disputes were investigated on monthly invoices. Some invoices included hundreds of transactions, but even a few disputes caused a remittance delay during the investigation period, which could last weeks. The time wasted involved, averaging one week, translated to $2 million a year for this company with $1 billion a year in revenues!

### Processing Expenses

Processing expenses are similarly important, as each transaction along the timeline—whether performed internally or outsourced—has a cost that directly affects your profitability.

A simple illustration is lockboxing, noted earlier. The all-in processing expense for a remittance handled internally by a company (without considering float) is about $2 (based on studies by the author performed for hundreds of clients). A retail lockbox application typically is priced by banks at about 25 cents.[2]

## Illustrative Total Potential Savings

Managing the float cost throughout the timeline can significantly impact the bottom line. Based on our client experience, the typical industrial business will waste more than 40 days because of its failure to critically examine the timeline and its activities.[3]

For example, a business experiencing $1 billion a year in revenue will receive $4 million in sales each business day (assuming 250 business days a year). At an assumed cost of capital of 10 percent, each day of delay in receiving, processing, and banking funds is equal to $400,000.

On the disbursement side of the timeline, each day probably involves two-thirds or so of the revenue received in salaries and wages, materials, and other accounts payable. That same $1 billion a year business will have about $2.7 million in daily outflows ($667 million ÷ 250 days), valued at about $270,000.

## Leisure Industry Working Capital Illustration

Traditional management of costs in the leisure industry has focused on the processing of consumer remittances and cash disbursements. Extending the search for cost management opportunities throughout the full business process timeline may yield savings far beyond those developed for specific portions of the timeline.

The benefits attained by a sample of companies in the consumer products/ leisure industry involve annual savings totaling over $2.2 million, with the companies included in the sample having annual revenues ranging to the hundreds of millions of dollars. These results are exclusive of recommendations that could not be quantified (e.g., improved control and security).

Consider an example of a theatrical supply company, focusing only on float costs. The business of Show Business Services is to supply theaters, circuses, and amusement parks with equipment, food, beverages, paper products, cleaning supplies, lighting, projection equipment, and other products. Working capital has been a continuing problem, and a study of payables practices seemed appropriate. Disbursements are made by check, with two major payables/check runs on the 8th and 23rd business day of each month.

The results for its largest vendors are shown in Exhibit 1.4, demonstrating an annual value of float costing nearly $800,000. The company immediately researched other vendor transactions and found similar problems. The total cost to Show Business Services from all vendors in lost payables float was determined to be about $1 million a year. In addition to these float savings, competitively bidding the disbursement function resulted in operating cost efficiencies of $200,000, resulting in an annual total benefit of $1.2 million. In Chapter 8 we will discuss specific actions that can be taken to accomplish those savings.

 ## APPLYING THESE IDEAS TO A REAL BUSINESS: BEST BUY

Thus far we've been considering the financials of fictional companies. Now we'll look at the working capital results for Best Buy (stock ticker symbol BBY), a leading consumer electronics retailer operating over a thousand stores primarily in the United States. Best Buy's business strategy centers on meeting individual consumer electronics needs with end-to-end solutions, which involves greater employee involvement and increased services than traditional outlets.

### What Is Best Buy's Industry?

In searching for Best Buy's industry and competition, we will use "electronics and appliance stores" (NAICS code 443115).[4] Most observers would agree that Best Buy had a direct (although smaller and far less successful) competitor in Circuit City, but that company ceased operations in 2008. Other retailers competing with Best Buy include Game Stop and Radio Shack.

**EXHIBIT 1.4** Show Business Services: Billing Activity of Largest Vendors (all invoices are received on the first or second of each month)

| 1 | 2 | 3 | 4 | 5 | 6 | 7 |
|---|---|---|---|---|---|---|
| Vendors (and Accompanying Notes) | Terms | Usual Pay Date | Days Paid Early vs. Net Terms | Discounts Offered* | Annual Purchases ($000) | Value of Foregone Float (at 10%) |
| Stagehands (a) | 1/10, n/30 | 8th | 20 | 1/10 | $6,800 | $ 0 |
| Playwrights (b) | net 20 | 8th | 12 | | $5,200 | $208,000 |
| Producers (c) | net 30 | 23rd | 7 | | $4,000 | $ 93,333 |
| Choreographers (d) | net 30 | 23rd | 7 | | $3,500 | $ 81,667 |
| Composers (e) | 2/10, n/30 | 8th | 0 | 2/10 | $2,725 | $ 0 |
| Librettists (f) | net 30 | 23rd | 7 | | $1,230 | $ 28,700 |
| Conductors (g) | 2/20, n/90 | 23rd | 67 | 2/20 | $1,000 | $223,333 |
| Aging Stars (h) | net 30 | 8th | 22 | | $ 835 | $ 61,233 |
| Stage Managers (i) | 1/20, n/30 | 23rd | 7 | 1/20 | $ 750 | $ 17,500 |
| Supporting Cast (j) | net 45 | 8th | 38 | | $ 680 | $ 86,133 |
| Annual Cost of Float Foregone (at 10%) | | | | | | $ 799,900 |

*Note:* An assumed 10% cost of capital is used in these calculations.
*Cash discount of 1% or 2% if the invoice is paid by the 10th day after receipt of invoice with payment due in 20, 30, or 45 days (see column 2), commonly stated in the format of "2/10, net 30." Chapter 6 provides a more complete explanation.
N/A = not applicable

*Notes:*

a. Stagehands: paid on the 8th day to take the 1% cash discount.
b. Playwrights: paid 12 days early because a brother-in-law of an owner worked at the company and saw no harm in issuing payments once the payables cycle was completed.
c. Producers: paid 7 days early because the next payables cycle would cause check issuance to be past the due date by 8 days.
d. Choreographers: paid on the 23rd because the next payables cycle would cause check issuance to be past the due date by 8 days.
e. Composers: paid on the 8th to take the 2% cash discount.
f. Librettists: paid on the 23rd because the next payables cycle would cause check issuance to be past the due date by 8 days.
g. Conductors: paid on the 23rd equivalent to 67 days before the appropriate date because its salesperson had once asked for an early check to make her monthly sales goal. The payables clerk embedded the check release date as an ongoing system instruction. In addition, the payment missed the cash discount by 3 days.
h. Aging Stars: paid on the 8th (not the next cycle) for no apparent reason.
i. Stage Managers: paid on the 23rd because the next payables cycle would cause check issuance to be past the due date by 8 days. In addition, the payment missed the cash discount by 3 days.
j. Supporting Cast: paid on the 8th (not in the 2nd following cycle) for no apparent reason.

13

Companies like Best Buy are experiencing severe price competition from discounters like Walmart, direct mail sellers like Amazon, and warehouse stores like Costco. There have been various Best Buy responses to this development, including the closing of marginal operations and the layoff of employees, more aggressive management of operations through leaner inventory and other actions, and the expansion into more profitable foreign markets like Asia (particularly China) and Canada. As an example of this last trend, Best Buy now does about one-fifth of its business in other countries. The company's stock traded in the high $40s (per share) as recently as 2010, but now sells at about $25 per share.

## Working Capital at Best Buy

The achievements of Best Buy can be traced to the retailing **category killer** concept,[5] which involves megastores with the size and general appearance of warehouses. These brick-and-mortar operations carry an enormous assortment of merchandise, low prices, and self-service supported by staff trained in specific electronics product lines.

Successful retailers have been able to seize market share from smaller operators who do not have the buying power to negotiate vendor discounts on inventory or the cash reserves to advertise aggressively or train staff. The consumer knows that prices are consistently low, so there is little reason to wait for special sales or to comparison shop.

Companies operating category killers have discovered that a key to this retail model is inventory, involving the ordering process, transportation, and warehousing. The process is highly automated in modern distribution centers through the use of bar coding equipment to scan and direct merchandise to holding bins or directly for delivery to stores.

As inventory is sold, computerized information notifies distribution to begin replenishment and marketing to match sales vs. projections. We see this in the 2009 ratios in Exhibit 1.5, with inventory turnover at 7.2 turns versus the industry median of 6.6. However, inventory turns have declined as Best Buy has been forced to adjust to competitive pressures and a weaker economy.

The other working capital ratios indicate similarly superior performance compared to the industry median. Furthermore, Best Buy managers understand that the capture of a market is a strategic process and cannot be accomplished in one quarter (the interval when public company earnings are reported). The compound growth rate for Best Buy over the 10 years prior to

**EXHIBIT 1.5**  Best Buy and Industry Working Capital Ratios

| | Best Buy | | Industry Median | |
|---|---|---|---|---|
| | **2012** | **2009** | **2012** | **2009** |
| Current ratio (to 1) | 1.3 | 1.0 | 1.2 | 1.3 |
| Quick ratio (to 1) | 0.6 | 0.4 | 0.6 | 0.6 |
| Receivables turnover (turns per year) | 19.8 | 22.9 | 10.2 | 19.6 |
| Inventory turnover (turns per year) | 5.7 | 7.2 | 7.2 | 6.6 |
| Return on equity (%) | 20.5 | 22.0 | 15.3 | 17.4 |

*Sources:* RMA, Annual Statement Studies; Leo Troy, *Almanac of Business and Industrial Financial Ratios;* and BBY Corporate Reports

the 2008 economic crisis was 16.5 percent, while competitors experienced flat or negative growth.

In terms of operating revenues, Best Buy now has some three-fourths of the volume reported by the consumer electronic retailing industry,[6] versus just over one-third 10 years earlier. It is likely that the current weak economy will continue to harm competitors, perhaps forcing them to terminate operations (such as Circuit City) or close stores, while Best Buy has substantial liquidity and can withstand slower consumer traffic. The company is currently experiencing strong growth in certain product categories (e.g., cell phones, televisions, and appliances).

 ## SUMMARY

Working capital involves two balance sheet aggregated accounts: current assets and current liabilities. There has been insufficient attention to this essential balance sheet metric due largely to the failure of most companies to assign manager or task force responsibility, allowing accountability to cross the various functions in the working capital timeline.

Working capital traditionally was viewed as a positive component in managing a business. The modern view is that it constitutes a drag on financial performance. Current assets that do not contribute to return on equity hinder the performance of the company, and may hide obsolete inventory that may not be salable and receivables that may not be collectible. The focus is now on reducing working capital accounts to the point that current obligations can be funded from the ongoing operations of a business.

**NOTES**

1. A **lockbox** is a collection mechanism in which mail containing payments bypasses a corporate office, going directly to a post office box maintained by the bank of deposit. After deposit of the mailed check, check copies, remittance advices, and other supporting material are forwarded to the company.
2. See above for a definition of lockboxing. **Retail lockbox** captures encoded MICR and/or OCR information from the bottom of the mailed documents and electronically transmits them to the client in a data file. **MICR** is magnetic ink character recognition; **OCR** is optical character recognition. Both formats are fonts or print characters that have a distinctive design recognizable by automated reader-sorter equipment.
3. See James Sagner, *Financial and Process Metrics for the New Economy* (New York: AMACOM, 2001), 75–95, esp. Exhibit 4.7 on p. 91.
4. NAICS is the North American Industry Classification System, and is used to classify business establishments according to type of economic activity (process of production). The Department of Commerce and the Office of Management and Budget (OMB) are the principal sponsoring federal agencies.
5. Examples of category killer retailers include the Home Depot and Lowe's (building supplies), Bed Bath & Beyond (home furnishings), Staples and Office Depot (office supplies), AutoZone (auto parts), and TJX Companies, the Gap, and Limited Brands (apparel). Although the category killer is not generally applied to companies that are in other industries, a few equivalent examples might include Apple (computer hardware); Goldman Sachs and T. Rowe Price (financial services); Coca-Cola, Colgate-Palmolive, and Pepsico (consumer nondurables); and Celgene, Gilead Sciences, and Teva Pharmaceuticals (biotechnology).
6. Using the definition of the industry used by S&P in its *Industry Surveys: Specialty Retailing—Computers and Electronics*. Within all of specialty retailing, only the Home Depot (at $71.3 billion) and Staples (at $23.1 billion) are of roughly similar size to Best Buy (at $45.0 billion).

2

# Working Capital Ratios and Other Metrics

This chapter covers these topics:

- Determination of how ratio analysis is used in understanding working capital.
- Appreciation of the calculation of the liquidity, activity, and profitability utilization ratios.
- Understanding of such other metrics as the statement of cash flows and the cash conversion cycle.
- Consideration of the advantages and disadvantages of benchmarking of working capital.
- Clarification of the general issues in using ratios and other metrics in managing working capital.

RATIO ANALYSIS AND OTHER METRICS are used to provide a comparative basis for a company against its industry and its experience in previous years. We use plastics manufacturing as the industry comparison, although the reader should understand that each industry is

**17**

unique. For example, companies that manufacture men's clothing experience a very long receivable cycle, often six months, while grocery stores and supermarkets are expected to pay their suppliers for certain food products in about one week.

We note certain metrics that present difficulties in finding appropriate industry comparisons. Toward the end of this chapter we will review some of the problems in using metrics to establish performance effectiveness.

 **RATIO ANALYSIS**

The various accounts on financial statements (the balance sheet and the income statement) can be used to provide critical information about a company to financial managers, bankers, investors and other interested parties. **Ratio analysis** allows us to quickly examine a company's financial statements to determine how performance has changed over time and/or against its competitors.

## How Ratios Are Constructed

To calculate a ratio, data are entered into a numerator and into a denominator, and then divided to allow the analysis of a relationship that is considered meaningful. We can compare these data to past years to see if a company's financial position is improving or deteriorating; this is called longitudinal analysis. We can also compare a company to others in the industry in the same timeframe; this is known as cross-sectional analysis.

Finding truly comparable companies is difficult because no two organizations are exactly alike. They may have different geographic coverage, varying product lines, significantly dissimilar economies of scale, and other distinguishing characteristics. In Chapter 1 we compared an actual company—Best Buy—to its industry while noting some of these discrepancies.

There are four sets of ratios in general use: liquidity, activity utilization, profitability, and financial leverage. We'll review the ratios that specifically impact working capital using Exhibit 1.1 data as supplemented by the income statement data shown in Exhibit 2.1. While we could calculate longitudinal ratios as we have two years of data, the ratio calculations will be for the most recent year, 2013. In the discussion that follows, it should be understood that these are the generally accepted "significant ratios" that have been applied to the analysis of companies for nearly 100 years.

**EXHIBIT 2.1** Rengas Company Income Statement (for the years ended December 31, 2012, and 2013)

|  | 2012 | 2013 |
|---|---|---|
| Sales | $125,000,000 | $150,000,000 |
| Less: Cost of goods sold | 85,000,000 | 100,000,000 |
| Gross profits | 40,000,000 | 50,000,000 |
| Less: Selling and administrative expense | 15,000,000 | 20,000,000 |
| Less: Depreciation expense | 3,000,000 | 5,000,000 |
| Operating profit | 22,000,000 | 25,000,000 |
| Less: Interest expense | 4,000,000 | 4,000,000 |
| Earnings before taxes | 18,000,000 | 21,000,000 |
| Less: Corporate taxes (at 35%) | 6,300,000 | 7,350,000 |
| Net income after taxes | $11,700,000 | $13,650,000 |
| Dividends paid | $ 6,000,000 | $ 7,400,000 |

## Liquidity

**Liquidity** refers to a company's cash position and its ability to pay its bills as they come due. The phrase "cash position" is not limited to cash on hand and in the bank; it includes access to bank loans and short-term investments. Liquidity should not be confused with profitability or net worth; a company could earn accounting income with significant assets, and yet go bankrupt for lack of working capital.

The two liquidity ratios are the current ratio and the quick (or acid test) ratio.

1. The **current ratio** is calculated as follows: Current assets ÷ Current liabilities. From Exhibit 1.1, the result is 2.9 ($65 million ÷ $22.5 million). This calculation supposedly provides an indication that a company has sufficient liquidity to make payments to employees, vendors, and other parties.

2. The **quick ratio** is considered more useful because it eliminates inventory in the numerator, on the theory that this asset could be stale, worn, or not salable except at bargain (perhaps below cost) prices. The quick ratio is calculated as follows: (Current assets – Inventory) ÷ Current liabilities, or 2.2 ([$65 million – $15 million] ÷ $22.5 million).

There are no significant ratios that solely measure the current assets of cash (or cash flow) or use working capital in a calculation. However, we will suggest useful cash and cash flow ratios later in this chapter, with more extensive commentary in Chapter 11.

## Activity Utilization

The **activity utilization** ratios indicate how efficiently the business is using its assets. The important working capital utilization ratios are receivables turnover (and its complement, average collection period) and inventory turnover (and its complement, inventory turnover days).

■ **Receivables turnover** is calculated as follows: Credit sales ÷ Accounts receivable.[1] For simplicity in this discussion, we'll assume that there are no cash sales, with the receivables turnover determined as $150,000,000 ÷ $27,500,000, or 5.5 times.

■ **Average collection period** (ACP) is calculated as follows: 360 days ÷ receivables turnover. In this example, we'd divide 360 days by 5.5 times, with the result of 65 days. The usefulness of the calculation of ACP is that the manager can quickly determine if the established credit period is being ignored. For example, if the terms to customers are net 30 (meaning payment is due 30 days after the receipt of an invoice), and the ACP is 65 days, many customers are disregarding the company's expectation for prompt payment. See Chapter 6 for a complete discussion of this issue.

■ **Inventory turnover** is calculated as follows: Cost of goods sold ÷ Inventory, or $100,000,000 ÷ $15,000,000, which is 6.7 times.

■ **Inventory turnover days** are calculated as follows: 360 days ÷ Inventory turnover. In this example, we'd divide 360 by 6.7, which is 54 days. As with ACP, the value is in understanding the number of days of inventory held by the company. While 54 days appears long, the ratio must be used in comparison with earlier years or the industry's results to be meaningful.

## Profitability

Although **profitability** is not an explicit component of working capital, it is included here because any change to working capital components directly impacts profits. In fact, if profit ratios have deteriorated or are below those of competitors, this may indicate working capital improvement problems and opportunities. Important profitability ratios are profits-to-sales and return-on-equity (ROE) ratios. The term *return* is another word for profits, and these ratios calculate the after-tax returns.

- **Net profits to sales** (sometimes called "profit margin" or ROS) is calculated as follows: Profits after taxes ÷ Sales, or $13,650,000 ÷ $150,000,000, or 9.1 percent.
- **Return on equity** (ROE) is calculated as follows: Profits after taxes ÷ Owners' equity, or $13,650,000 ÷ $62,500,000, or 21.8 percent. The ROE is a unique metric as it can be used in comparison with all other possible investments. While 21.8 percent is a healthy result, a manager who realizes a significantly lesser amount, perhaps 12 percent or so, should be considering other uses for the investment in a business.
- There are a few industries where the ROE is considered of secondary importance to the ratio that measures the **return on assets** (ROA). For example, this ratio is widely used in banking to determine the profitability of a bank based on its asset base. The calculation of return on assets (ROA) is as follows: Profits after taxes ÷ Total assets, or $13,650,000 ÷ $125,000,000, or 10.9 percent. (In a typical American bank, the ROA is about 1 percent.)

## Leverage

There is a fourth important category of ratios—financial leverage—that measures the extent to which a company uses debt as a source of its capital. The primary **financial leverage** ratio is calculated as follows: Total debt ÷ Total assets. An alternative leverage ratio is Total debt ÷ Total equity, which is how certain sources of ratios report this result.

Another important leverage ratio, **times interest earned**, measures the number of times that income covers the obligation of paying interest on debt. This ratio is calculated as follows: Operating income before interest and taxes (EBIT) ÷ Interest expense.

These ratios are not considered as relevant in measuring working capital because the components do not appear in the current portion of the balance sheet. However, any change in working capital affects the "free" debt portion of current liabilities—that is, such accounts as payables or accruals, which do not carry an explicit interest charge, as well as the requirement for financing the business and the resulting interest and equity cost.

**OTHER RATIOS AND THEIR APPLICATION**

The term *significant ratios* exists largely because of historical usage, rather than because there has been a thoughtful analysis of the current usefulness of specific ratios. For example, cash is often considered the lifeblood of a business, and yet we noted that no significant ratio measures cash or other forms of liquidity such as bank lines of credit (to be discussed in Chapter 4).

### Troy and RMA

The following ratios from Troy and RMA may be useful in determining the working capital of a company in comparison with its industry.[2] These ratios are in addition to the significant ratios that have been discussed.

- Troy
  - Net sales to working capital
  - Current assets to working capital
  - Current liabilities to working capital
  - Working capital to net sales
  - Inventory to working capital
  - Total receipts to cash flow
  - Cost of goods (sold) to cash flow
  - Cash flow to total debt

The term *total receipts* primarily refers to revenues, but also includes cash inflows from interest income, rental receipts, royalties, net capital gains, and dividends. *Cash flow* is calculated as cash receipts less cash disbursements.

- RMA ratios
  - Cost of sales (cost of goods sold) to (accounts) payable
  - (Net) sales to working capital

The definitions of several of these Troy ratios probably do not require explanation, although the logic should be noted. The working capital measures (Troy and RMA) are forms of activity utilization, with a low ratio indicating a less efficient use of the current portion of balance sheet accounts. The cash flow ratios are a form of the liquidity ratios. The total receipts-to-cash-flow ratio is particularly useful in measuring liquidity, and we will return to a discussion of its application in Chapter 11.

## How Ratios Are Used

We can compare a calculated current ratio of 2.9:1 (read as "2.9 to 1") to the industry's statistic or the result from previous years. The general rule when using industry comparisons is that any result within the interquartile range is considered normal, and that any result outside of that range is unusual and worthy of further analysis.

▪ The **interquartile range** refers to the area in an array of results from the 25th to the 75th percentiles (or the first to the third quartiles).
▪ An **array** is a listing of the members of a group in either ascending or descending order.
▪ The middle item in an array is the **median** (the 50th percentile), while the **mean** is the arithmetic average of the total of all items divided by the number of items.

In our situation, 2.9:1 can be too low compared to the industry, which is unlikely, or too high, which is quite possible. In other words, there may be an efficiency problem when ratios are too high, usually indicating that too much of a numerator (such as an asset or a group of assets) is being used to support a denominator (such as a liability or a group of liabilities). It may be a more serious problem when there is too little of a numerator supporting a denominator, as this could indicate a possible future liquidity, activity utilization, or profitability problem.

Exhibit 2.2 compares Rengas with the median result for plastic manufacturers. We could also list the interquartile results for the industry. The company is conservatively managed based on its higher liquidity ratios and times interest earned. Although Rengas is certainly profitable compared to its peers, there could be improvements in receivables collection. This is a valuable "snapshot" of a company's performance as long as the comparison is with equivalent companies.

 **OTHER METRICS**

There are numerous other metrics that can be used to measure the performance of a company's working capital management. Arguably the most important of these is the statement of cash flows, which is a mandatory document for publicly traded companies.[3] The statement uses balance sheet accounts and income that affects cash and cash equivalents, and analyzes operating, investing, and financing activities.

**EXHIBIT 2.2** Rengas Company and Plastic Manufacturing Industry Ratios

|  | Rengas | Industry |
| --- | --- | --- |
| Current ratio | 2.9 | 1.6 |
| Quick ratio | 3.3 | 0.9 |
| Debt ratio | 50.0% | 50.0% |
| Times interest earned | 6.3 | 3.6 |
| Receivables turnover | 5.5 | 7.3 |
| Average collection period days | 66.0 | 49.3 |
| Inventory turnover | 6.7 | 7.1 |
| Days in inventory | 54.8 | 50.7 |
| Return-on-equity | 21.8% | 10.9% |
| Return-on-sales | 9.0% | 3.0% |

*Source:* RMA, Annual Statement Studies, Industry NAICS 326122, for companies with greater than $25 million in sales

The first section calculates operating cash by restating accrual income as adjusted for changes in the financial statements during the year. A source of funds is any increase in cash, while a use of funds is any decrease in cash. Strategic decisions in a company involve capital investing, permanent financing, and the calculation of the net cash position.

The obvious concern of working capital management is the operating cash section. Although a negative net operating cash position in a particular year can be offset by financing or investing decisions, a continuing cash loss from ongoing operations cannot be indefinitely continued. For the Rengas Company's Statement of Cash Flows, see Exhibit 2.3.

Rengas has a healthy amount of working capital from operations, which has been used for capital investing and the payment of dividends. The statement of cash flows is particularly helpful to bankers and investors who need to know that the company is producing sufficient cash to conduct longer-term strategies without compromising its position. This financial metric can be compared to results in previous periods to determine whether improvement or deterioration has occurred.

## Cash Conversion Cycle

The **cash conversion cycle** (CCC) is defined as the number of days between disbursing cash and collecting cash in connection with undertaking a discrete unit of operations. The calculation is in Exhibit 2.4.

**EXHIBIT 2.3**  The Rengas Company Statement of Cash Flows ($ millions)

| Part A: Cash Flow from Operations | | |
|---|---|---|
| Net sales | $150.0 | Source |
| Chg. in accounts receivable | –2.0 | Use |
| Cash receipts from sales | 148.0 | Net |
| Cost of goods sold | –100.0 | Use |
| Chg. in inventory | -3.0 | Use |
| Chg. in accounts payable | 3.5 | Source |
| Cash purchases | –99.5 | Net |
| Cash margin | 48.5 | Aggregated Net |
| Total selling, gen. and admin. expenses | –20.0 | Use |
| Depreciation expense | 5.0 | Source |
| Chg. in prepaid expenses | 0.5 | Source |
| Chg. in accrued expenses | 0.5 | Source |
| Cash operating expenses | –14.0 | Net |
| Cash operating profit | 34.5 | Aggregated Net |
| Interest expense | –4.0 | Use |
| Income taxes | –7.3 | Use |
| Cash flow from operations | $ 23.2 | Net |
| **Part B: Cash Used for Capital Investing** | | |
| Net fixed assets 2013 | $ 60.0 | Net Use |
| Less: Net fixed assets 2012 | –50.0 | |
| Cash used for capital investments | –$ 10.0 | Aggregated Net |
| **Part C: Payments for Financing** | | |
| Chg. in notes payable | $ 2.0 | Source |
| Chg. in bonds payable | 0 | No Change |
| Chg. in mortgage payable | 3.5 | Source |
| Cash paid for dividends | 7.4 | Use |
| Payments for financing | –$12.9 | Aggregated Net |
| **Part D: Summary and Reconciliation vs. Balance Sheet Cash** | | |
| Cash flow from operations | $ 23.2 | |
| Cash used for capital investing | –10.0 | |
| Payments for financing | –12.9 | |
| Net cash and short-term investments | $ 0.3 | |
| Reconciliation: Chg. in cash and short-term investments from balance sheet (2013 vs. 2012) | $ 0.3 | |

Chg. = Change.

**EXHIBIT 2.4**  Cash Conversion Cycle

| = | Inventory conversion period | + | Receivables conversion period | − | Payables conversion period |
|---|---|---|---|---|---|
| = | $\dfrac{\text{Average inventory}}{\text{Cost of goods sold}/365}$ | + | $\dfrac{\text{Average accounts receivable}}{\text{Revenue}/365}$ | − | $\dfrac{\text{Average accounts payable}}{\text{Cost of goods sold}/365}$ |

Dell Computer and several other companies have effectively implemented the modern approach to working capital management discussed in Chapter 1.

## Dell Computer's CCC

Dell has actually attained a quarterly cash conversion cycle of *minus* eight days! Dell accepts ownership of components shortly before the start of manufacturing, driving raw materials inventory to minimal levels. Products for consumers are sold and a collection transaction is concurrently initiated, using credit card or payment through electronic mechanisms, eliminating most accounts receivable.

Managing working capital to nearly eliminate current assets and liabilities requires that cash not be expended to prepay for inventory or other operating costs, that vendors hold title to goods until delivery is requested, and that redundant expenses be eliminated where possible. A considerable inventory position is warehoused by cooperating vendors within minutes of delivery to a Dell factory, and is requisitioned once a customer sale is booked.

Since some suppliers are reluctant to do business with these requirements, Dell buys from fewer than 50 companies, down by 75 percent from a decade earlier. Another innovation is the direct shipment of video displays to customers by the vendor based on an e-commerce instruction from Dell. This saves the cost of a second shipment, worth $30 per display.

As the result of these various actions, Dell's inventory turnover (for the year ending in January 2009) was an astonishing 57.8 times and 32.4 times in 2013, versus a median 6.3 times for the computer manufacturing industry, and its receivables turnover is 9.5 versus a median 8.0 for the industry. How does working capital affect Dell's financial statements? In the most recent reporting period, Dell's ROE was 58.0 percent, while the industry was earning

16.1 percent. And over the five-year period prior to the credit crisis that began in 2008, the ROE of Dell was 63.1 percent versus the industry's 32.2 percent.

##  BENCHMARKING

Benchmarking compares the processes of a business and selected performance metrics to industry best practices or those from other industries. The theory of benchmarking is that the "best" companies in an industry have processes that are worth studying and perhaps replicating in the effort to stay competitive, increase market share, and improve profitability.

### Methodology

The following is an example of a typical benchmarking effort:

- **Selection of problem(s) to study.** Benchmarking can be applied to any business process or function, and so a range of research techniques may be required. They include informal conversations with customers, employees, or suppliers; exploratory research techniques such as focus groups, in-depth marketing research, quantitative research, surveys, questionnaires, reengineering analysis, process mapping, quality control variance reports, or financial ratio analysis; or the review of cycle times or other performance indicators.
- **Identification of other companies and industries that have similar processes.** It is essential to use comparable companies and industries to establish reasonable standards. It is only valid to compare performance against similar size organizations in analogous lines of business and at equivalent stages of technological innovation, research and development, and maturity of channels of distribution.
- **Determination of organizations that are considered industry leaders.** Consult customers, bankers, suppliers, financial analysts, trade associations, and industry publications to determine which companies are worthy of study.
- **Surveying and visitation of companies for metrics and practices.** Companies target specific business processes using detailed surveys of metrics and practices used to identify alternative practices.
- **Implementation of improved business practices.** Using the superior business practices, develop implementation plans, which include identification of specific opportunities, funding of the project, and marketing the ideas to the organization for the purpose of gaining demonstrated value from the process.

## Working Capital Benchmarking

Much of the effort in benchmarking of working capital processes has been through advisory firms and association sponsorship, rather than through publicly available sources; leading firms include the following:

- AnalyticResults
- Hackett Group
- Citibank Treasury Diagnostics
- Deutsche Bank (Treasury Pulse)
- CEB

Organizations sponsoring benchmarking studies include the Association for Financial Professionals, the Benchmarking Network, and the Knowledge Management Benchmarking Association. These sources have provided data for comparison and improvement for several years, and are now adding connections to mainframe ERP systems [4] (such as Oracle and SAP) to extract information on costs, cycle times, error rates, and cash conversion cycles.

Working capital benchmarking applications usually focus on metrics that provide logical comparisons and opportunities for cost savings. These include:

- **Full-time-equivalent (FTE) staff levels:** measured as FTEs per dollar of sales
- **Cost:** measured as cost per dollar of sales
- **Throughput:** measured as units processed per FTE for standard activities (such as payment transactions)
- **Cycle times:** measured as days required to complete such activities as reconciling bank account discrepancies, developing cash budgets, and calculating the correct timing and amount of inventory to order (the EOQ position; see Chapter 7)
- **Policies and procedures:** measured as the existence of policies and procedures

A typical focus is efficiency and cost savings, as shown in the purported savings opportunities in Exhibit 2.5.

### Benchmarking Concerns

The cynical Jaques states in *As You Like It* (Act II, Scene 7, William Shakespeare), that "I met a fool i' the forest, A motley fool." Benchmarking is one of the current popular management buzzwords. Some of these fads have relevance to an improved business organization, and some of the concepts are clearly flawed.[5]

**EXHIBIT 2.5**   Savings from Benchmarking (per transaction)

| Process | Measure | Cost Average Company | Cost "Best" Company |
|---|---|---|---|
| Payables | Invoice | $3.55 | $0.35 |
| Receivables | Remittance | $0.67 | $0.04 |
| Fixed Assets | Asset Tracked | $4.55 | $0.64 |

*Source:* The Hackett Group

Business managers do not operate on an assembly line, standardized product world. Based on experience with hundreds of companies, it is the author's conclusion that there are significant variations in activities by industry, organizational structure, business role within the organization, extent of technological maturity, and participation in global markets. In fact, about the only standard activities are those that involve purchased services from banks and vendors through a process of competitive bidding.

Companies that count the number of transactions completed or the equivalent cost, rather than emphasizing the content of those transactions, are forcing employees to focus on quantity rather than quality. In our work we have observed companies where the process has turned into a team competition, where the winning group receives recognition at the end of the month. In those situations, the result is speed, but at the sacrifice of the work product.

This is a form of microanalysis, which involves the examination of a very specific element that exists within the larger context of the cash flow timeline. The essence of the timeline concept is an entire process, not a single step or action within that process. If the focus is on specific elements rather than the process, managers may find that not all alternative approaches are identified, that timeline element interactions are not considered, and that not all elements within each alternative are examined.

## GENERAL PROBLEMS IN THE USE OF RATIOS AND METRICS

The main difficulty in using financial statement data from an aggregated source like Troy or RMA is that each business has its own unique characteristics, and when aggregated into an industry, data lose meaning. There are certain commonalities in such data, such as vendors and labor costs (in accounts payable), prices paid for materials (in inventory), cash and liquidity sources, and perhaps others. Specific accounting problems in the data are noted next.

## Fiscal Year

Balance sheets are published on an "as of" date, and do not represent a year's financial results (in contrast to the income statement). A fiscal year is a period used for publishing a company's annual financial statements as required by regulation in most countries. The choice of the actual fiscal year-end closing is at the discretion of management.

The general practice is to choose a time when any seasonality effect is minimized. As an example, retailing firms often close their fiscal years after Christmas and January sales have ended. There is no direct way to interpret the results from a balance sheet in terms of events during the fiscal year, and any ratio constructed from the balance may not truly represent the borrower's actual situation.

## Accrual Accounting

Nearly all companies use accrual accounting, which attempts to match revenues and the expenses that were incurred to generate that activity. This involves the use of such conventions as depreciation that artificially assign a portion of the cost of a fixed asset against sales, possibly over- or understating the true cost of the asset, the economic or physical life or period until obsolescence, and any resulting reported profits. Similar accrual conventions include amortization (for intellectual property) and depletion (for natural resources). These choices affect the comparability of company results.

In both accrual and cash accounting,[6] there are other necessary judgments as to specific protocols used. For example, inventory costing may be LIFO (last in, first out), FIFO (first in, first out), or average cost. Depreciation expense may be calculated over the life of the asset as straight-line (level amounts), or accelerated.[7]

## Window Dressing

Because of the fiscal year problem, companies may be tempted to present results consistent with investor, banker, and analyst expectations. Unfortunately, there have been numerous instances of short-term adjustments to critical balance sheet accounts that are reversed the following business day. Various frauds have been sustained by such practices. The Sarbanes-Oxley Act of 2002 was enacted to induce greater honesty and transparency in the presentation of financial results by U.S. public companies.[8]

## Aggregated Data

Various accounts use aggregated data in ratios, such as the following:

- Current ratio
  - Current assets, including cash, accounts receivable, and inventory
  - Current liabilities, including accounts payable, notes payable, and accruals
- Working capital (as current assets and current liabilities are netted)
- Leverage (as current liabilities and long-term liabilities are summed)
- Profitability (as net profits are the net result of the income statement calculation)

Such data may misrepresent the actual position of the company with respect to specific working capital accounts.

## Off–Balance Sheet Obligations

Companies may be obligated for or have arrangements for debts that are not recorded on the balance sheet, including leases, contingent liabilities, unused lines of credit, and special purpose entities (SPEs) (sometimes known as special purpose vehicles [SPVs]) that may be construed as a responsibility of the entity. SPEs became a key element in the failure of Enron, when investments that were losing money were moved off of the balance sheet and into SPEs.[9] Contingent liabilities or off–balance sheet obligations arise from either of the following:

- Past events, the existence of which will be confirmed only by the occurrence of one or more uncertain future events not wholly within the entity's control, such as a lawsuit.
- A present obligation, such as an operating lease, that arises from past events but is not recognized because either it is not probable that a transfer of economic benefits will be required to settle the obligation or because current accounting conventions do not require its recognition.

Off–balance obligations can significantly alter the profitability and net worth of the borrower.

**SUMMARY**

The performance of working capital accounts is traditionally measured using significant ratios to examine a company's financial statements, allowing the determination of how performance has changed over time and/or against competitors. The four sets of ratios in general use calculate liquidity, activity utilization, financial leverage, and profitability as compared to such standard sources as RMA and *Troy's Almanac*. There are various other ratios that these two sources publish. In addition, there are benchmarking metrics that can be used to measure a company's performance against "best" industry practices.

 **NOTES**

1. Only credit sales are used because any cash sales would be collected immediately; therefore, no receivable would be created. The term *receivables* refers to accounts receivable.
2. Leo Troy, *Almanac of Business and Industrial Financial Ratios* (Commerce Clearing House [CCH]), and RMA (Risk Management Association), *Annual Statement Studies*. Both sources are published annually. Selected ratios are also at *Value Line* (published by Value Line Inc.), Standard and Poor's Industry Surveys, Dun & Bradstreet, and financial websites like hoovers.com. The sources discussed in this chapter are available in the business reference sections of many libraries. See Appendix II for a listing of useful references and websites. Troy can also be located at http://books.google.com/books?id = 5nEsDHfsfFwC&printsec = frontcover&dq = almanac+of+business+and+industrial+financial+ratios&hl = en&sa = X&ei = YOwwU6K7GKiIyAG6_IHIDQ&ved = 0CEYQ6AEwAA#v = onepage&q = almanac%20of%20business%20and%20industrial%20 financial%20ratios&f = false. The various industry sources derive their data from the Internal Revenue Service (U.S. Department of the Treasury), which provides a statistical sampling of the tax returns of all companies.
3. In 1987, FASB (Financial Accounting Standards Board) Statement No. 95 (FAS 95) established this requirement.
4. ERP systems are discussed in Chapter 11.
5. A leading expert on the fallacies of strategic planning is Henry Mintzberg, who wrote *The Rise and Fall of Strategic Planning* (New York: Free Press, 1994). A more recent exposé is his *Strategy Safari*, coauthored with Joseph Lampel and Bruce Ahlstrand (New York: Free Press, 2005).
6. In contrast to accrual accounting, **cash accounting** records revenues when they are received and expenses when they are actually paid. No attempt is made to match revenues and costs incurred as in accrual accounting.

7. The two accelerated depreciation methods in general use are double-declining and sum-of-years digits. **Double-declining** uses the formula: Depreciation expense = 2 × Straight-line depreciation percent × [(Book value at beginning of period – Salvage value) – Accumulated depreciation)]. **Sum-of-the-years digits** takes the asset's expected life and adds together the digits for each year. If the asset was expected to last for four years, the sum of the years' digits would be obtained by adding: 4 + 3 + 2 + 1 to get a total of 10. Each digit is then divided by this sum to determine the percentage by which the asset should be depreciated each year, starting with the highest number in year 1.

8. For a discussion of accounting window dressing, see Herve Stlowy and Gaetan Breton, "Accounts Manipulation: A Literature Review and Proposed Conceptual Framework," *Review of Accounting & Finance* 3 (2004): 5–68; and Lyn M. Fraser, *Understanding the Corporate Annual Report: Nuts, Bolts and a Few Loose Screws* (Upper Saddle River, NJ: Prentice-Hall, 2002).

9. For a discussion of this situation, see Steven L. Schwarcz, "Enron and the Use and Abuse of Special Purpose Entities in Corporate Structures," *University of Cincinnati Law Review* 70 (2006): 1309–1318.

CHAPTER THREE

# Cash—Management and Fraud Prevention

This chapter covers these topics:

- Understanding the significant components of cash.
- Appreciation of the bank products useful in managing paper and electronic forms of cash.
- Determination of how to reduce float and processing costs associated with cash.
- Consideration of various techniques of managing the risk of theft and fraud affecting cash.
- Reviewing the application of cost management to an actual cash collection cycle.

C ASH INCLUDES ANY GENERALLY ACCEPTED form of payment, including coin and currency, checks, and the electronic mechanisms of Fedwire and ACH. In this chapter we focus on these cash transaction forms, as they are in the widest use in business. The use of cash to complete business transactions is the obvious essential element in operating any company. We expect to be paid in cash or its equivalent when we sell our goods and services, and we know our employees and vendors will only accept similar methods of compensation when we pay our bills.

 ## FORMS OF CASH

There are three forms of cash, each of which has to be *proactively* managed to attain the optimal working capital position:

1. Bank cash, or cash in the process of collection or disbursement (which we referred to as float in Chapter 1).
2. Cash to which access has been arranged through a bank line of credit, accessible whenever a shortfall of cash from operations is forecast.
3. Cash invested in short-term investments in order to earn a return, but which can be quickly turned into actual cash through the liquidation (sale) of the asset.

The management of each of these forms of cash constitutes a separate set of procedures and skills, and overreliance on any one form may significantly increase the cost associated with cash and/or the risk of not having adequate liquidity to pay bills when due. In this chapter we emphasize bank cash and float. In Chapter 4 we discuss the other forms of cash.

### Reactive Cash Management

Consider some actual examples of companies that were *reactive* in managing cash—that is, they permitted long-established routines to continue and ignored appropriate working capital practices.

**Actual Situation I.** A company received checks in the mail, created a deposit ticket, and had one of the older female employees walk the deposit to the bank on her way to lunch. The bank was located in an office plaza adjacent to the company's offices. This activity occurred every day at about the same time, so passersby could watch her on her journey.

One of these observers realized that the woman was fairly defenseless, so he grabbed her bag containing the deposit, knocking her down and injuring her in the process, and easily got away. The deposit, including checks and some cash, was never recovered.

**Actual Situation II.** Checks for monthly retail services were sent to a company whose name included the word "the" (as in "The Wiley Group"). The checks were received in the mailroom, where clerks opened all mail and directed it to the appropriate area of the organization. Any checks were supposed to be sent to the finance group for copying and deposit. One of the mailroom clerks noticed that some company names in the "pay to the order of" line left quite a bit of space between the words "the" and the company's name.

When that occurred, the clerk inserted an "O" or an "A" in matching ink to change the recipient's name to Theo or Thea, then stole the check and deposited it in a bank account he had opened in that name (as in Theo Wiley Group). Months passed before customers realized that they had never received credit for their payments and notified the company.

**Actual Situation III.** An insurance company issued a check for $70 to settle a claim for property damaged by its policyholder in an auto accident. The check was altered to $7,000 using inexpensive desktop technology and then cashed. Three months passed before the fraud was discovered, and by that time the check recipient had disappeared.

Each of these situations resulted from sticking to accepted routines, failing to consider risk, and ignoring modern cash management procedures. Situations I and II could have been avoided through the use of lockbox; situation III could have been prevented through controlled disbursement. We will examine those products in this chapter.

## Essential Cash Management Elements

As noted in Chapter 1, the two critical factors in the optimization of cash are float and processing expenses:

1. An understanding of float is critical because all elements in the timeline of collections and disbursements have inherent delays, and delays cost a company. Although we cannot eliminate float, we can examine every step of the working capital timeline to search for savings opportunities.
2. Processing expenses are similarly important as each transaction—whether performed internally or outsourced—has a cost, and that cost directly impacts profitability.

Both factors can be managed through the use of various bank and vendor products.[1]

**PAPER TRANSACTIONS: LOCKBOXING**

The United States is a nation of check writers; although the volume has fallen from the peak of about 55 billion several years ago, some 18 billion checks are written every year by companies, individuals, and governments.[2] The origin of our use of so many checks—which is very different from other countries—goes back to our national banking system, which prohibited interstate banking from 1927 (the McFadden Act) until the middle 1990s (the Riegle-Neal Act of 1994, fully implemented in 1997). During those seven decades, banks were generally restricted to performing transactional activities in their states (and in some states, such as Illinois, the counties in which they were domiciled).

Interstate transactions involve a time-consuming check-clearing process, with the Federal Reserve and private clearinghouses exchanging physical checks from the bank of first deposit to the drawee bank (the bank on which the check was drawn). There has been a significant move to electronic imaging of checks by banks as permitted by the Check Clearing for the 21st Century Act (or Check 21), which took effect in 2004. The law allows the creation of a digital version of the original check, eliminating the need for further handling of the physical document and expediting its clearing.

### Lockboxing Procedures

**Lockboxing** is a service that comprises several elements:

- Customers direct mail remittances to a bank-controlled post office box in major cities.
- Banks pick up mail numerous times each day beginning in the early morning.
- Mail is delivered to the bank's processing site.
- The lockbox area opens the mail, pulling checks and remittance advices.
- The lockbox determines whether any checks should not be deposited based on instructions from the company (such as the wrong payee or a postdated payment, one dated past the current date).
- A copy or image of each check is created.
- Acceptable checks are encoded[3] and deposited.
- **Availability** is assigned, showing how rapidly the checks will be considered as collected funds based on the drawee bank, the bank on which the check is drawn.

▪ Summary information is sent to the company about the remittances, followed by electronic or paper versions of remittance documents and copies of the checks.

Lockboxing relieves companies of the burden and delay of handling mail and check deposits. The original form of lockbox services—known as **wholesale lockbox**—was established to handle low-volume, high-dollar checks. Critical data fields are manually key-entered from the remittance document such as the customer and/or invoice number. A **retail lockbox** is based on automated processing of scanlines (known as magnetic character ink recognition or MICR-lines) of documents and is used primarily for consumer payments.

**Imaging** is a technology that permits the digitized scanning, sorting, cataloging, and retrieval of paper documents, including checks, remittances, envelopes, and correspondence. The manipulation of an image replaces the labor-intensive process of handling wholesale lockbox items, while increasing the flexibility of the data captured and the scope and speed of receivables information transmitted to the company.

## How Does Lockboxing Reduce Float?

Lockboxing eliminates the delays experienced when checks are directed to a business. The sources of these delays include the following:

▪ **Late delivery of mail to suburban locations.** Mail may be one-half to more than one day slower arriving at a noncentral city location, say on Tuesday at noon instead of Monday at 10 a.m., because of additional sorts and longer routes to reach the final destination.

▪ **Holdover of mail due to internal processing steps.** As an example, one company had a 24-hour turnaround rule, meaning that mail had to be processed and moved along within a day. The problem was that there were four separate workstations and four days (at best) before the checks were deposited!

▪ **Depositing of checks at suburban banks.** For convenience, many companies use nearby branches of their banks for deposits. The problem is that the bank courier stops by once a day at each branch, often as early as noon. Missing the courier's pickup means a one-day delay in starting the check-clearing process.

▪ **Check clearing.** Availability float is the term banks use to assign "good" or collected funds to checks that are deposited. Availability is based on a bank's recent experience in clearing the checks it receives, and is measured in zero days (for U.S. Treasury and on-us checks),[4] one day (for major city and nearby suburban checks), two days (for distant locations), and three or more days (for checks written on nonbank financial institutions and foreign checks). Locating a depository bank distant from where checks are drawn can increase availability float by one-half day or more.

Lockbox speeds all of these activities, and can result in a savings of up to one-half of current total collection time, which can be six or more days. Costs vary, depending on the services provided by the bank, but they are never more than about $1 per transaction for wholesale lockbox and 25 cents for retail lockbox.

## How Does Lockboxing Prevent Fraud?

Fraud may occur when cash and accounting functions are performed by the same individuals in a business office. Lockboxing places all cash handling under the management of a bank, which takes full responsibility for opening mail, pulling checks and other documents received, and making deposits of monies received. Notification is sent to client companies by any of various media as to each day's activity. Any loss due to bank error or theft is the responsibility of that financial institution.

In this situation, the only checks that are not under the direct supervision of the bank are those that are mailed or couriered to an office address rather than to the lockbox, and those handed to sales representatives rather than mailed. If a company aggressively pursues these practices, the possibility of theft is largely eliminated.

## PAPER TRANSACTIONS: DEPOSITORY ACCOUNTS

Many companies continue to use regular depository accounts (demand deposit accounts or DDAs) for any checks received in their offices. This practice is inefficient (due to float considerations) and potentially risky (due to the possibility of theft and fraud).

## Control of Access

Regular bank accounts are difficult to monitor in terms of access, as companies often allow several authorized check signers to disburse deposited funds. The purpose of such payments may be entirely legitimate, but controls are often weaker than on lockbox and controlled disbursement accounts managed by the treasury staff, and internal auditors may only review the bank statements every two or three years. Furthermore, a disgruntled former employee who has taken check stock may write those checks to a phony business and then pocket the funds.

## Multipurpose Accounts

Bank accounts are frequently opened at each facility of an organization for the convenience of staff, check encashment (cashing employee checks), or other reasons. Large companies with widely separated operations may receive requests to have access to local banks, and if funds are collected by a branch office, may simply open a local account, deposit these receipts, and disperse the funds for local expenses. All openings of bank accounts should require a board of directors resolution, and any such violations should be treated as a serious breach of company policy.

In Chapter 4, we examine the management of the bank relationship, including the mobilization of funds from depository accounts to the major banking relationship. It is perhaps sufficient to note that multiple bank accounts require time-consuming, active management, with associated processing costs, or the manager could choose to leave the funds in the depositories, which will cost float.

## Too Many Accounts

As merger activity resumes, the surviving company may find that the number of their bank accounts is excessive and expensive. However, it may be reluctant to close accounts against which checks may have been written or which receive deposits. It is difficult to manage a large account configuration, particularly as accounts may have different purposes, authorized signatories, and other characteristics. Some accounts may be dormant, yet are costing monthly bank fees. The entire banking system should be investigated and accounts closed wherever possible.

 **PAPER TRANSACTIONS: CONTROLLED DISBURSEMENT**

**Controlled disbursement** became a viable product in the early 1980s when the Federal Reserve System began to provide banks with early morning information on check clearings to be made that day. Like lockboxing, the product offers both float and control features that are superior to regular checking. In a regular disbursement account, checks can be presented until the time of the bank's closing, usually 4 p.m. This requires that idle cash balances be maintained in those accounts to cover such checks.

## Controlled Disbursement Procedures

Controlled disbursement accounts are located at large bank suburban or country locations specifically established for the purpose of receiving the presentment of a cash letter once or twice daily in the early morning hours.[5] The bank notifies its corporate customers by midmorning of that day's check clearing (or debit) against the account. The customer then funds the debit once daily, eliminating the need to leave balances awaiting possible later clearings. Banks offering this product hold checks received later in the day or make clearing adjustments the next day for debiting to the account, eliminating the need for supplemental funds transfers to cover any shortfall.

Funding options include an internal bank transfer and an electronic transfer through Fedwire or ACH, both of which are discussed in the next section. The ACH credit does not become good funds until the next business day, so the bank will require the equivalent of the average check clearings of one or more days to be maintained in the account to cover the ACH float. Controlled disbursement costs about 15 cents per item.

## Account Reconciliation

Any disbursement account must be reconciled monthly to match the bank's records with the company's own books and so that neither party has made an error that goes uncorrected. Banks now provide automated partial or full reconciliation to the company within 5 to 10 days of month-end. **Partial reconciliation** is simply a list of paid or cleared items, including check numbers and dollar amounts, that the company must then reconcile against its own ledgers. The cost is about three cents per item.

An affiliated (and recommended) bank product is **full reconciliation**, which takes the issued and cleared item files and matches them monthly. Companies are notified of matches, checks still outstanding, items cleared but not issued (when the bank did not receive the issued file or notice of a late exception item), duplicate items (*forced postings*), and other problems. This step can ensure that only checks properly issued are charged against the account. Full reconciliation costs about five cents per item.

## How Does Controlled Disbursement Improve Float?

Controlled disbursement can improve float by extending the clearing time required for a check to travel from the deposit bank back to the drawee bank. This occurs because the drawee bank is located outside of major cities where clearing times are expedited by access to transportation, and because there are only one or two morning presentments of cash letters. The extension of float is typically about one-half day.

## How Does Controlled Disbursement Prevent Fraud?

Controlled disbursement contains no fraud prevention controls, but associated products do allow financial managers to discover suspect checks. Many companies support controlled disbursement with **positive (or match) pay**, which requires that a file be sent to the bank containing the number and amount of each check issued that day. As the issued checks clear, the bank matches the number and amount to the check issued file. If any mismatches occur to either factor, the bank asks the company for *accept* or *reject* decisions. The daily files of issued check information can be accumulated by the bank into a file for monthly account reconciliation purposes.

Assuming that the protocols are followed, the honoring of any fraudulent check is prevented, such as those resulting from alteration or counterfeiting (e.g., the entire check is phony, which may result from using manipulated check images). Some banks now offer payee positive pay, which matches the payee's name on clearing checks to the issued file along with the check number and amount. Positive pay costs about five cents per item.

 **ELECTRONIC TRANSACTIONS**

There are two electronic bank products in wide usage for business-to-business transactions: Fedwire and ACH. We are not including credit and debit cards, ATMs (automated teller machine), or value-added cards in this discussion, as they are used almost entirely for business-to-consumer transactions.[6]

### Federal Wire Transfer

**Federal wire transfer** (Fedwire) is processed on a same-day basis without settlement risk to the participant, as the Federal Reserve System guarantees payment. Most businesses do not often have need for Fedwire, because there are few situations where funds must be moved that day. Financial services companies are the largest users of this system due to the volume of the funds and their value, and because regulations governing these industries force the immediate crediting of funds to investors' accounts.

Fedwire advantages are the following:

- **Value:** Companies receive immediate, same-day value.
- **Speed:** Transfers are very fast. However, a few hours' delay might occur at peak operating times.
- **Security:** Fedwire is reliable and secure.

Disadvantages are the following:

- **Cost:** Fedwire is expensive to use relative to other payment types. At about $15 at each end of the transaction, or $30 or more, Fedwire is 200 times the cost of ACH.
- **Limited automation linkages:** Not all financial institutions are online with the Fed and so have to make alternative arrangements, which can slow the process and introduce errors.

**Automated Clearing House (ACH)** networks offer an electronic alternative to checks.[7] The ACH system was established to effect inexpensive settlement of low-value, high-volume and repetitive payments on an electronic, batch, overnight basis. Credit transactions are used for direct deposit of payroll, pension, and annuity payments. Debit transactions, also known as direct debits, are used for consumer bill payments, such as utility bills, phone bills, and insurance premiums. Corporate use has been largely for cash mobilization and payroll. The total number of ACH transactions is now about 22 billion a year, slightly more than the number of checks written.

ACH advantages include the following:

- **Value:** Payments can be made on precise settlement dates.
- **Reliability and efficiency:** Compared with checks, ACH collections follow a more predictable pattern.
- **Electronic processing and interfaces:** ACH allows for automated interfaces to reconciliation and cash application systems.
- **Payment options:** ACH handles debit as well as credit transactions, providing opportunities for improved collection processes.

- **Information:** Large amounts of information can be transferred with the payment.
- **Cost:** The typical ACH charge is 15 cents (or less for high volumes).

ACH disadvantages include the following:

- **Delayed settlement:** ACH payments generally settle the day following the payment's initiation; in contrast, Fedwire settles same-day.
- **Finality:** ACH does not offer the same guarantee of finality as Fedwire, as debits can be returned if not honored by the bank due to insufficient funds.

## Terminal-Based Electronic Payments

Banks have long provided access to Fedwire transfers for their business customers through terminal-based electronic systems; we'll discuss information products in Chapter 10. Fedwire transactions have various levels of approval, requiring that separate, designated financial managers set up, sign off on, and release any disbursements. In this way, fraud can occur only through the collusion of several individuals. Companies can now send and receive ACH transactions through the Internet with equivalent safeguards.

## Why Do Frauds Still Occur?

We have spent some time in this chapter discussing ways to prevent fraud. Despite the proven efficacy of bank products, frauds do occur to the extent of some $10 billion a year or more in the United States. Here are some the common reasons companies give for not instituting stronger fraud protection:

- **"We're too small."** Companies that have about $500 million or less in annual sales have a higher rate of fraud than large businesses. Smaller companies often do not separate accounting and cash handling responsibilities. This situation is an invitation to employee fraud and should be avoided. This is a particular problem with long-term, trusted employees who are "above suspicion" of larceny or other criminal behavior.
- **"Our bank doesn't have these products."** Bankers may not call on smaller companies to explain cash management products, either because potential revenues are too small or because the banker does not understand or does not have the product. The solution is for the financial manager to become educated about these products and contact community and/or regional banks that can provide them.

- **"Our auditors never told us."** Auditors may not be familiar with the very products that can protect their clients! While the accounting profession does require continuing education for CPAs to retain their licenses, there may not be adequate education on fraud problems and solutions outside of traditional accounting.
- **"These are our longtime, trusted employees!"** Studies of patterns of fraud indicate that it is precisely the longtime, trusted employee who may commit the fraud. There are various factors that may be in effect: a family situation requiring access to money, resentment at a newer employee who may be perceived as being favored, an addiction that costs more than a paycheck can support, and so on. Regardless, the solution is to transfer as much of the cash-handling function to a bank as possible.

 **FLOAT AND COST ISSUES**

As we noted in Chapter 1 and at the beginning of this chapter, the critical issue in managing working capital is cost, the critical components of which are float and processing expenses. Here is a simple illustration of how these costs occur in a collection transaction cycle, along with the opportunities for savings.

## Base Case

A company with $50 million a year in sales uses a bank to deposit its cash receipts—assume $200,000 per day in 500 payments (including checks and other forms of collection) from the sale of product and associated revenues. We'll look at each component of the collection cycle later; for now, just consider those checks received at an office in the regular mail delivery at 11:30 a.m.

As the USPS mailperson is leaving, the office staff heads off to lunch, not to return until 12:30 p.m. The mail is then distributed and opened, checks are pulled and copied, and the treasury manager prepares a deposit ticket. It is now 1:30 p.m. The office assistant drives the deposit to a bank located in a shopping center perhaps two miles away.

What are the costs so far or are yet to be incurred? The answer may be surprising but is critical in understanding the working capital opportunities.

1. Time in the mail from the customer to the office address (mail float): 3.5 days.
2. Time lost before the deposit begins to be processed by the bank (holdover float): 1.0 day.

3. Time to convert the deposit to "good" funds (availability float): 1.5 days.
4. Total staff time to prepare and make the deposit: 3.5 hours.

What happens next is the application of receipts to accounts receivable, resolving any discrepancies, and the verification of the stamped deposit ticket copy against the bank's deposit report. Decisions must be made regarding the use of the "good" funds we receive—invest, reduce existing loans, or pay incoming invoices or payroll. (*Good funds* are those to which the bank allows access, and have completed the availability process.) Those costs are added in as well:

5. Time to apply receipts to receivables and verify the deposit: 3.5 hours
6. Time to manage good funds: 1.0 hour.

Finally, the bank must be paid for its services:

7. Bank fees to handle deposit and report on the daily transaction: 25 cents per check (plus $2 per deposit and $1 per daily report).

This all adds to a surprising amount of annual cost.

## Baseline

| | |
|---|---|
| Float: | Cost of capital is 10 percent of (6 days @ $200,000 per day) = $120,000 |
| Staff time: | 1 day @ $200 × 250 business days = $50,000 |
| Bank charges: | $125 × 250 business days = $31,250 |
| Total: | $120,000 (float) + $50,000 (staff time) + $31,250 (bank fees) = more than $200,000! |

Note: All staff hourly costs are valued at $25, including benefits.

While we cannot eliminate the $200,000, we can manage this amount down to a somewhat smaller cost.

## Possible Improvements

Based on the ideas discussed in this chapter, the float time can be reduced to 3.5 days and the staff time can be managed down to 3.5 hours. The float reductions are in mail, holdover, and availability float. The staff time is in processing the mail, creating the bank deposit, and taking the deposit to the bank. The bank charges will rise by the lockbox cost, which will include an incremental $75 per month for the product and 75 cents per lockbox deposit.

## First Scenario

| | |
|---|---|
| Revised float: | Cost of capital is 10 percent of (3.5 days @ $200,000 per day) = $70,000 |
| Revised staff time: | 3.5 hours @ $25 per hour × 250 business days = $21,875 |
| Revised bank charges: | $31,250 (deposit and other charges); $75 per month × 12 months; 75 cents per lockbox item × 500 items × 250 business days = $93,750 |
| Revised total: | $70,000 (float) + $21,875 (staff time) + $93,750 (bank fees) = $185,625 |

The savings so far are $15,000 annually.

## Second Scenario

This alternative assumes that we can convert one-fourth of our mailed payments to ACH electronic transactions.

| | |
|---|---|
| Revised float 2: | The float will continue for the 75 percent of the items that are checks, or $52,500; for the 25 percent that are converted to electronic, the float is one day, or $50,000 calculated at a 10 percent cost of capital = $57,500 |
| Revised staff time 2: | No change from first revised staff time = $21,875 |
| Revised bank charges 2: | $31,250 charge continues; the lockbox costs are 75 percent of the first revision, or $46,875; the electronic receipts typically cost about 15 cents each, or $7,500 = $85,625 |
| Revised total 2: | $57,500 (float) + $21,875 (staff time) + $85,625 (bank fees) = $165,000 |

The savings are now $25,000 a year. And there are other benefits that we did not have earlier:

- **Control:** All payments are directed to a lockbox or are paid electronically, so employees do not handle the cash.
- **Convenience:** The bank handles tasks that can require several hours each day of employee time.
- **Credit and collection information:** The credit manager can know the same day whether customers have paid their invoices and if it is appropriate to ship them new merchandise.

The true savings are certainly greater than $30,000, because the company has avoided theft, saved employee time, and learned as soon as possible whether customers have paid. Each company must determine the value of these savings, but $50,000 a year (on an original cost of $200,000) is certainly within the experience of U.S. companies.

 ## SUMMARY

The two critical factors in managing cash are float and processing expenses. Float is significant because nearly all business elements have inherent delays that increase costs. Although float cannot be eliminated, every step of the working capital timeline should be examined in the search for savings opportunities. Processing expenses are important because each transaction has a cost and an impact on profitability. Both float and processing expenses can be managed through the use of bank products, the most important of which are lockboxing and controlled disbursement. Electronic transactions are managed using Fedwire and the ACH.

 ## NOTES

1. For complete information on bank products including features and costs, contact a bank. For the names of selected commercial banks, see Appendix II or contact the national organization for cash and treasury management, the Association of Financial Professionals (www.afponline.org).
2. See "The 2013 Federal Reserve Payments Study," at rbservices.org/files/ communications/pdf/research/2013_payments_study_summary.pdf.
3. **Encoding** is the process of entering the dollar amount of the check on the bottom of the face of the check.
4. "On-us" are checks written on and deposited into the same bank.
5. The Fed actually delivers a **cash letter** (or grouping) of clearing checks to a bank operation in a noncity location (known as a Regional Check Processing Center [RCPC], or a country point). Recent changes in check processing allow the electronic delivery to these banks of check images, significantly speeding the processing.
6. However, see the discussion of procurement (purchasing) cards in Chapter 8. These transaction formats are credit cards with special characteristics useful to companies.
7. There are various ACH rules governing payment formats; the interested reader should refer to the website of the Electronic Payments Association at www .nacha.org.

# CHAPTER FOUR

# Cash—Credit and Short-Term Financial Instruments

This chapter covers these topics:

- Matching of cash collections and disbursements in an integrated process.
- Understanding how to construct cash forecasts and cash budgets.
- Learning about lines of credit and asset-based financing.
- Evaluation of alternatives in the investment of excess short-term funds.
- Importance of policies on the short-term investment of excess funds.

THE PREVIOUS CHAPTER DISCUSSED PROCEDURES to manage cash as it is received and disbursed. In this chapter we analyze the choices financial managers have when short-term liquidity requirements do not match cash from operations and bank accounts. The process involves three steps, which we will review in this chapter.

1. Developing a short-term forecast
2. Preparing a cash budget

3A. Arranging for a line of credit or other financing for temporary cash deficiencies *or*

3B. Investing any excess cash in securities with short-term maturities

 ## DEVELOPING A SHORT-TERM FORECAST

Statistics can be applied to business forecasting through various processes. One technique is regression analysis, which measures how much of a factor (the dependent variable) is caused by other factors (the independent variables). An example is estimating sales based on experience with such causal factors as advertising, sales calls, and recent sales experience. Another useful technique is time series analysis using the moving-average method, which forecasts future events (like sales for the next half year) based on known past events (like recent sales).[1]

The **distribution method** is a technique that is simple yet useful. With sufficient historical data on patterns of inflows, cash forecasts can be prepared based on day-of-the-week and day-of-the-month patterns of activity. This technique is effective for companies with a fairly regular sales pattern and is helpful in estimating disbursement check clearings.

### How to Use the Distribution Method

In order to analyze cash flows using the distribution method, a company must accumulate data on patterns of receipts for at least three or four months. Exhibit 4.1 illustrates a schedule that results from this history, allowing us to predict the receipt of payments for retail sales.

Based on forecast sales for the coming month of June of an assumed $500,000, the amount for any particular date can be calculated. Assume that

**EXHIBIT 4.1**   Illustrative Distribution Method (by Business Day)

| Receipts by Day-of-the-Week | | Receipts by Day-of-the-Month | |
|---|---|---|---|
| Mondays | 15% | 1st, 15th, 30th (includes the 31st) | 7% |
| Tuesdays | 10% | 2nd, 16th | 6% |
| Wednesdays | 15% | 3rd, 17th | 5% |
| Thursdays | 15% | 4th | 4% |
| Fridays | 20% | 5th, 6th, 7th, 8th, 9th, 10th, 18th | 3% |
| Saturdays | 25% | 19th, 20th, 21st, 29th | 3% |
| *Average day* | 16⅔% | All other days | 2% |

Monday, June 17, is the 15th business day (as there is no activity on Sundays). We can forecast the activity of that day using the day-of-the-week factor as adjusted, times the day-of-the-month factor times the monthly sales forecast.

The adjustment changes the day-of-the-week factor by dividing it by the average day amount; a six-day week is adjusted using $16\frac{2}{3}$ percent, while a five-day week is adjusted using 20 percent (100 percent ÷ 5 days). For June 17, the calculation is as follows:

$$(15 \text{ percent} \div 16\tfrac{2}{3} \text{ percent}) \times 7 \text{ percent} \times \$500{,}000 = \$31{,}500$$

This calculation is useful in planning for our daily business activities, but our real working capital need is for cash.

 ## CASH BUDGETING

The second step in determining appropriate short-term financing actions is to forecast the cash position through a process known as **cash budgeting**. While the example that follows uses monthly data that may be acceptable for a small business, many large companies prepare daily cash budgets while those in the middle market prepare such analyses twice a week.

### Information Required for the Cash Budget

A cash budget is based on **accrual accounting**[2] data such as sales, expenses, and other income statement accounts. We convert sales into expected cash collections by assigning the historical experience of customer payment histories as applied to actual sales. In a similar manner, we transform expenses into cash disbursements. We then add nonrecurring cash events, including dividends, taxes, capital investments, and similar activities.

Assume that sales and expense forecasts for a company are as follows:

|  | Sales ($000) | Expenses ($000) |
|---|---|---|
| April | $30,000 | $32,000 |
| May | $40,000 | $35,000 |
| June | $50,000 | $43,000 |
| July | $60,000 | $52,000 |
| August | $50,000 | $43,000 |
| September | $40,000 | $35,000 |
| October | $30,000 | $30,000 |
| November | $30,000 | $28,000 |

Of course, these are forecasts based on statistical estimates and actual results will vary from our projections.

Assume that all sales are credit, with 20 percent collected in the month of the sale, 60 percent collected in the following month, and the remainder collected in the second following month. All expenses are paid during the month they are incurred; in addition, a tax payment of $4 million is due in July and again in September. The beginning cash balance in June is $6 million.

## How to Prepare the Cash Budget

We'll prepare a cash flow statement for June through August; see Exhibit 4.2. Assuming the company's minimum allowable cash balance is $5 million, we'll prepare a surplus/deficit cash projection for those three months. We begin with the cash collections for June, which involve some monies collected that month

**EXHIBIT 4.2** Illustrative Cash Budget ($000)

|  | June | July | August | September |
|---|---|---|---|---|
| *Sales* | *$50,000* | *$60,000* | *$50,000* | *$40,000* |
| Collections |  |  |  |  |
| That month (20%) | 10,000 | 12,000 | 10,000 | 8,000 |
| Month after (60%) | 24,000 | 30,000 | 36,000 | 30,000 |
| Two months after (20%) | 6,000 | 8,000 | 10,000 | 12,000 |
| Total cash In | 40,000 | 50,000 | 56,000 | 50,000 |
| Payments |  |  |  |  |
| Expenses | 43,000 | 52,000 | 43,000 | 35,000 |
| Taxes | 0 | 4,000 | 0 | 4,000 |
| Total cash out | 43,000 | 56,000 | 43,000 | 39,000 |
| Net cash in/out | −3,000 | −6,000 | 13,000 | 11,000 |
| Beginning cash | 6,000 | 3,000 | −3,000 | 10,000 |
| Ending cash | 3,000 | −3,000 | 10,000 | 21,000 |
| Minimum cash required | 5,000 | 5,000 | 5,000 | 5,000 |
| Surplus/deficit (denoted by minus sign) | −2,000 | −8,000 | 5,000 | 16,000 |
| Bank borrowings | 2,000 | 8,000 | 0 | 0 |
| Cumulative borrowings | 2,000 | 10,000 | 5,000 | 0 |
| Short-term investing | – | – | – | 11,000 |

Italics = Accrual accounting data; all other data are based on conversion to cash accounting.

(20 percent of sales, or $10 million), 60 percent of sales in the previous month (60 percent of May's sales, or $24 million), and 20 percent of sales in the second previous month (20 percent of April's sales, or $6 million). The total of "cash in" for June, then, is $10 million + $24 million + $6 million = $40 million. We can calculate July through September in a similar manner.

The payments are all made in the month incurred, but we must remember to include taxes of $4 million in July and in September. The total of "cash out" is entered, and the net of "cash in" and "cash out" is calculated, a negative $3 million for June. We began June with $6 million, and we expect to end June and begin July with $3 million. However, our minimum cash is $5 million, so we are "short" $2 million in June.

To obtain this amount, we could arrange for bank borrowings, sell short-term investments, or use other financial strategies. As we work these calculations through the remaining months, we determine total borrowings and the amount available to invest after the borrowings are repaid. The decision that results is to arrange to finance $2 million in June and $8 million in July, and to use the surpluses of $5 million in August and $11 million in September. We'll explore our options in the next sections.

## CREDIT FINANCING

The next step is the consideration of the various credit arrangements provided by banks (and such other lenders as commercial finance companies), including lines of credit and asset-based financing.

### Arranging for Bank Credit

When arranging for a line of credit or any type of bank loan, the borrower should come fully prepared to meet with a banker. Essential documents are the cash budget and pro forma financial statements (an income statement and a balance sheet). The term **pro forma** refers to projected or in the form of, and reflects expected results for coming periods. In addition, bank loan officers require audited financial statements from recent reporting periods.

Other data that should be provided include specific sources of sales, including customer names and their likely purchases; marketing plans, including advertising and promotional activities; likely employee hiring and terminations; and justification for major expenses, such as new equipment, the rental of additional production capacity, outsourcing arrangements, and other initiatives. Expect to discuss contingency arrangements in the event of a failure to meet business goals.

The banker will indicate the frequency and form of the future exchange of data to keep him or her updated on current developments. Any expectations regarding the use of other bank services, such as the products discussed in Chapter 3, will be strongly suggested. (Because of the illegality of tying arrangements, bankers cannot require that a borrower buy noncredit services in order to obtain credit.) In the interim, maintain contact with the banker—he or she does not want to be unpleasantly surprised!

## Lines of Credit

A company may arrange with a bank for access to a **line of credit**, a specified amount of money accessible for a specified time period, usually one year.[3] The line may be drawn as needed during seasonal shortages of cash resulting from normal operations. In the cash budget example, the company needs $2 million in June and $8 million in July, and we could use the credit line to meet those temporary needs.

The bank guarantees the line if it is **committed** so long as the borrowers meet all of the conditions of the agreement. An **uncommitted** line is not guaranteed but is almost always granted (assuming the terms of the lending arrangement are met). Depending on the credit risk and condition of the company, banks will typically charge a fee of about ½ of 1 percent for a committed facility; there is no fee for an uncommitted line. Typical pricing of the used portion of the line is about 2 to 4 percent above Fed funds, LIBOR, or the prime rate, depending on the perceived credit risk of the borrower.[4] Because of the complexities of bank lending, a discussion in some detail is provided in Chapter 5.

## Bank Returns on Lines of Credit

Banks in the United States can make a reasonable return on credit above their costs of capital when a nominal commitment fee is earned, about 5½ percent.[5] The return on uncommitted lines is about 3 percent less, making the provision of this version of the product marginal. These results are *before* default losses on nonperforming losses are included. The decision of banks to provide lines of credit without commitment fees has been due to three factors:

1. Banks profitability models have been available only since about 1985, and the assumptions in these models are questionable given the strong negotiating position of large corporate borrowers, at least until the present credit crisis. In other words, a strong corporation may negotiate away

commitment fees and other loan covenant conditions, and banks have been unwilling to hold the line on cost-recovery strategies.

2. In the past, noncredit products have subsidized credit such as those discussed in Chapter 2. Banks may knowingly (or unknowingly) provide no- or low-return credit products such as credit lines in order to have the opportunity to sell higher-return noncredit products.

3. Credit *is* profitable for banks for certain groups of companies. These include some middle markets and most small businesses, and situations where reasonable returns can be earned in specific industries due to the absence of lending competition.

There is no assurance that banks will be willing to provide free uncommitted lines or committed lines for a nominal fee of perhaps ½ of 1 percent given the recent problems of the banking industry. Furthermore, financial managers do not act prudently when they fail to lock in committed lines. The natural impulse is to bargain aggressively for a reduction in this fee, to shop for better pricing from a competitor, or to accept an uncommitted, "free" line of credit. Bargaining and shopping are certainly acceptable, but settling for an uncommitted line could be a mistake for the following reasons:

1. In normal economic times, a middle-market business may have a balance sheet composed of total assets of $150 million, with about 10 percent in cash and short-term investments. In addition, lines of credit provide access to financing that represents an additional 5–5½ percent. Assuming current commitment fee pricing of ½ of 1 percent, the cost of an assured line would be about $40,000 a year. While companies may be reluctant to spend this amount to guarantee access to credit, it should be considered to be as essential for business survival as insurance or risk management.

2. As has been noted, banks cannot make an adequate return on uncommitted credit lines, and are beginning to carefully review and expunge those activities and others that do not earn target returns. This is not a new phenomenon; banks have been ending unprofitable relationships for at least a decade. The likelihood is that further terminations will occur.

3. Credit-rating agencies are enhancing their forecasting models to include off–balance sheet financing such as lines of credit. Acceptable credit ratings are essential to maintaining good supplier relationships, particularly as more vendors look to asset-based financing for working capital, which is subject to lender approval. The borrower's creditworthiness and the agreement of companies to sell to it depend on having a committed line of credit.

Lines of credit are essential sources of liquidity for any business. A treasurer does not want to receive a telephone call from his or her banker that an uncommitted line of credit is no longer available.

## Asset-Based Financing

**Asset-based financing** uses a company's accounts receivable and/or inventory as collateral in situations where the lender is uncertain of the borrower's creditworthiness. Typical costs are 4 to 5 percent higher than arranging a line of credit.

- **Factoring** of receivables involves the direct collection from the borrower's customers, who are instructed on the invoice to remit to a specified address controlled by the lender.
- **Inventory financing** is used in industries with expensive equipment and medium-length sales cycles. The lender uses the equipment as collateral, and the loan is paid as sales are made to customers of the borrower.

We will discuss asset-based lending in more detail in Chapters 6 and 7.

 ## SHORT-TERM INVESTMENTS

In our cash budget, we had excess cash of $11 million in September. This section discusses the final step in our cash decision: choosing investments appropriate for any temporary excess of cash. We paid down our borrowing with the excess cash in August for two reasons:

1. It is always more expensive to borrow than to invest, often by three or four percentage points.
2. The bank expects its borrowers to repay lines of credit as soon as cash is available.

### "No Effort Investments" and Equivalents

There are two investment vehicles that do not require any action by the financial manager: ECRs and sweeps. Although we could just leave any unneeded money in the bank, the earnings we would receive on such "no effort investments" are minimal.

## Earnings Credit Rates

The Federal Reserve's Regulation Q prohibits the payment of interest on corporate checking accounts (called demand deposit accounts, or DDAs). While there has been discussion for about two decades of changing this rule, the restriction continues.[6] As a result, banks have long used the concept of the **earnings credit rate (ECR)**, which is applied to average balances left on deposit and used to offset any service charges.

The calculation is shown on the bank's monthly invoice, called the **account analysis**. Assuming an ECR of 2 percent, a company would earn $375 for a month on an average earnings balance of $225,000; see Exhibit 4.3. We will be discussing the account analysis further in Chapter 5.

Companies desiring to earn this credit simply do nothing, and the bank will automatically apply the earnings against any bank service charges. However, the effective return is only 1.8 percent ($375 × 12) ÷ $250,000 when the ECR is 2 percent. (The ECR rate is calculated by the bank against a benchmark rate, usually the yield on short-term U.S. Treasury securities.)

## Sweeps

Banks and investment companies introduced **sweeps** in the 1980s, when high interest rates were a strong incentive for financial managers to aggressively

**EXHIBIT 4.3**  Illustrative ECR Calculation (based on a typical bank account analysis)

| Description | Purpose | Amount |
|---|---|---|
| Average ledger balance | Reflects the ledger amount of debits and credit in the bank | $2,000,000 |
| Less: Average float | Shows the funds in the process of collection through the assignment of availability[7] | $1,750,000 |
| Equals: Average collected balances | Indicates the average funds that can be used for transactions | $250,000 |
| Less: Federal Reserve requirement (currently 10%) | Is the amount set by Federal Reserve rules that banks must hold to maintain liquidity | $25,000 |
| Equals: Average earnings balance | Shows the amount on which the company earns an ECR credit | $225,000 |
| Earnings credit rate (ECR) | Applies the current earnings rate | 2% |
| ECR allowance | Provides the earnings allowance for the month | $375.00[8] |

invest short-term. A **sweep** automatically moves any DDA (demand deposit account or checking account) balances into an interest-bearing account outside of the bank. There is a fairly wide choice of investments for companies that use sweeps, including government and corporate securities and offshore higher-yielding opportunities. Balances are returned the next morning to the DDA.

The all-in charge for a sweep account is about $100 a month, so interest income must significantly exceed that cost, which may be difficult in the current low-interest environment. For example, 2½ percent earned on $50,000 produces only about $100 in monthly interest income and is not worth the effort to create a sweep account. A concern with sweeps is that there is no Federal Deposit Insurance Corporation (FDIC) insurance on the amount swept while it is outside of the bank.[9]

## "Some Effort" Investments and Equivalents

Many companies use telephone or Internet instructions to their banks or securities firms to make safe investments with reasonable returns. While financial managers may receive advice, they must actively choose among the instruments and maturities. Furthermore, these investments may charge a transaction fee, and there is a cost for the movement of funds to pay for the investment. See Exhibit 4.4 for short-term investment rates just before the 2008–2009 credit crisis, a period generally considered as "normal," and in

**EXHIBIT 4.4** Comparison of Rates on Debt Instruments (pre- and post-credit crisis) (in percent of annual interest)

|  | March 2008 | March 2014 |
|---|---|---|
| Federal funds | 2.4 | 0.1 |
| U.S. Treasury bills | 1.4 | 0.1 |
| LIBOR | 2.7 | 0.15–0.3 |
| Prime rate | 5.3 | 3.25 |
| Broker call | 4.0 | 2.0 |
| Commercial paper (nonfinancial) | 2.3 | 0.1 |
| Money market mutual funds | 2.0–3.0 | 0.1 |
| U.S. Treasury notes | 3.0 | 0.5–2.0 |
| U.S. Treasury bonds | 4.0 | 2.75 |

There are several published sources of rates on debt instruments, including the *Wall Street Journal*, *New York Times*, and *Barron's* (in the "Market Week" section and at www.barrons.com/data).

early 2014, during an unusual period in our economic history due to the policies of the Federal Reserve.

- **Banker's acceptance.** A banker's acceptance (BA) is an instrument created when a bank guarantees an international transaction using a letter of credit. The bank sells the BA to investors at a discount and accepts the responsibility for repaying the loan, protecting the investor from default risk. BAs are generally issued for up to six months.
- **Repos.** A repo (repurchase agreement) is an investment contract between a brokerage firm or bank and an investor (usually a financial institution or large corporation). The repo is sold with an agreement for repurchase at a future date at a set price, with most settling overnight. There is minimal risk with repos, although companies interested in this investment should ascertain that there is adequate collateral supporting the repo.
- **Commercial paper (CP).** Commercial paper involves unsecured notes issued by companies with high credit ratings. Maturities are from a few days to 270 days. Most issuers use CP as a continuing financing source and reissue the CP at the time of redemption. Sales are either direct to investors or through dealers (securities firms). Much of the outstanding CP is backed by bank credit lines, minimizing any risk to investors. CP typically carries ratings by leading credit rating agencies and is graded as A-1, P-1, or A-2, P-2.
- **Money market mutual funds (MMFs).** Money market mutual funds are pools of various types of short-term investments that offer shares to corporate investors. A significant benefit of MMFs is that relatively small units of funds can be placed, allowing the earning of some yield even to the small corporate investor. The diversification in these funds mitigates any risk from the decline in value of a particular holding.
- **U.S. Treasury securities.** Securities of the U.S. government include Treasury bills and notes (those with maturities from 1 to 10 years); and **Treasury bonds**, with maturities from 10 to 30 years. These instruments are highly liquid and risk-free, although the longer the maturity, the greater the risk that inflation could impact the real return.
- **U.S. agencies.** Although not generally well known, there are various federal agencies that issue securities to fund their operations. Two of these agencies are backed by the full faith and credit of the government: Ginnie Mae (the Government National Mortgage Association) and Vinnie Mac (the Department of Veterans Affairs). Other agencies include Fannie Mae (the Federal National Mortgage Association), Freddie Mac (the Federal

Home Loan Mortgage Corporation) and the CoBank ACB, a component of the U.S. farm credit system that funds agribusinesses.[10]

▪ **Municipal securities.** State and local government municipal securities (**munis**) have the attraction of having their interest payment exempt from taxes, although yields are less than those of other instruments. The investor has various options in selecting among municipals, including revenue securities, which are backed by revenue streams from specific projects; and general obligation securities, which are backed by the income sources of the issuer.

## Policies on Short-Term Investing

Many companies have written policies that clearly define acceptable risks, instruments, and maturities for investments. Such policies should reflect the appropriate profile on risk and expectations on return. The purpose of these policies is to protect the company against bad investment decisions and the possible loss of principal. This is not a trivial issue due both to the large amounts at risk and to catastrophic losses experienced by apparently "safe" money managers.[11]

A committee made up of the board of directors and financial managers will normally draft an investment policy. Exhibit 4.5 outlines the issues that

**EXHIBIT 4.5**   Investment Policy Issues

| | |
|---|---|
| Investment objective | What is the company's acceptable level of risk and yield? How important is yield, given the safety of principal and liquidity? |
| Investment authority | Who is authorized to implement the investment policy and make investments on behalf of the company, and to what limits and in which instruments? |
| Audit trails | What type and frequency of reporting and audit trails will be available to monitor compliance with the investment policy? |
| Permitted or restricted instruments | Which investment instruments are permitted or prohibited in the portfolio? What is the accepted credit quality and marketability? |
| Maturity | What maturities are acceptable in terms of risk and liquidity? |
| Diversification of investments | What are the allowable positions in different types of investments, with regard to issuers, industry, and the country of the issuer? |
| Securities dealers | Who are the acceptable dealers with whom the company is prepared to deal? In what amounts? |
| Safekeeping | What custodial arrangements are required, both to safeguard the company's investment and to facilitate audit requirements? |

an investment policy should address. The typical policy will limit short-term investments to certain classes of securities, such as highest-rated U.S. Treasury instruments and commercial paper (A-1 by Moody's and P-1 by Standard & Poor's). These are particularly important in the context of the collapse of Bear Stearns in 2008 and the possibility of the loss of invested funds.

## SUMMARY

Financial managers have a sequence of decisions when short-term liquidity requirements do not match cash from operations and bank accounts. These involve: (1) developing a short-term forecast; (2) preparing a cash budget; and (3) arranging for a line of credit or other financing for temporary cash deficiencies *or* investing any excess cash in securities with short-term maturities.

Various techniques are available to prepare short-term forecasts; our focus in this chapter was on the distribution method, which uses day-of-the-week and day-of-the-month factors. Cash budgeting restates accrual accounting data to cash accounting terms and then determines the beginning and ending cash for each forecast period. Lines of credit (and other financial arrangements) provide temporary sources of cash during expected deficiencies. Various short-term investment alternatives offer opportunities to earn returns on excess cash, with the choice based on yield, risk, and the effort required to make and manage the investment.

## NOTES

1. See any standard text; e.g. Douglas Lind, William G. Marchal, and Samuel Wathen, *Statistical Techniques in Business and Economics*, 15th ed. (New York: McGraw-Hill, 2011).
2. **Accrual accounting** attempts to match revenues (sales) to the costs of developing those revenues. Nearly all large companies use accrual accounting and its conventions, such as depreciation. **Cash accounting,** used primarily by small businesses, recognizes revenues as cash is received and expenses as cash is disbursed.
3. Loans for longer periods are known as **revolving term loans** (sometimes called "revolvers") for periods of one to five years. These types of loans are not appropriate for working capital; instead, they are used for capital needs involving investments with lives of more than one year.

4. Federal fund (**Fed funds**) is the rate that U.S. commercial banks charge each other for overnight borrowing. **LIBOR** (the London Interbank Offered Rate) represents that arrangement outside of the United States. Many U.S. loans are based on one of these rates. Some banks charge for lines of credit using the **prime rate**, which is the rate charged by banks to their best small and middle market customers.

5. The analysis and discussion in this section are explored in depth in James Sagner and Herbert Jacobs, *Handbook of Corporate Lending*, rev. ed. (New York: Bank Credit Training Partners, 2014), 157–159.

6. Not-for-profit organizations are exempted from this rule.

7. **Availability** is a bank-assigned factor that reflects the expected number of days required to receive collected funds for checks deposited.

8. Calculated as (2% × $225,000) ÷ 12 months.

9. The FDIC provides deposit insurance that guarantees the safety of a depositor's accounts in member banks up to $250,000 for each deposit ownership category. For additional information, visit www.fdic.gov.

10. Fannie Mae and Freddie Mac are government-sponsored enterprises (GSE) of the U.S. government. As GSEs, they are privately owned corporations authorized to make loans and loan guarantees, with the implied guarantee of the government. The failure of these two agencies in September 2008 forced the Federal Housing Finance Agency to place them under its conservatorship. The eventual disposition will likely be a sale of the assets, a recomposition, or nationalization for the purpose of pursuing their mission of providing home ownership to low-income Americans.

11. The situation with Bernard Madoff is too well known to require repetition in this chapter. However, there have been other cases involving massive investor losses. For example, Orange County, California, declared Chapter 9 bankruptcy in December 1994, due to the investment strategies of County Treasurer Robert Citron. In an effort to earn high returns for the county without raising taxes, he entered into risky, leveraged fixed income positions. A liquidity default occurred when interest rates increased and bankers for the county required increased collateral.

CHAPTER FIVE

# Managing Bank Relationships

This chapter covers these topics:

- Analysis of current trends in banking relationship management.
- Mobilization of cash in a multibank network.
- General terms of credit agreements.
- Specific issues of importance in arrangements for credit.
- Ongoing bank relationship concerns.

CHAPTERS 2 AND 3 DISCUSSED considerations relating to cash and credit. Those working capital concerns are closely aligned with decisions about banking—which financial institution to use, how to make the selection, how to determine if your prices and services are what your business needs, and how to manage the relationship with your banker. We'll review those issues in this chapter.

THE CHANGING FINANCIAL LANDSCAPE

At some point in a company's history, a bank account was opened that began either a happy or a troubled relationship. A predecessor in the company's finance group may have walked over to the closest bank office, or knew someone from high school who was working at a bank, or asked a friend, relative, or associate for a recommendation. Those days are over; changes in the regulation of financial institutions have completely altered the competitive landscape and, as a result, how a bank treats its customers.

### Financial Deregulation

There were prohibitions on interstate banking in the United States from the 1920s until the mid-1990s.[1] Congress also imposed strict limitations on the business activities of banks, with the most restrictive being the forced separation of investment and commercial banking from 1933 to 1999.[2] The current financial services structure of the United States is significantly smaller in terms of the number of institutions; for example, there were nearly 15,000 commercial banks in 1980; there are now about 6,800.[3]

The friendly neighborhood banker has suffered as the result of this competitive change. Fewer banks, more products, the integration of technology into the delivery of services (see Chapter 10), and the globalization of business have forced banks to merge or become more knowledgeable, and a handshake has given way to a formal relationship. If a company is still using a bank from 10 or 20 years ago, it may be time to reexamine the situation. In the next sections we will review the functions of the principal banking relationship; in the chapter appendix we will discuss a process frequently used in reviewing banks and financial institutions.

 BANK RELATIONSHIP MANAGEMENT

**Bank relationship management** is a comprehensive approach to the bank-corporate partnership, involving all of the credit and noncredit services[4] offered by financial institutions and required by their business customers. Elements of relationship management include the following:

- ■ Credit arrangements to meet short- and longer-term financing requirements.

- Appropriate noncredit services for U.S. and global transactions.
- Reasonable pricing.
- Acceptable service quality.
- Consideration for financial institution risk.

Prior to recent financial deregulation, companies often had affiliations with several banks to provide the services they required. To some extent, it was a "buyer's market," with bankers selling their products through every possible marketing device, including but not limited to the following:

- Constant calling to build brand recognition.
- Entertainment to build personal contact and a sense of "obligation."
- Aggressive pricing, often at or even below fully loaded costs.
- A regular rollout of new product offerings.
- The intertwining of the bank's systems with the company's systems, to make separation as difficult as possible.

## Twenty-First-Century Banking

The traditional bank calling strategy worked as long as banks could generate adequate revenues from all of their corporate business, particularly as most financial institutions had a poor understanding of profitability by customer or product line. Furthermore, commercial banks were restricted in the use of capital, and could not pursue more lucrative financial business, such as investment banking or insurance.

The new regulatory environment allows banks and other financial service companies to pursue a much broader range of opportunities, reducing their reliance on marginally profitable services. Like all for-profit shareholder-owned companies, banks require a reasonable return-on-equity from each customer and may terminate a relationship if there is little prospect of acceptable returns in the long run. A proactive relationship management plan is necessary for companies to satisfy their financial institutions and for bankers to justify the business to their management.[5]

## Finance as the Gatekeeper to Banking Services

Bank contact with companies has traditionally been through the treasurer, whose responsibilities include the safeguarding of the cash and near-cash assets of the company. However, access has been extended through other business functions in recent years as banks have broadened their product offerings. Too often, treasury staff remains unaware of the resulting dilution of its responsibility. For example:

- Purchasing and accounts payable are often the entry for e-commerce and purchasing cards.
- The payroll department or human resources may invite discussions concerning the direct deposit of payroll and payroll ATM cards (paycard).
- The investment or real estate departments may be interested in such specialized services as stock loan, custody, and escrow or tax services.
- Systems or information technology (IT) often initiates discussions about any of the more technology-oriented bank services.

Given the current credit environment, it is essential that the finance organization be the gatekeeper for all financial institution contact. This will ensure that an attractive package of profitable business is assembled for the relationship banks, and prevent unauthorized negotiations or contracting between the company and other banks.

 ## CASH MOBILIZATION IN A MULTIBANK NETWORK

Where multiple collection and disbursement accounts exist, cash needs to be mobilized into and funded from a principal bank relationship.[6] That bank is the main provider of credit and noncredit services to a company, but other banks may be used in field or office locations due to long-standing relationships or because no national bank yet covers certain regions. Companies in this situation may use one of the U.S. national banks with wide market coverage.[7]

Example of industries with a multibank structure include retailing and branch offices that require local financial depositories to receive checks, currency, and credit card receipts. As a result, funds often accumulate in collection accounts. In order to use the funds most effectively, the financial manager needs to mobilize the balances.

### Funds Mobilization

There are a number of options for a company to move funds into the principal account:

- **Company-initiated.** Large companies may develop their own reporting systems for cash mobilization. The technology used involves computer processing, with automated notification from the local office to company headquarters using specified protocols. For example, the stock brokerage industry uses proprietary systems to report each day's activity at branches. Some of these systems require the branch to input the transit routing numbers[8] of client checks to determine when collected funds will be received at the local depository for inclusion in cash mobilization. Financial managers prepare the necessary wire transfers or ACHs based on a cost–benefit calculation for each method.

■ **Standing instructions.** The administrative effort necessary to concentrate funds can be minimized by the issuance of instructions to the depository or principal banks to effect transfers based on specific rules. These criteria could be based on:

  ■ Frequency: for example, daily or at some other time interval
  ■ Amount: for example, any collected funds or only funds exceeding a predetermined target

■ **Deposit reporting services.** A deposit reporting service (DRS) assists in the mobilization of funds in local accounts to the principal bank account. The office manager contacts the DRS through a toll-free telephone number or a point-of-sale (POS) terminal and, following a series of prompts, reports the location number, the time and amount of the deposit, and any detail required by the company (such as the coin and currency subtotal).

The DRS accumulates all of the calls for the company, creates an ACH file to draw down the deposited funds, and transmits the ACH through the banking system. The all-in daily cost per store is approximately $1. The effectiveness of a DRS system relies on the local manager to report accurate and timely information, and to actually make the bank deposit! The company can be notified if any store does not contact the DRS, allowing a rapid follow-up to determine the reason for the failure.

## Too Many Bank Accounts?

A company's financial staff may have only limited data on daily receipts and deposits in local accounts. The complexity and cost of a cash mobilization system, including the burden placed on the local office manager for notifying the home office and making the deposit, must be weighed against the value of funds transferred. Rather than a minor change to the banking system, it may pay to consider a complete redesign to eliminate local banks and the funds mobilization process.

Companies with more than 25 bank accounts should examine why these accounts are open. Idle accounts often exist that are infrequently used, and their balances can be moved into a single bank account earning a higher return. The idle accounts can then be closed, saving the monthly maintenance charge and other fees. Each idle bank account closed, assuming the balances are $15,000, is worth about $1,500 a year ($1,000 for the value of the earnings and $500 a year for maintenance and other charges). Closing 15 accounts could save between $20,000 and $25,000 a year and significantly reduce the possibility of fraud.

If a credit line is constantly being used for working capital (as discussed in Chapter 4), move money back to the lender whenever there is an excess of cash to minimize interest costs. Having the same bank for credit and cash management services allows excess funds to repay borrowing through an intrabank transfer, saving about four percentage points (the difference between the bank's ECR and the line of credit borrowing cost). These transfers cost about 50 cents.

## Selecting the Bank

The importance of carefully selecting a bank cannot be overemphasized. A company should want a financial institution that has well-trained staff, the right mix of products, adequate credit facilities, and any noncredit services that your business will require to succeed. The consolidation within the banking industry and more difficult regulatory requirements has turned the banking/ corporate relationship into a seller's market, with companies finding it somewhat more difficult to find willing lenders.

▪ Is the company selling in global markets? Letters of credit and foreign exchange will be required (discussed in Chapter 9).
▪ Should the bank handle collection and disbursement activity? The company will need lockbox and/or controlled disbursing (discussed in Chapter 3).
▪ Is there consideration of outsourcing of the payables function? The company will need comprehensive payables (discussed in Chapter 8).
▪ Is bond or equity financing being considered? The company will want to work with a bank with access to and expertise in the capital markets.
▪ Does a company just need good, objective advice? The banker and the resources that support him or her are critical to businesspeople in these difficult economic times.

Issues relating to noncredit services are reviewed in the appendix to this chapter.

**GENERAL TERMS OF CREDIT FACILITIES**

Credit facilities are normally not bid through an organized bidding process; the company usually requests a loan from a financial institution based on past and projected financial statements, a business plan, booked and anticipated sales, and other relevant data. Lenders review various information from prospective corporate borrowers, as noted in Exhibit 5.1.

## The Basic Provisions

The first portion of a loan agreement details the type of loan being made, its amount of the bank's commitment, fees and interest to be paid, the repayment schedule, and any restrictions that may be applied on the use of loan proceeds by the borrower. For example, in Exhibit 5.3 it is stated that the purpose of the loan is to finance the working capital requirements of the borrower, and the amount is $10 million with a maturity date one year from the execution date of the agreement. Payments are due monthly by long-standing practice. For purposes of this book, the types of loans that will be used are lines of credit (up to one year in duration but renewable), and term loans and revolving credits that can convert to term loans with durations of three years or more.

---

**EXHIBIT 5.1**    Information Required in Establishing a Credit Facility

- Audited financial statements for three years
- Pro forma (projected) financial statements for the next two years
- Cash budget showing sources and uses of cash for the next year
- Names of major customers and anticipated sales activity
- Statement of strategic plans and possible capital investments
- Collateral for the loan (if required), usually involving a perfected first security interest in:
  - Leasehold improvements
  - Accounts receivable
  - Inventory
  - Equipment, furniture, and fixtures
- List of current debt, other financing obligations, and long-term leases
- Statement regarding existing banking relationships
- Unresolved or pending legal issues such as lawsuits and contract negotiations
- Information regarding senior managers including experience and education
- Required filings with government agencies (such as the Securities and Exchange Commission)
- Resolution of the board of directors authorizing the loan

The second part of a loan agreement, reflecting its essentially contractual nature, details "conditions precedent" whereby one party, namely the bank, is not required to perform its duties and obligations—namely, lend the borrower the money, until the borrower has satisfied certain requirements, namely the conditions precedent to allow the loan to be executed.

Obviously, depending on the structuring features of the loan agreement, the conditions precedent will vary (e.g., is the loan to be guaranteed?). If so, then a satisfactory guarantee and a satisfactory legal opinion about its enforceability will be required as a condition precedent before loan proceeds can be disbursed.

### Representations and Warranties

Following the conditions precedent section, there is a detailed listing of representations and warranties to be made by the borrower. These "reps and warranties" involve commentary on the borrower's legal status—that is, its ability to enter into said obligations. Other representations often involve statements on litigation and defaults; a listing of subsidiaries of the borrower, where they are incorporated and what percentage of ownership the borrower has for those subsidiaries; outstanding liens; and the borrower's compliance with the Employee Retirement Income Security Act (ERISA).[9] Representations can also be stated regarding the borrower and its subsidiaries filing tax returns and having paid taxes owed.

### Restrictions in Lines of Credit

**Loan covenants** apply to lines of credit and other types of credit agreements, which are affirmative or negative restrictions that require certain performance by borrowers. These may include limitations on new debt beyond current borrowings, changes in business strategies or senior management, and various financial compliance requirements, often as measured by standard ratios in such categories as liquidity, leverage, activity, and profitability. Exhibit 5.2 lists illustrative loan covenants.

 ## SPECIFIC TERMS IN CREDIT FACILITIES

In situations where the credit is questionable, the bank may demand collateral and protective covenants to secure the loan. Exhibit 5.3 provides the details of a loan agreement. In this example, the bank has a security interest in leasehold improvements, accounts receivable, inventory, equipment, furniture and fixtures, and all cash and noncash proceeds. In addition, banks require that their borrowers stay out of the bank—that is, not use the line—for a minimum

**EXHIBIT 5.2** Illustrative Loan Covenants

Affirmative
- Certified financial statements must be provided within 60 days of the end of the fiscal year.
- Borrower will maintain appropriate company records.
- Borrower will insure company chief executive officer (and other senior executives) using key man insurance, with the bank named as beneficiary.
- Bank will have the right to access borrower's premises to inspect its property.
- Borrower will be in compliance with all federal and state laws.
- Borrower will pay all taxes due and government fees.
- Borrower will maintain all property in good condition.
- Borrower will provide lender with any notice of litigation or other legal action.

Negative
- Borrower cannot allow financial ratios to fall below specified amounts (e.g., a current ratio cannot be less than 2:1). Note that the precise value assigned to the ratio or metric is usually determined by industry experience. Other ratio or metrics that are used in loan agreements include the following:
  - Days receivables outstanding
  - Inventory turnover
  - Total debt-to-total assets
  - Total net worth (in U.S. dollars or other currency)
  - Fixed charge coverage
  - Cash flow from operations must exceed payments for dividends and debt service
- Outlays on capital expenditures cannot exceed $2.5 million (or other selected amount).
- Cash dividends cannot exceed one-half of earnings (or other selected amount).
- Officers' salaries cannot exceed $500,000 (or other selected amount).
- No acquisition or merger activity can be considered without prior bank approval.
- No assets may be sold (or leased) that exceed 15 percent of the value of existing assets (or other selected amount).
- No change in senior management may occur without bank concurrence.
- No additional long-term debt may be incurred without bank approval.

number of months each year, usually two consecutive months, so that the line is not part of its permanent financing.

## Pricing the Loan

Banking continues to be a highly competitive business despite the substantial reduction in the number of financial institutions in recent years. As a result, loan pricing is based on a cost-plus calculation, with the benchmark rate used

**EXHIBIT 5.3**   Illustrative Bank Loan Agreement

This letter will serve as the offer of the Last National Bank (the Bank) to provide financing on the following terms and conditions:

| | |
|---|---|
| Purpose: | Working capital line of credit |
| Amount: | $10,000,000 |
| Maturity: | One year |
| Interest rate: | Prime rate of bank plus one percent (1%) per annum |
| Payments: | Monthly payments of accrued interest, outstanding balance and accrued interest due and payable in full at maturity |
| Collateral: | A valid, perfected first security interest in all leasehold improvements, accounts receivable, inventory, equipment, furniture and fixtures, and all cash and noncash proceeds thereof, now owned or hereafter acquired by Borrower |
| Financial statements: | The Borrower shall furnish to the Bank within 45 days of the end of each quarter one copy of the financial statements prepared by the Borrower. The Borrower will also furnish to the Bank within 90 days of the end of each fiscal year one copy of the financial statements audited by an independent public accountant. Borrower shall furnish to the Bank within 15 days after the end of each month an aging of the Borrower's accounts receivable in 30-day incremental agings.[1] |
| Financial covenants: | During the term of the note, Borrower shall comply with the following financial covenants: |

Net Worth. Maintain a Net Worth of not less than the sum of $15,000,000 at all times.

Debt to Assets. Maintain a ratio of Total Debt to Total Assets equal to or less than 40%.

| | |
|---|---|
| Expiration: | This commitment shall automatically expire upon the occurrence of any of the following events: |

Borrower's failure to close the loan by April 15, 20XX, or such later date as Bank may agree to in writing.

Any material adverse change[2] in Borrower's financial condition or any occurrence that would constitute a default under Bank's normal lending documentation, or any warranty or representation made by Borrower herein is false, incorrect, or misleading in any material respect.

The foregoing terms and conditions are not inclusive and the loan documents may include additional provisions specifying events of default, remedies and financial and collateral maintenance covenants. This commitment is conditional upon Bank and the Borrower agreeing upon such terms and conditions.

Oral agreements or commitments to loan money, extend credit or forbear from enforcing repayment of a debt, including promises to extend or renew such debt, are not enforceable. To protect the borrower(s) and the bank from misunderstanding or disappointment, any agreements reached covering such matters are contained in this document, which is the complete and exclusive statement of the agreement between the parties. The bank may later agree in writing to modify the agreement.

Additional requirements of the borrower are as follows:

1. Resolution of the board of directors authorizing the loan.
2. Warranties by the borrower as normally required, including that the business is duly incorporated, that it is not a party to substantive litigation, and that it is current with all tax payments.

---

[1] An aging schedule shows the quality of a company's receivables by listing the amount of outstanding invoices by groupings of days. A schedule may show a large amount of unpaid receivables more than 30 or 60 days old, which would be of concern to a lender dependent on that revenue source. See Chapter 6 for a more complete explanation.

[2] A material adverse change is a provision often found in financing agreements (and merger and acquisition contracts) that enables the lender to refuse to complete the financing if the borrower suffers such a change. The rationale is to protect the lender from major adverse events that make the borrower a less attractive client.

as the underlying cost of funds (CF), to which are added increments for the bank's operating costs, including the necessary spread above the benchmark rate (OC), the risk of the borrower (RB), and the designated profit margin for the bank (PM). This formula can be expressed as:

$$\text{Loan interest rate} = CF + OC + RB + PM$$

A typical situation prior to the 2008 credit crisis may have involved a CF of 4 percent, OC of 1¾ percent, RB of 1 percent, and PM of ¾ of 1 percent, for total pricing of 7½ percent. Pricing in 2014 would be significantly less due to the low cost of funds, with a rate of perhaps 4 percent depending on the risk of the borrower. The standard reference on loan pricing is a Thomson Reuters publication called *Gold Sheets*, which provides reporting and analysis of the global loan markets.[10] As we discussed in Chapter 4, the cost-plus approach to loan pricing has little to do with establishing a rate that will fully compensate the bank on a comprehensive basis.

##  ONGOING BANK RELATIONSHIP CONCERNS

Once the loan has been completed, the company must actively monitor compliance, maintain accurate records on bank activity, and arrange for periodic reviews of current activities and business conditions.

## Monitoring Compliance

Borrower and lenders must constantly monitor compliance to avoid default; if business deteriorates, the financial institution should immediately be informed of the situation. The bank has the right to call the loan any time that the borrower is not in compliance with a loan provision, such as a lower current ratio (or other ratio) than the loan agreement requires. Banks will work with borrowers to adjust expectations as required, but expect to be notified of any material change in business activity.

## Control of Banking Records

The company should assign the task of updating banking records to a specific manager. Finance staff is often lax in performing this duty. It was previously noted that covenants in loan agreements must be constantly monitored for compliance. Here are other examples:

- Companies often fail to delete approved signatures from their bank's records, even though an employee may have long departed the company.
- Lockbox requirements may change, such as new company names or the preferred processing of nonstandard items (such as foreign currency checks), but no one informs the bank.
- Controls may be weak on the use of confidential data and access codes from remote locations. Your financial managers may be entering or downloading this information from home or a branch office, but are there any logs or other controls to protect the company?

It is important to keep such information up-to-date and secure, to protect the company *and* the bank.

## Periodic Relationship Reviews

Given the partnership orientation of banks and companies, there has been a growing trend toward periodic relationship reviews. There are several objectives of the review:

- Ensure that the relationship is profitable to the bank while providing added value to the company.
- Develop a consultative attitude between the bank and the company to improve current processes and increase efficiencies.

- Deliver quality customer service and the timely implementation of new products and services.
- Understand the future requirements of the company.

The review is often supported by a document discussing the expectations of each party during the coming period, usually one year, and supported by specific calendar targets. A typical annual review cycle might consist of the following:

- **First quarter**: Formal meeting of company management and bank officers to:
  - Discuss the strategic and financial results for the previous year.
  - Outline the next year's goals and objectives.
  - Schedule the implementation of new initiatives.
- **Second quarter**: Calling by the bank's relationship manager to:
  - Update the company on service and technology initiatives.
  - Introduce product specialists.
- **Third quarter**: Informal meeting of company management and bank officers to:
  - Review the status of the year's goals.
  - Determine which initiatives to emphasize to meet critical objectives.
- **Fourth quarter**: Senior-level social event to:
  - Discuss current year.
  - Plan for the next year and beyond.

At each step in the cycle, adjustments can be made by either party to meet the requirements of the "partnership" between the company and the bank.

 ## SUMMARY

The recent credit crisis and changes in the regulation of financial institutions have altered the competitive landscape and how banks treat their customers. There are now fewer banks and more bank products, resulting in the development of relationship management as a comprehensive approach to the bank–corporate partnership, including all of the credit and noncredit services offered by financial institutions. Banking involves situations where multiple collection and disbursement accounts exist and cash must be mobilized into and funded from a main bank account. A company must be vigilant in managing its banking relationship(s) to ensure a continuing partnership and access to credit.

 **NOTES**

1. Interstate banking prohibitions were discussed in Chapter 2. There were some exceptions to this prohibition. For example, Bank of America was "grandfathered" into business activities in several western states. The Federal Reserve occasionally would permit an exception when a bank was in danger of failing. For example, Citibank was able to enter Illinois when a local Chicago-based financial institution failed and the Fed asked for Citi's help to prevent losses to depositors and borrowers.
2. The Glass-Steagall Act of 1933 separated commercial and investment banking; this law was repealed by the Gramm-Leach-Bliley Act of 1999. As with interstate banking (see the previous footnote), exceptions to this prohibition occurred. For example, Merrill Lynch began offering a comprehensive retail financial services product—the CMA account—in 1977.
3. U.S. Federal Deposit Insurance Corporation, *The FDIC Quarterly Banking Profile, Historical Statistics on Banking*, annual, www2.fdic.gov/qbp; *Statistics on Banking*, 2012), www2.fdic.gov/SDI/SOB.
4. Noncredit services are all of the for-fee products offered to corporate customers, including cash management, trust, shareholder services, custody, trade finance, foreign exchange, and derivative instruments.
5. In extending credit, banks must allocate scarce capital to support the loan. The Basel 2 (and proposed Basel 3) accords require that all lending be supported by senior debt and equity with risk weights for certain types of credit risk. The standard risk weight categories are 0 percent for short-term government bonds, 20 percent for exposures to developed country banks, 50 percent for residential mortgages, and 100 percent weighting on unsecured commercial loans. The minimum capital requirement (the percentage of risk-weighted assets to be held as capital) is 8 percent. For additional information, see www .bis.org.
6. The term *concentration bank* was previously used to refer to a company's principal bank(s). This term has largely disappeared due to the deregulation that permits full interstate banking in the United States.
7. These banks include Citibank, JPMorgan Chase, Bank of America, and Wells Fargo. Their market coverage is extensive but not complete. For example, Wells Fargo does not have locations in New England or the lower Midwest.
8. A transit routing number (or American Banking Association [ABA] number) is the nine-digit MICR-line number found at the bottom of a check. It is used to route a check to the drawee bank, and essentially constitutes an address.

9. ERISA establishes standards for pension plans in industry. The law was enacted to protect the interests of employee benefit plan participants and their beneficiaries through the disclosure to them of information concerning the plan; the establishment of standards of conduct for plan fiduciaries; and provisions for access to the federal courts.

10. *Gold Sheets* are published by Thomson Reuters LPC for various regions and market segments. For additional information, see www.loanpricing.com/products.

# Selecting Noncredit Banking Services

B EFORE THE GREAT RECESSION that began in 2008, companies often used a competitive bidding process to select noncredit banking and vendor services necessary for the management of working capital. This situation has changed as banks have rationed credit to corporate borrowers while expecting that noncredit service business would be included in any banking package. While it is illegal to "tie" banking credit and noncredit services, bankers can strongly "suggest" combining these activities.

At some point, the situation may revert to the earlier practice of competitive bidding. The process starts with a request for proposal (RFP) sent by the company to banks or vendors. Note that several reputable vendors provide the services previously only available from banks. In this discussion, the term *bank* is meant to include vendors.

# THE REQUEST FOR PROPOSAL

An initial step used by many companies is to issue a request-for-information (RFI) letter to candidate service providers. The RFI is used to determine which banks are qualified and interested in providing banking services. A list of potential bank bidders can be developed from previous calling efforts; contacts at conferences and meetings; and referrals from accountants, attorneys, and business colleagues. The responses to the RFI are used to select the banks to be included in the request-for-proposal process.

Companies began using RFPs in the 1980s to formalize purchasing decisions that had become too casual. Existing bank relationships tended to be given extensions of old business and any new opportunities under consideration without a formal bidding process. See Exhibit A5.1 for a list of available banking RFPs.

## Issues Covered in RFPs

The request for proposal (RFP) is usually organized as lists of questions pertaining to general banking concerns and to specific attributes relating to each service. Specific conditions for contracting for services are included. For example, what are the logistics of the bidding process? Who is authorized to speak for the bank and the company? Will the bids be treated with confidentiality?

General issues pertain to any noncredit service being considered, and apply to the bank's financial stability and creditworthiness, approach to management of the organization for and delivery of services, quality control, and similar issues. This is the section of the RFP where references should be requested.

**EXHIBIT A5.1**　RFP Templates for Banking Service

| | |
|---|---|
| 401K plan bundled provider | Paycard (payroll through ATM cards) |
| Automated clearinghouse (ACH) | Purchasing card services |
| Controlled disbursing | Remote deposit services |
| Custody services | Retail lockbox |
| Depository services | Short-term investment management |
| Disbursement (payables) outsourcing | Treasury technology |
| E-banking and information reporting | Wholesale lockbox |
| Global treasury services | Wire transfer |
| Merchant card services | |

*Source:* www.afponline.org/pub/res/brm/rfp/rfp.html.

In this regard, it is useful to require names of companies in the same industry that are of equivalent size.

## Specific Service Issues

The issues pertaining to each noncredit service will vary by product. Some examples follow in Exhibit A5.2.

## Review of Pricing

We defined the account analysis and reviewed the earning credit rate in Chapter 4. In this appendix, we examine how companies are charged for noncredit services. The lower portion of the account analysis will vary by

**EXHIBIT A5.2**   Examples of Bank RFP Questions on Noncredit Services

| | |
|---|---|
| Wholesale Lockbox | List the bank's schedule for post office pickups of wholesale lockbox mail for weekdays, weekends, and holidays. |
| | Does the bank have a unique five-digit zip code assigned exclusively for receipt of wholesale lockbox items? |
| | Who performs the fine sort per box number, the bank or the post office? If the bank sorts the lockbox mail, describe the mail sorting operation. Include manual and automated handling, ability to read bar codes, and peak volume capabilities. |
| Controlled Disbursement | What is the published time at which customers are notified of their daily controlled disbursement clearings? How many notifications of clearings are made each day? |
| | If more than one notification is made, what percentage of the dollars and items was included in each notification? |
| | What are the accepted procedures that are used to fund the debit from each day's clearings? |
| ACH | What procedures are used to verify accurate and secure receipt of data transmissions through a secure Internet server? |
| | Can the bank automatically redeposit items returned for insufficient or uncollected funds? When items are redeposited, are any entries posted to the customer's account? |
| | What are the hardware and software requirements for PC-based services? Does the application support use of a LAN (local area network) or cloud computing? Will assistance with software installation be provided? |

bank; an illustrative configuration is shown in Exhibit A5.3. It is useful to calculate the complete cost of each noncredit service and to determine if any unusual or incorrect fees are being charged. For a directory of more than 200 bank services and their standard codes, see www.afponline.org/pub/sc/srvc.html.

Although pricing has long been the consideration in selecting a domestic cash management bank, recent experience has seen a decline in its importance and a rise in the following factors.

**EXHIBIT A5.3**    Bank Account Analysis: Illustrative Noncredit Service Presentation

| Service | Reference | Quantity | Unit Price | Price Extension |
|---|---|---|---|---|
| Account maintenance | 1 | 2 | $25.00 | $  50 |
| Deposits—unencoded | 2A | 140 | $ 0.18 | $  25 |
| Deposits—encoded | 2B | 600 | $ 0.12 | $  72 |
| Returned items | 3 | 50 | $10.00 | $ 500 |
| Checks paid | 4 | 400 | $ 0.15 | $  60 |
| ACH debits/credits | 5 | 100 | $ 0.13 | $  13 |
| Fedwires | 6 | 4 | $20.00 | $  80 |
| Total charges | 7 | | | $ 800 |
| Net due for services | 8 | | | $425* |

References
1. *Account maintenance* is the fixed charge assessed to cover the bank's overhead costs associated with a DDA.
2. *Deposits* are checks presented for deposit. *Unencoded* checks do not have the dollar amount encoded in the MICR line; *encoded* checks have been imprinted by the corporate depositor with the dollar amount using an encoding machine. Encoded checks usually have a lower unit price.
3. *Returned items* are checks not honored by the drawee bank, either due to insufficient funds or a stopped payment by the maker.
4. *Checks paid* are disbursements written against the account.
5. *ACH debits/credits* are automated clearinghouse debits and credits to the account.
6. *Fedwires* are same-day electronic transfers of funds through the Federal Reserve system.
7. *Total charges* are the sum of the price extensions for all cash management services.
8. *Net due for services* is the difference between total charges and the ECR allowance based on the balances in the account.

*Based on the Exhibit 4.4 calculation of an ECR allowance of $375, which has been deducted from Total Charges.

- **Product cycle.** Because many bank products are in the mature phase of the product cycle, there is minimal variation in the price charged by most banks. Furthermore, information on pricing is published in the *Phoenix-Hecht Blue Book of Pricing* (www.phoenixhecht.com), making pricing data fairly widely available to all interested parties.
- **Unbundling.** Banks have unbundled pricing for noncredit services, making line-by-line comparisons meaningless. Some banks charge for each specific service, while others include the service in the fee for the underlying product. For example, controlled disbursing may include positive pay, or it may be priced separately.

**Quality.** It is generally recognized that any quality or service problems relating to a specific bank product can cost many times the price per unit of the service. As a result, the savings of a few cents per item is not important when compared to the cost to resolve an error, a communication or transmission problem, or other bank issues.

##  RFP EVALUATION

Because of the sheer number of potential questions and answers in a set of proposals, it is very difficult to simply read through and make any sense of the material. For this reason, one technique that has been helpful is to organize each set of responses into a table, listing the bank names in the columns and the important answers in the rows.

It is necessary to array the responses for each question with the intention of assigning points based on a template of average answers. For example, despite the maturity of the lockbox product, there are often significant differences in the responses. The application of points to these RFP answers allows for the objective ranking of each bank.

### Weighted Scoring of Proposals

The final step in evaluating the banks' proposals is to assign weights to each response based on the perceived importance of the question. The total weight should add to 100 percent, but any individual question can have a weighting ranging from a value of 0 percent to as much as 15 or 20 percent. The weights are based on the company's perception of the importance of each question.

An illustrative weighted scoring for lockbox services is provided in Exhibit A5.4 for four banks. The responses are displayed as unweighted, that

**EXHIBIT A5.4** Evaluation Score Sheet for Lockbox Services

| | Weight (%) | Unweighted Scores | | | | Weighted Scores | | | |
|---|---|---|---|---|---|---|---|---|---|
| | | Bank A | Bank B | Bank C | Bank D | Bank A | Bank B | Bank C | Bank D |
| Unique zip code | 8 | 2 | 0.5 | 2 | 3 | 16 | 4 | 16 | 24 |
| Number of mail pickups at post office | 12 | 2 | 1 | 2.5 | 2.5 | 24 | 12 | 30 | 30 |
| Quality assurance program | 22 | 2.5 | 2 | 1 | 3 | 55 | 44 | 22 | 66 |
| Customer service | 20 | 3 | 2 | 2 | 1.5 | 60 | 40 | 40 | 30 |
| Error rate per 10,000 transactions | 14 | 2.5 | 1.5 | 1.5 | 3 | 35 | 21 | 21 | 42 |
| Availability assignment | 8 | 3 | 2 | 2.5 | 3 | 24 | 16 | 20 | 24 |
| Volume for price discount | 8 | 3 | 1 | 0 | 2.5 | 24 | 8 | 0 | 20 |
| Period of price guarantee | 8 | 2.5 | 2 | 3 | 2 | 20 | 16 | 24 | 16 |
| Total weighted points | 100 | | | | | 258 | 161 | 173 | 252 |

is the raw point assignments; and weighted, with the value specified for each response applied to the point assignment. The final results show Bank A with 258 points and Bank D with 252 points, both of which are significantly better than Banks B and C.

These scores allow the company to consider whether the expected results are consistent with the analysis, or if some adjustment in the weightings is necessary. Should the results stand, the company can visit the two finalists to ask difficult questions, meet the client team assigned by each bank, and develop a sense that the bank wants to be a long-term partner. Contact all references and probe to see if the bank has met its credit and noncredit obligations with its other clients. The scores can also be used to inform the banks that were not awarded the business why they lost, to show that the analysis was objective.

## Managing Banking Relationships

Once the decision has been made, the next activity is to review the contracts the bank(s) will require as an essential part of the relationship. Each service is governed by agreements that address the various requirements of each party to protect both the bank and the company in the event of a dispute. The contracts have been drafted by the bank's attorneys, and are based on long-standing precedent as established in the federal banking statutes and the Uniform Commercial Code (UCC) adopted by all states.

Service level agreements cover terms of service for each noncredit product, and will vary depending on specific operating issues. Banks specify standard processing arrangements for the price that is quoted; any variation is considered as an exception, resulting in additional charges. Typical concerns in service agreements include acceptable and unacceptable payee names on checks for a lockbox; names of initiators and approvers for wire transfers; approved account signatories; and approved users and access restrictions for treasury information systems.

The bank requires these documents to instruct it on how to handle any transactions that are initiated, and to protect itself in the event of an error or an attempted fraud. Furthermore, the bank will require its customers to indemnify and hold it harmless from and against any liability, loss, or costs arising from each service provided.

# CHAPTER SIX

# Accounts Receivable and Working Capital Issues

This chapter covers these topics:

- Consideration of appropriate policies for receivables management.
- Evaluation of the impact of float on receivables.
- Understanding of how to use ratios and aging schedules in managing receivables.
- Learning about specific receivables issues, including sales financing and credit reporting.
- Evaluations of terms of sale, invoicing practices, and factoring in receivables decisions.

OUR DISCUSSION SO FAR has focused on cash as the first issue to address in managing working capital. This chapter discusses accounts receivable while Chapter 7 reviews inventory, the two significant current asset accounts besides cash. Finally, in Chapter 8 we review accounts payable, the significant working capital current liability.

Managing receivables would appear to be a relatively simple matter: Send out a bill and get paid. If payment is not made, plead, threaten, or—when all else fails—sue! However, the float consequences of poor receivables management are potentially so devastating that this should be a high priority for a company. With cash, we measured float improvement in days. With receivables, it is often measured in weeks.

 ## ELEMENTS OF RECEIVABLES MANAGEMENT

There are various important elements in establishing a program to manage accounts receivables, including establishing policies and organizing a business for the implementation of these policies, both of which are discussed in this section. We will then explain how to monitor results. Many companies have some components of this receivables program. However, the typical situation is that there has been little review or change to long-established procedures, and this inattention might not be a major focus given the current difficult business climate.

### Developing Receivables Policies

Policies on receivables formalize decisions on the extension of credit to customers. Rules should be established on various issues:

- How much credit will be granted to specific groups of customers?
- What are the credit terms that will be extended? That is, how many days will be the standard for payment of invoices or statements?
- Will discounts—called **cash discounts**—be granted for early payment? Will other types of discounts be offered?
- How will the company pursue slow and no payers? What mechanisms will be used, and what will trigger each action?
- What forms of financing will be used to assist our customers in making purchasing decisions?
- Should we use a financial intermediary to lend to us on our receivables while we await payment in a process called asset-based lending? Should we sell our receivables—called factoring?
- Are we monitoring our company's salespeople to prevent their making unauthorized credit promises to customers in order to generate sales?
- Should we use the services of a debt collection agency?

Written policies ensure consistency in decision making and avoid the possibility of discrimination against certain customers. In situations where preferential treatment is extended, the policy should specify the conditions for such treatment. These conditions could occur when a business relationship has existed for five or more years, or when a customer is consistently current on its payments.

Similarly, when punitive treatment is indicated, there should be a policy. For example, a customer consistently late in paying could be disciplined by requiring some cash in advance or by executing a **lien** (a legal claim to the property) on certain assets such as the inventory or equipment that was delivered.[1]

Furthermore, policies establish required practice for all parties that cannot be modified except by senior management. This is important when a customer or a prospect asks for special terms, such as a longer time to pay or a smaller down payment. Any violation should be considered as a serious breach of behavior triggering appropriate penalties.

## Getting to Know You—Getting to Know Your Company![2]

Financial managers typically do not go on customer calls with their salespeople. As a result, it is impossible to have any idea of what they may be promising to win business. For example, are they offering pricing concessions, lenient credit terms, or a delay in payment? Salespeople are usually compensated by commission or a salary and a bonus for superior performance. Commissions and superior performance are driven by sales and not by concern for profits. Without adequate supervision, sales could be occurring at the expense of financial returns.

Incidentally, manufacturing often responds to the same motivation— production at the expense of efficiency and profitability. Unfortunately, these functional areas typically do not coordinate their decisions except at the level of the company president, and real turf wars can inhibit cooperation and appropriate procedure. Managers should leave the "friendly confines" of the finance office and go on a few sales calls or tour the factory floor. They may be surprised at what really goes on!

 **FLOAT OPPORTUNITIES IN MANAGING RECEIVABLES**

Does a company have a receivables manager? Probably not, because most businesses divide that responsibility among each of the parts of the collections section of the working capital timeline that affect receivables: sales (in marketing), credit and collections (also in marketing), invoice generation (probably in information technology), cash receipt (in finance), and cash application (in accounting). Although this traditional approach is acceptable, it does not deal with the interrelationship of the various functions to accomplish optimal efficiency.

Here's an example: An electronics company bills $500 million per year in mailed invoices prepared through two information systems. Credit terms are "net 30," that is, payments are considered late if received more than 30 days after the invoice is received by the customer. Consistent with industry practice, no cash discounts are offered.

Weekly system runs print invoices an average of 15 days after the sale date. The due date for payment is 30 days after the target date for the customer to receive the invoice (the customer invoice receive date). Given typical mail times in the geographic areas served by the company, customers receive these invoices approximately 12 days prior to the due date. The timeline sequence for a typical transaction involving these events is as follows:

- Sale of product: April 1
- Target issuance of invoice: As soon as possible after April 1; assume April 6
- Target customer receipt of invoice: April 9
- Actual issuance of invoice: April 15
- Actual customer receipt of invoice: April 18
- Target date to receive payment: May 6
- Actual due date: May 28

## Calculating Receivables Float

The slippage or float lost between the target and actual due dates is 22 days. The value of the lost days, at an assumed 10 percent cost of capital, is calculated as $500 million × 22 lost days ÷ 360 calendar days × 10 percent cost of capital = $3.1 million. Research determined that the delay in invoicing was caused primarily by various scheduling issues within the information technology function, with invoicing cycles run at certain weekly intervals at the convenience of that department.

Once senior management became aware of the potential value of the lost float, it was a relatively simple matter to mandate the rescheduling of processing runs. Although some customers did notice the change in the timing of their monthly invoices and held checks until the usual release date, many paid once the bill was approved.

The various steps in the receivables cycle result in a loss of more than three weeks and $3 million a year, yet no one function is responsible. The rational

CEO would demand that this situation be fixed, but who would he or she turn to? Unfortunately, the answer is a group of managers (probably vice presidents), each of whom could blame the others. What is needed is a dedicated senior manager (or committee) who can analyze the situation and initiate whatever changes are required, from earlier assembly of invoice data through the issuance of invoices.

The receivables manager/committee would also be responsible for specific activities that assist marketing, such as sales financing and cash or trade discounts; that trigger receivables, including invoicing; and that provide working capital to the company as it awaits payment, such as factoring. In the absence of a receivables manager, a company could establish a committee or task force on receivables with the power to examine and decide on possible changes in procedures.

 ## RECEIVABLES CYCLE MONITORING: RATIOS

In some instances, it is relatively easy to determine if a company is attaining acceptable results. For example, did we eliminate the 22 days of float for the electronics company? We can develop logs of invoice dates and mailings, and determine if all of the appropriate functions are cooperating. In other cases we will need to manage our company against the performance of others in our industry to attempt to meet or beat our peers. There are two types of analyses that are useful in this monitoring effort, and we review these next.

### Receivables Ratio Analysis

Ratios were discussed in Chapter 2 using receivables turnover (calculated as Credit sales ÷ Receivables) and a variation of that ratio, average collection period (calculated as 360 days ÷ Receivables turnover). In comparing ratios, we noted that we would measure the company's result to that of its industry using the interquartile range as normal. Our calculation for receivables turnover was 5.5 times and 66 days for average collection period.

Now let's examine an actual set of ratios using a standard source; as an example, we'll use plastics manufacturing (NAICS 326121–22).[3] As reported by RMA for 2008–2009, receivables turnover (in turns) was 11 (3rd quartile), 9 (median), and 7 (1st quartile); average collection period (in days) was 32, 43, and 55. This means that results outside of the 11 to 7 turns or the 32 to 55 days should be reviewed for their inadequate performance.

## Interpretation of Receivables Ratios

Certainly our results fall well outside of that range (at 5.5 turns and 66 days), but are they due to insufficient sales (the numerator) or poor receivables management (the denominator)? Because receivables directly result from sales, the culprit is certainly receivables management. But is the problem throughout receivables, or is it caused by a small subgroup, likely the slow and no-paying group of customers?

It should be noted that for most ratios we would have to carefully analyze every ratio among the significant ratios to draw firm conclusions about the source of a problem. For example, a poor current ratio can result from problems with current assets, current liabilities, or both. With receivables, summarized balance sheet data may mask collection problems with certain of our customers. The solution is to review an aging schedule.

##  RECEIVABLES CYCLE MONITORING: THE AGING SCHEDULE

The ratios that we examined are aggregated numbers—that is, they include customers who are current in their remittances (whether early or on time) and those who are delinquent (whether slow, very slow, or not paying at all). An **aging schedule** is a useful method to determine the extent of each of these practices, and follows the expectation that the longer a bill in unpaid, the less likely it will ever be paid.

The procedure is relatively simple:

1. Sort accounts receivable by age, such as in groupings of months unpaid.
2. Total the sorted groups.
3. Multiply the totals by a factor representing the likelihood of payment, based on previous experience.

Assume that there are five major customers with a recent payment history, as shown in Exhibit 6.1. The application of the expectation (probability) of payment calculation is in Exhibit 6.2.

## Interpretation of the Aging Schedule

The result is an aging schedule that provides a reasonable estimate of doubtful accounts, which are subtracted from accounts receivable on the balance

**EXHIBIT 6.1**   Receivables Aging by Customer

| Days Outstanding | 0–30 Days | 31–60 Days | 61–120 Days | 121–182 Days | Over 6 Months | Receivables Balance |
|---|---|---|---|---|---|---|
| Anchovy Inc. | $200,000 | $200,000 | | | | $400,000 |
| Cheese Brothers | | | | | $100,000 | 100,000 |
| Onion Company | | | $150,000 | $150,000 | | 300,000 |
| Pepperoni Group | 400,000 | | | | | 400,000 |
| Sausage Ltd. | 300,000 | 200,000 | 100,000 | | 50,000 | 650,000 |
| Total | $900,000 | $400,000 | $250,000 | $150,000 | $150,000 | $1,850,000 |

sheet to arrive at a net figure. In addition, payment patterns are revealed by customers and, when compared against previous results (say from last month), by aging group to show improving or deteriorating experience.

For example, the $150,000 in the 121 to 182 days group is about 8 percent of all receivables. If the previous report showed that group at 6 percent, we'd assume that the credit and collection manager was becoming less aggressive about pursuing overdues. And if similar statistics are found elsewhere in the aging schedules, that could be the source of the poor ratio performance.

Aging helps to determine if a company's credit analysis is being properly handled, or if exceptions have become too frequent. A credit report (to be discussed later in this chapter) may suggest that a good customer is becoming slow in paying others, but the marketing manager has not noticed a fall in its credit rating or may want to help the customer and not lose sales. However, a company may be shipping to a customer who will never pay if its business

**EXHIBIT 6.2**   Receivables Aging by Group with Estimated Doubtful Accounts

| | Total in Each Aging Group | Percentage Doubtful* | Total Doubtful in $ |
|---|---|---|---|
| 0–30 Days | $900,000 | 1.5% | $ 13,500 |
| 31–60 Days | $400,000 | 4.0% | 16,000 |
| 61–120 Days | $250,000 | 12.0% | 30,000 |
| 121–182 Days | $150,000 | 25.0% | 37,500 |
| Over 6 Months | $150,000 | 50.0% | 75,000 |
| Total Doubtful (in $) | | | $172,000 |

*Based on previous accounts receivable experience.

situation has deteriorated.[4] Finally, aging identifies specific problems that are difficult to see in aggregated ratios.

##  SALES FINANCING

**Sales financing** assists customers that may require credit assistance or long payment terms in their purchase activity—with an interest charge assessed, particularly when the product involves a considerable cash outlay.[5] In those situations, sales financing (or leasing) programs, more than pricing or product features, can determine success or failure in making the sale.

Financial managers should be involved in sales financing in the development of pricing models based on timing of payment, anticipated charges (such as late payment fees), and the spread earned on finance charges over the cost of capital. Transaction specifics include the credit terms and interest charges offered to customers, and depend on customer creditworthiness, the life of the asset, and industry experience with financing programs.

Although maintaining the overhead of an internal sales financing program can be a significant expense, a major benefit is the ability to directly control response time and "deal" particulars for each transaction considered. Certain customers may be especially desirable given their business potential or status, justifying a coordinated sales financing effort. Other customers may be repeat business and the level of effort may be less demanding.

### Outsourcing Sales Financing

If this is too difficult, the sales financing process can be outsourced to a finance company or other lender in three possible formats:

1. Full recourse sales financing (allowing lowest interest rates), with the lender becoming the source of funds and offering advice on customer creditworthiness.
2. Limited liability or ultimate-net-loss, allowing a limitation on the extent of the recourse, with the seller and lender each absorbing some credit risk.
3. No risk, with the lender independently determining the creditworthiness of the customer.

When lenders assume some or all of the risk, approvals can be delayed up to a few weeks, depending on the information provided by the customer and on his or her credit rating.

While an outsourcing program avoids certain credit group and legal overhead, customer service could be adversely affected. Certain lenders focus on transaction activity, and may not understand the importance of service to the customers of the selling company. Problems might arise when questions are directed to the lender regarding such matters as the logistics and crediting of payments.

 ## CREDIT REPORTING

Credit information services provide numerical grades of the creditworthiness of companies based on experience reported by vendors and other parties in a business relationship. In making credit sales to a company, the goal is to find evidence of stability, creditworthiness, and the capacity to meet its obligations. Credit report grades are based on the time to pay and amount of recent transactions, as supported by financial statements, public records, liens, lawsuits, number of years in business, and management.

The primary providers of this service are Dun & Bradstreet (D&B), Experian, TransUnion, and Equifax, with reports available on businesses in North America, Europe, and selected Asian countries. Associated marketing analytics include data on customer requirements and typical purchase activity. The credit reporting industry is a huge, sophisticated business; for example, Equifax had revenues in 2010 of nearly $2 billion.

### Reporting on Business Creditworthiness

Reporting data include a complete dossier on a company's credit and business history, and a credit score based on a complex proprietary statistical model. While the score simplifies the credit decision down to a single number, it is often too ambiguous to enable a simple "sell or don't sell" decision. In our illustration (Exhibit 6.3), the score is 55 (medium risk), making the "credit or no credit" decision a judgment call. However, the assemblage of data provided could not be accomplished by any company at any price, so many businesses subscribe to and use these services. Individual reports typically cost about $40, and subscriptions start at about $50 a month.

### Fixing a Company's Credit Score

In Chapter 4 we discussed various sources of credit for a company. This chapter discusses customer credit scores. Just as a finance manager is

**EXHIBIT 6.3**    Business Credit Report

| Summary of Business Activity | |
| --- | --- |
| Key Personnel | Years in Business |
| SIC Code/Description | Total Employees |
| Business Type | Sales |
| Experian File Established | Filing Data Provided by SOURCE |
| Experian Years on File | Date of Incorporation |

| Recent Credit History (DBT = remittances paid in days beyond terms) | |
| --- | --- |
| Current DBT | Business Inquiries |
| Predicted DBT (for next period) | Highest 6-Month Balance |
| Average Industry DBT | Current Total Account Balance |
| Payment Trend Indicator | Highest Credit Amount Extended |
| Lowest 6-Month Balance | Median Credit Amount Extended |

| Credit Score |
| --- |
| 55 (Medium Risk)—A credit score predicts payment behavior, with high risk (approaching 100) indicating that there is a significant possibility of delinquent payment and low risk (approaching 0), meaning that there is a good probability of on-time payment. |

| Credit Trend Charts (changes in payment history over time) |
| --- |
| Monthly and quarterly payment trends |
| Continuous, newly reported and combined payment trends |
| Trade payment experiences by vendor category |
| Actions on collection disputes including judgments, by date and amount |
| Fixed debt obligations (such as leases) |

*Note:* These credit and business history categories are similar in all credit reporting companies.

vitally concerned about the credit scores of customers, he or she should pay attention to the credit scores of his or her company. Here are several recommended steps:

- Check the credit report of the business regularly and verify that the information in it is accurate and up to date.
- Establish credit with businesses that report trades. Not all business creditors report their trade information, so inquiries will have to be made of vendor practices.
- Pay creditors on time; past payment behavior with vendors plays a major role in calculating a business credit score.

- Remember that credit scoring uses several variables in its calculation, and none of the mathematics is disclosed. The finance manager should try to manage everything, but most particularly outstanding balances; payment habits; the extent of credit used; actions against a company for collection; and demographics such as years on file, NAICS codes,[6] and business size.

##  TERMS OF SALE

Vendors normally follow industry practice in establishing terms of sale, which is the length of time allowed before payment is expected. Terms are stated as "net" and the number of days, usually beginning on the date of the receipt of the invoice or statement, as in "net 30" or "n30." Terms follow the normal selling cycle of a business, so companies that require about 60 days to sell goods would receive terms of "net 60."

### Cash Discount Basics

Although many texts discuss cash discounts, actual experience today is that only about 10 percent of vendors offer such price reductions to their customers. The discount is specified as the amount of the discount and the last date on which the discount is offered. The cash discount "2/10" means that 2 percent may be deducted from the invoiced amount if the payment is received no later than 10 days after the bill is received. A full set of commonly used terms is "2/10, n30." Terms are printed near the top of the invoice or statement.

The selling company and its customer should be aware of the value of the cash discount in order to make appropriate decisions. Terms of "2/10, net 30" calculate to 36 percent of value annually, determined as follows:

- Calculate the "nondiscount" days in the credit cycle; e.g., 30 days less 10 days = 20 days.
- Divide the result into 360 days; e.g., 360 days ÷ 20 days = 18 annual payment cycles.
- Multiply the number of cycles times the cash discount; e.g., 18 cycles times the 2 percent cash discount = 36 percent,[7] which is the annual value of the discount.
- Compare the annual discount to the cost of capital; e.g., 36 percent (the value of the discount) vs. 10 percent (the cost of capital we've used throughout this book).
- If the discount exceeds the cost of capital, accept. Otherwise, reject.

### Cash Discount Decision Factors

In this situation, we would take the discount if we were customers, as it is more than 3½ times the cost of capital. On the other hand, the selling company possibly should not offer such a generous incentive, as its financial cost is likely far greater than any sales benefit. Another consideration is that a customer regularly taking the discount and then passing it might be suspect to the vendor, who might assume that the customer's financial situation has deteriorated.

Cash discounts create a dilemma for companies when their customers take the discount but pay after the discount period. Should the customer be billed for the discount or should the policy infraction be ignored? If this is ignored once, the customer will simply repeat its action with each invoice. If the customer is billed for the discount, bad feelings could result.

### Other Discounts

The most common types of discounts offered to induce customer sales are noted in Exhibit 6.4. However, none of these improve working capital management, and, in fact, may result in reduced cash collections.

 ## INVOICE GENERATION

Invoice generation is usually a shared responsibility of sales, receivables, and information technology, with critical decisions on invoice design and the timing of the billing cycle often made at the convenience of systems managers. Invoice runs may be scheduled when time is available in the processing cycle without regard to the optimal timing of the printing and mailing process.

### Invoice Design

Simplifying the invoice or statement eliminates unnecessary verbiage and multiple addresses. A bill should be easy to read and pay, with a clean look. A single return address forces the customer to mail payments to the proper address rather than to a location that may delay processing. (One company had four addresses on each bill—the home office, the regional office, the office of the sales representative, and the lockbox address! Little wonder that many items were sent to the incorrect location.)

Invoice design may involve developing formats readable by automated equipment, including those in MICR and OCR fonts.[8] MICR and OCR characters

**EXHIBIT 6.4**  Discounts Other than Cash Discounts

There are various types of discounts offered to motivate customer purchasing. The two most important discounts (other than cash) for business-to-business transactions are those based on trade and on quantity (volume).

1. *Trade discounts.* These are payments to wholesalers, retailers, and other members of a marketing channel for performing a marketing function. For example, a trade discount 18/10/4 would indicate a 18% discount for warehousing the product, a further 10% discount for shipping the product, and an additional 4% discount for stocking the shelves. Trade discounts are most frequent in industries where retailers hold the majority of the power in the distribution channel.
2. *Quantity discounts.* These are price reductions given for large purchases. The rationale is to obtain economies of scale and pass some of these savings on to the customer. In some industries, buyer groups and cooperatives have formed to take advantage of these discounts. The two types of quantity discounts are:
   ▪ *Cumulative quantity discounts:* based on purchases over time
   ▪ *Noncumulative quantity discounts:* based on the quantity of a single order

are printed in special ink at designated positions on checks and remittance documents, usually at the bottom of the page.

## Invoice and Statement Timing

Research has been conducted over the past decades to examine alternative invoice or statement mailing dates and the resulting payment "receive" date for both corporate and retail payments. For most industries, the optimal time for the customer to receive a monthly invoice or statement is 25 days prior to the due date for receipt of funds by the date due.

However, many companies are sending bills 10 to 15 days later than optimal, say two weeks prior to the due date, with the result that their days' sales *outstanding* (DSO) is longer than average for their industry. Equivalent relationships hold for industries billing on cycles other than monthly.

There are several factors that drive this situation:

▪ The invoice or statement must be received at the correct location (see the previous section on "Invoice Design") and forwarded to a payables clerk.
▪ The payables clerk must verify that the invoice or statement is correct. Although we defer discussion of the payables cycle to Chapter 8, it is sufficient to note that time is required to gather the necessary purchase order, receiving report, and other documents or approvals.

- Any disputes must be manually entered and deducted from the net payment.
- The approved invoice or statement must enter the disbursement cycle, which runs only once or twice a week in many companies.

The total time that has elapsed can be longer than two weeks. By the time the check is received and the collected funds are credited, three weeks may elapse, meaning effective payment is one week later than the due date.

### Invoices versus Statements

Some companies issue both invoices and monthly statements (or other types of bills). Unless requested by customers, delivering multiple types of bills can confuse accounts payable clerks, particularly when there is a disagreement in the documents, and may provide an excuse for delaying remittances. Choose one of these forms of billing, probably basing the decision on industry practice and customer preference, and drop the other type.

##  ASSET-BASED FINANCING

Asset-based financing (ABF) became an important supplement to normal bank credit during the credit crisis that began in 2008. It is currently estimated that $750 billion of such lending is outstanding in the United States. Participants include large banks, regional and smaller banks, and commercial finance companies. The two primary assets used in these programs are receivables, discussed in this section, and inventory, discussed in Chapter 7.

Lenders need to understand the collateral at stake and the characteristics of the industry. ABF bankers are in contact with their clients nearly every day and many of them spend time in the field checking up on their clients and their collateral. Cooperation by information technology is essential in feeding data on receivables (or inventory) to lenders so that precise data are available on whether credit sales have been paid (and which items have been sold).

### Receivables Factoring

**Factoring** involves the sale of accounts receivable.[9] By selling invoices for future payment, cash is generated sooner than waiting to collect cash from customers. The factor that purchases a company's receivables takes title to the invoices and directs that payment be made to a post office box (usually a lockbox) when due. Factoring is expensive, because the cash paid for a receivable is discounted by about 5 percent.

**EXHIBIT 6.5**   Representative Factoring
Organizations

| | |
|---|---|
| Aquent | Marquette Financial |
| Barclays | Natixis |
| BB&T Corporation | Wells Fargo Trade Capital |
| CIT Group | |

Aging is important in receivables financing, as the older the account, the less value it has. For example, lenders may lend 80 percent of the face value for outstandings less than 45 days old but only 50 percent on older receivables. A monthly interest rate on receivables is calculated by applying a daily percentage rate to the receivables outstanding each day.

As in sales financing, a possible consideration in factoring is the harm to customer relations, as any collection actions taken may endanger an ongoing business relationship with customers. There may be situations where a company would compromise a debt, extend payment deadlines to a preferred customer, or employ a more lenient collection approach for a specific customer. A factor has little interest in preserving a future relationship with the debtor. See Exhibit 6.5 for a list of factors.

 **DEBT COLLECTION AGENCIES**

A **debt collection agency** pursues payments on unpaid debts owed by individuals or businesses. Few companies operate their own debt collection activities for accounts older than about 90 days. In that situation, a third-party collector is recommended to pursue no-pay customers. These firms typically accept assignments on a contingency fee basis, and receive a fee—typically 15 percent—only on amounts received. See Exhibit 6.6 for a list of leading debt collection companies.

**EXHIBIT 6.6**   Representative Debt Collection Agencies

| | |
|---|---|
| Asset Acceptance Capital Corp. | NCO Group, Inc. |
| Chamberlin Edmonds | Policy Studies Inc. |
| Encore Capital Group, Inc. | Portfolio Recovery Associates, Inc. |
| ER Solutions, Inc. | Transcom WorldWide S.A. |
| Green Tree Servicing | West Corporation |

## SUMMARY

Managing accounts receivable involves establishing policies and procedures, and organizing a business for their implementation. An aging schedule is a method to determine the effectiveness of these practices, and follows the expectation that the longer a bill in unpaid, the less likely it will ever be paid. Credit information services provide numerical grades of the creditworthiness of companies based on experience reported by vendors and other parties in business relationships.

Vendors normally follow industry practice in establishing terms of sale, which is the length of time allowed before payment is expected, with terms stated as "net" and the number of days (as in "net 30" or "n30"). Invoice generation is usually a shared responsibility of various company functions, with critical decisions on invoice design and the timing of the billing cycle often made suboptimally at the convenience of information technology. Asset-based financing (ABF) based on receivables (factoring) is now an important supplement to traditional bank credit.

## NOTES

1. A lien is a legal claim that attaches to property. A creditor who holds a lien often can have property sold to satisfy the lien.
2. With apologies to Rodgers and Hammerstein: "Getting to Know You" is sung by Mrs. Anna in Act I of their musical *The King and I* (1951).
3. Ratios are provided by industry in the standard sources noted in Chapter 2. For our purposes, we are simply choosing one industry of the some 600 that are reported by RMA. NAICS is the North American Industry Classification System, and is the standard used by federal statistical agencies in classifying business establishments for the purpose of collecting, analyzing, and publishing statistical data related to the U.S. business economy. For further information, see www.census.gov/eos/www/naics.
4. It is sobering to note a few of the established U.S. companies that have declared bankruptcy in the past decade: Linens 'n Things (small appliances), Circuit City (electronics), Fortunoff (jewelry and home furnishings), and Bennigan's (restaurants).
5. Examples of sales financing include automobile and truck dealers (e.g., through GMAC or Ford Motor Credit), aircraft engines and electrical machinery (e.g., through GE Capital), and industrial equipment (e.g., through CIT Group).

6. NAICS is a six-digit code assigned to each industry by the U.S. Department of Commerce for classification purposes. It replaced the SIC four-digit code.
7. The actual calculation is $(2\% \div 98\%)(18) = (0.0204 \times 18) = 36.72\%$. This assumes a 360-day year. A 365-day year results in a rate of 41.37 percent.
8. See Chapter 1, note 2, for an explanation of MICR and OCR.
9. However, see the previous section in this chapter on "Outsourcing Sales Financing" for recourse versus nonrecourse alternatives. Marginal credit risks may be rejected by a factor, leaving the sales/credit decision to the selling company.

# CHAPTER SEVEN

# Inventory and Working Capital Issues

This chapter covers these topics:

- Consideration of appropriate policies and organization for inventory management
- Understanding how ratios and other metrics assist in inventory management
- Learning about problems in purchasing and work-in-process inventory
- Evaluation of new techniques such as EOQ, JIT, and SCM
- Review of such financing alternatives for inventory as asset-based lending

N CHAPTER 6, WE NOTED THE MANY issues involved in managing a seemingly simple working capital activity, accounts receivable. As we discussed, the process is far more complicated than sell and wait for payment. Managing inventory is similar, in that finance managers typically do not become involved in inventory decisions, traditionally the responsibility of manufacturing. Furthermore, the concept of "inventory" makes sense on the balance sheet but is too vague in dealing with the realities of working capital issues. There are two aspects of inventory management:

1. The purchasing of materials and components.
2. The management of those materials and components as they are retrieved and used to produce goods for sale, referred to as **work-in-process (WIP)**.

Various economic and financial factors should be considered in managing inventory, including economic order quantity—that is, how much should be ordered at any particular time; price, volume purchasing, and the possibility of pricing concessions; the timing of delivery of material prior to the beginning of manufacturing; and several other considerations that have come to be integrated into the concept of supply chain management (which we will define shortly).

 ## ELEMENTS OF INVENTORY MANAGEMENT

As with receivables, there are important elements in establishing a program to manage inventory, including establishing policies, organizing for policy implementation, and monitoring results.

### Developing Inventory Policies

Inventory policies formalize decisions on the acquisition and use of inventory, and the write-off or scrapping of stale materials. Rules should be established on several issues, based on answers to the following questions:

- Who is managing our purchasing? Should this function be handled on a decentralized or centralized basis?
- How strictly do we require adherence to inventory and purchasing cycle documentation such as purchase orders (POs) and receiving reports?
- How aggressively should inventory be managed? That is, should we consider a just-in-time (JIT) approach or is it more prudent to maintain a reasonable amount of inventory of raw materials, work-in-process (WIP), and/or finished goods?
- How forcefully will we address vendor errors? Should we demand some control and/or access to our vendors' sites and procedures, or simply request replacements and/or billing credit?

- Should we allow vendors to buy lunches, drinks, or similar entertainment for our purchasing staff? If this is allowed, what limits are appropriate?
- Should we attempt to forecast our inventory requirements, or is purchasing as our needs are determined adequate to deal with possible price increases or shortages in the future?
- Would using a supply chain management system enhance our ability to compete and satisfy our customers?

Policies establish required practice for all parties that cannot be modified except by senior management. This is important when a vendor offers a special accommodation, when POs and/or receiving reports are not prepared, when faulty materials are delivered, and in many other situations directly affecting manufacturing quality and delivery promises. Any violation may trigger appropriate responses by management.

## Organizing for Inventory Management

Optimal inventory management requires a dedicated manager, committee, or a task force approach. Unfortunately, most companies defer to purchasing and production managers in making decisions regarding inventory acquisition and use. However, there are large float and cost implications of inventory, and inappropriate decisions or inefficient procedures can add significant costs, adversely impacting working capital. A company might consider appointing a senior inventory manager or a task force composed of manufacturing, marketing, finance, and information technology.

 **INVENTORY CYCLE MONITORING: RATIOS**

In Chapter 2, we calculated the inventory turnover (Cost of goods sold ÷ Inventory) of the Rengas Company as 6.7 times; its variation inventory turnover (360 days ÷ Inventory turnover) was 54 days. Continuing the actual data for the interquartile range for plastics manufacturing from RMA, we find that the result is 10 (3rd quartile), 7 (median), and 5 (1st quartile) turns, and 35, 52, and 76 days.

Our company (at 6.7 turns and 54 days) is close to the median result for both ratios. This is good news—right? A closer look might be in order, as both of these ratios aggregate considerable data. All of inventory is included, and cost of goods sold—where inventory is placed on the income statement—is the second-largest account after sales.

## Supplemental Data

There are several additional data that should be examined:

- **Common-size financial statement data.** RMA (and some other sources like *Troy's Almanac*) publish data by industry that set total assets (and total liabilities and owners' equity) equal to 100 percent, allowing the calculation of the percentage for each significant account. Inventory is 24.9 percent of total assets for this industry, while our company has 12.0 percent in inventory ($15 million ÷ $125 million).
- **Additional ratio data.** As noted in Chapter 2, *Troy's Almanac* publishes ratios that support additional analysis of the basic ratios. For inventory, an inventory-to-working capital ratio is provided, which is 1.0 times for the industry. Our company has a ratio of 0.353 times ($15 million ÷ [$65 million – $22.5 million]).

We would certainly wonder why we are carrying so much less in inventory than the industry. Are we doing a superior job of managing this asset, or is this an indication that we may have to forgo future sales because we do not have enough to sell? We would want to determine how aggressively we are using our suppliers to deliver materials just prior to the beginning of a production cycle and whether sales are being missed.

 **INVENTORY CYCLE MONITORING: METRICS**

Better-managed companies develop internal metrics as a form of control against deterioration in financial and operating performance. Like an aging schedule (discussed in Chapter 6), these measures are used to chart the functioning of relevant activities over time. For inventory, the most important of these metrics are listed in Exhibit 7.1.

**EXHIBIT 7.1**  Inventory Metrics

Days in Raw Materials and in WIP
> Inventories of raw materials and WIP, measured in days, may show substantial variation of actual results from target (or budgeted) estimates. Trends of holding-period days for raw materials and purchased components highlight excess materials purchased, which forces the commitment of working capital. These metrics indicate the efficiency of material requirements, scheduling, and expediting (delivering inventory to required locations).

*(continued)*

### Vendor Errors

Mistakes by suppliers are usually resolved from data in purchase orders (POs) and receiving reports as matched against invoices or statements. (Purchase orders authorize vendors to ship specific items to a buying company at predetermined prices. A receiving report shows the quantity and condition of material and components as received from vendors.) However, companies typically do not keep detailed records of such errors (except as remembered history).

It is useful to record the percentage of material shortages, overages, and below-specified quality standards by vendor, as well as the items in error, particularly as these occurrences may adversely affect production schedules or result in excess inventory. These measures can be useful in evaluating the performance of current suppliers when new POs are being negotiated.

### Materials Movement Time

The period required to move materials to production is an important manufacturing metric when measured over time. Any deterioration in this metric should be investigated to determine whether there are vertical or horizontal movement obstacles that can delay production scheduling, or whether problems exist in developing or delivering instructions for pulling material from storage. (Vertical movement refers to multistory factories, requiring freight elevators or gravity movement. Horizontal movement involves delivery of inventory across a level platform, although problems can arise when significant distances are involved.)

### Commodity Analysis

The cost of many raw materials used in a production cycle can be hedged using publicly traded commodities futures contracts or options. A useful measure in determining price volatility is the ratio of the expected purchase price to the actual purchase price plotted over time. The hedging utilization metric tracks the percentage of purchases hedged compared to total purchased dollars. Materials that cannot be protected by hedging contracts may be managed by long-term contracts with pricing guarantees.

### Completion of Purchasing Cycle

The completion of the purchase order/receiver file is an important element in the management of inventory. Many companies permit the bypassing of established purchasing procedures. A particular problem is failure to follow PO requirements or to prepare receiving reports prior to authorizing payments to vendors. This metric determines the percentage of complete files for purchases that require these documents.

### Damage in Movement

Inventory can be damaged in movement at any point in the manufacturing process. Careful handling is essential to minimize destruction, rework, and scrap. Metrics should be maintained on such damage to determine whether adequate care is being

(*continued*)

exercised. Such measures include percent of materials damaged prior to production; number of rework orders compared to production orders; and percentage of materials scrapped compared to the percentage entered into production.

**Assembly Line or Machinery Downtime**
Production downtime may result from scheduled maintenance, staffing adjustments, insufficient materials or WIP, machinery repairs, or other causes. It is important to chart the percentage of downtime to total manufacturing time to determine trends and to investigate the cause of any deterioration.

 ## THE PURCHASING FUNCTION

As we noted in our introduction to this chapter, traditional inventory management is controlled by two sets of staff: production managers who focus on securing the necessary materials and components to manufacture goods that can be sold, and purchasing managers who search for the least-cost, highest-quality supplies and equipment. Sounds logical, but who is watching working capital?

The cost of funds is seldom considered when these decisions are made, and few financial managers have ever really reviewed the processes used or the decision rules followed. It is only in recent years that some enlightened manufacturing companies (i.e., United Technologies) are encouraging their production managers and engineers to study financial techniques. Furthermore, staff organizations (e.g., finance, accounting, personnel, law, and information technology) almost always defer to line organizations (sales and manufacturing) in these types of decisions.

### The Purchasing Cycle

Despite years of e-commerce (and its predecessor EDI or electronic data interchange), there continues to be a significant extent of manual activity in purchasing: finding vendors, issuing requests for bids, preparing purchase orders (POs), sending POs, awaiting delivery of materials, preparing reports on items delivered and any defects or shortages (receiving reports), awaiting invoices or statements, matching the PO to the receiver to the bill, reviewing budget codes for payment authorization, preparing vouchers approving payment, and disbursing funds. If payment is by check, bank balances must be reconciled and the clearing debit must be funded.

Whew! It's no wonder that careful analysis of a single purchasing cycle takes weeks, costs $50 to $75 per PO (according to various studies), and appears to be beyond fixing. Let us assume the situation of a large company with significant buying needs, perhaps $200 million a year. If each purchase averages $20,000, this company has 10,000 purchasing cycles a year, costing about $650,000! Even if there are repetitive purchases within a single PO, the cost can still be hundreds of thousands of dollars.

## Purchasing Cycle Problems

In this cycle, can any element go wrong? Here are some of the problems we've seen at companies:

- **High vendor prices and too much expended on inventory.** There are various sources of these situations:
  - Suppliers could simply be charging too much. This could be due to sweetheart arrangements between the vendor and a company's managers, or because services have not been recently rebid to more competitive vendors; see the appendix to Chapter 5.
  - Local buying, often permitted to empower branch managers, to meet unexpected needs, and to maintain goodwill with the local business community. A centralized purchasing function may be perceived as unresponsive and bureaucratic, and local purchasing managers may be rewarded with lunches, golf games, and baseball tickets.

    The extra cost of this behavior has been variously estimated at 15 percent to 25 percent through higher prices, lower order quantity, and tacit acceptance of lessened quality. Reducing or better management of local purchasing can improve the forecasting of future requirements and the determination of economic order quantity (to be discussed later).
  - Manufacturing processes are inefficient. A company may be using production techniques that have not been reengineered or reconfigured. Making products the same way as in 1980 may be forcing the company to spend too much.
  - Swings in the price of materials. Certain purchases can be traded as commodities futures contracts, and it is possible to hedge[1]—a form of risk management—by buying these contracts to lock in a price for later delivery. **Futures** are derivative contracts that give the buyer the right but not the obligation to buy or sell specified amounts of commodities, interest rates, and other physical or financial assets.

For example, farmers use futures to be guaranteed a price when their produce goes to market, perhaps six months or more after planting. By selling a futures contract in March for delivery in October, they know that adequate revenue will be received at harvest to cover the costs of labor, seed, equipment, and energy, in addition to other expenses. Buyers of futures contracts include speculators and actual users of the asset (such as baking companies for wheat and airlines for aviation fuel).

▪ **POs and receiving reports may not be issued.** In our experience, about one-third of all buying does not conform to these procedures. If there is no PO, unauthorized company employees can make and approve a purchase. If there is no receiving report (sometimes referred to as a *receiver*), defects and missing items may be overlooked.

Purchasing following established rules usually occurs with essential, repetitive buys, such as raw materials, paper, shipping materials, and office supplies. The process is most often incomplete for technical or specialized products, such as technology and engineering instruments. Without proper documentation, the treasurer might as well hand over his or her company's checkbook to its vendors!

▪ Bills may not be reviewed for authorization or matched to POs and receivers. The accounts payable department receives an invoice or a statement and verifies that appropriate approvals have been attached. But where are the PO and/or the receiver? We'll discuss payables in Chapter 8. For the present discussion, note that most payables functions go ahead and pay the vendor even if the PO and/or receiver are missing.

 ## ANALYZING PURCHASING ACTIVITIES

While there is no standard method of analysis, a situation encountered at a large manufacturing company may illustrate how to conduct a purchasing cycle review.

### A Situation of Decentralized Purchasing

The CFO of the company in question discovered that parts were being purchased in anticipation of pricing increases or shortages. This problem surfaced when metrics were developed on materials utilization that showed a significant increase in the days of materials held in inventory. The first step in this effort was to analyze the company's purchasing activities, which were managed at each manufacturing site. Vendor selection was made by the local production managers with advice from his or her supervisors. Maintenance of local vendor relations was considered important to ensure delivery of critical supplies.

The review noted that several appointments with local production decision makers were postponed due to vendor lunches and a few golf games. The CFO requested that any available data on prices paid for the various items purchased be forwarded to his office. However, none of the sites maintained such data, and no statistics could be provided on competitive bids, quantities purchased, pricing discounts, or net prices paid.

As a result, it was decided to pull vendor invoices for a four-month period on 40 significant inventory items, a portion of which appears in Exhibit 7.2. It was discovered that the average price paid was substantially above fair market and that the range of prices was significant. It became quite obvious that local purchasing was redundant, inefficient, and expensive, and that favored vendors regularly entertained the purchasing managers.

The excess cost above fair market value *for the items studied* would have amounted to about $100,000. On seeing these results, senior management centralized purchasing, changed procedures for selecting vendors, and established stringent policies on vendor entertainment of the company's purchasing managers.

## Investigating a Company's Payables History

Here's how to conduct a purchasing cycle review. Hire temps (perhaps college students) to pull three months of paid invoices from the home and branch offices. Have the following data logged onto a spreadsheet:

■ Dollar amount
■ Whether the cash discount was taken

**EXHIBIT 7.2**   Selected Materials Purchasing Activity

| Material | Unit | Fair Market Price | Average Price Paid | Number of Purchases |
|---|---|---|---|---|
| Steel rods | Ton | $100 | $140 | 50 |
| Steel sheets | Unit | $4 | $6 | 700 |
| Pig iron | Ton | $70 | $85 | 100 |
| Exotic metals | Ounce | $700 | $850 | 85 |
| Lumber | 1,000 board feet | $300 | $400 | 60 |

- Invoice date and date of payment
- Vendor's name including address and tax identification number
- Items purchased, by budget code or category
- Authorized approver's name

Have the data summarized. Based on our client experiences, here's what may be discovered:

- Dollars spent exceed budget authorization.
- Multiple vendors were used for the same type of item or service.
- Invoices lacked appropriate approvals.
- Some vendors are phony (although we hope not, as this indicates fraud).
- Some purchases were for questionable services (fancy meals, trips to Las Vegas, etc.).
- Some cash discounts were missed (discussed in Chapter 8).
- Some invoices were paid early (discussed in Chapter 8).

 **EOQ AND JIT**

**Supply chain management** (SCM) attempts to optimize all of the components of a manufacturing process, including purchasing, inventory management, and transportation-logistics.[2] Two key concepts in SCM are EOQ and JIT.

### Economic Order Quantity

**Economic order quantity** (EOQ) is a mathematical model that calculates the optimal size of a materials or components purchase. It is also used in making production lot size decisions. Buying decisions may fail to consider the cost of carrying inventory, the real value of volume discounts offered, or the potential loss from stale inventory. For example, one large manufacturing company frequently acquired materials and components far in advance of the start of its production cycle, resulting in excessive carrying costs and some unusable materials due to changes in production requirements and the natural decay of inventory.

The average holding period for this company was 70 days, which reduced the realized gross margin (sales less cost of goods sold) by 1.5 percent, from 10 percent to 8.5 percent. The impact on the company's return on equity (ROE) was 2 percent, with the target ROE of 16 percent declining to 14 percent.[3] The role of finance in this situation is to determine the EOQ, calculate the value and costs of volume discounts based on recent experience, and support decisions that optimize results.

## Calculation of EOQ

The optimal order quantity can be determined from the following calculation:

$$Q^* = \sqrt{\frac{2TF}{CC}}$$

where

$Q^*$ = EOQ
$T$ = total sales in units
$F$ = fixed purchase order (PO) cost
$CC$ = carrying cost of inventory per unit

Assume that we expect 5,000 units in sales, a purchase order cost of $50, a price per unit of $10, and a carrying cost per unit of $1.[4] The resulting EOQ is calculated as about 700 units, with an average inventory on hand of 350 units (or one-half). Few companies actually do these calculations, and, in fact, do not know their PO costs or the carrying cost of inventory. Instead, orders are either based on sales forecasts, which are usually optimistic, or the inventory carried is minimized, following the Japanese concept of just-in-time.

## Just-in-Time

**Just-in-time** (JIT) attempts to set the minimum required inventory of materials through careful planning and management of production cycles. JIT means having the right materials, parts, and products in the right place at the right time, on the theory that excess inventory means waste and cost. Successful JIT programs rely on the ability of vendors to meet tight delivery schedules and a high level of quality control. The example of Dell Computer from Chapter 2 should be reread as an application of JIT.

However, if a disaster affects a vendor, such as a weather situation or a fire, a company's activities may be adversely affected. Even a delay in transporting materials, a frequent event in winter months, can be a problem. In the current economic environment, companies have failed, and a JIT supplier may have been forced into bankruptcy. In that situation, the economics of JIT may look fairly insignificant when there are no materials or components for production lines.

 **WORK-IN-PROCESS**

As noted at the start of this chapter, the work-in-process (WIP) cycle involves the second component of inventory, and includes the management of materials and components as they are retrieved and used to produce goods for sale. From an accounting perspective, the costing of WIP requires an inspection of inventory as it progresses through a manufacturing cycle and an estimate of the approximate stage (or percent) of completion.

## WIP Cycle Management

It is important to analyze WIP because of the inherent inefficiencies in many manufacturing situations. According to various observers, only a small portion of manufacturing cycle time is actually spent in the production of a good, with considerable delays for queuing, inspection of physical movement to the next production activity, temporary packaging and storage, and similar activities.[5] These delays are aggravated by changes due to customer requirements, engineering specifications, maintenance, and manufacturing processes.

Long WIP cycles contribute to rigidity in manufacturing and reduce a company's flexibility to alter production routines to meet unique customer demands. While consumer products are usually not subject to unusual requirements, large systems and some business products nearly always have a particular configuration. This problem indirectly affects a company's capability to respond to the pressure from global competitors and likely raises delivered prices.

In most companies, it is extremely costly to institute a manufacturing change. The strategy traditionally considered to be the most economical is mass production and long production runs. As an alternative approach, some producers acquire equipment that can produce different products by simply changing fabrication tools and manufacturing configurations. The strategy should be to foster flexible and customized production with decentralized control, with the goals of reducing setup time and smoothing the production schedule on the basis of customer demands.

## Benefits of Supply Chain Management

A manufacturer of consumer electrics confronted variations in demand and inefficiencies in SCM that strained resources, delayed time-to-market, and increased supply chain costs. The company decided to outsource to a SCM software vendor, enabling it to focus its scarce internal resources on furthering its core competencies of research and the development of innovative products. Several elements were required for a workable solution:

- Implementation of a flexible supply chain capable of meeting peak demand spikes without service disruption or other delays.
- Initiation of efficient logistics programs to improve repair cycle times and customer satisfaction.
- Creation of an infrastructure that accommodated anticipated distributor and consumer sales growth of more than 300 percent in the next two years with minimal risk and capital expenditure by the company.

Results included the following:

- Improvement in production efficiencies with close to 100 percent of orders shipped on time to end users.
- Consistent achievement of 99 percent order accuracy.
- Reduction in sales returns program cycle time, achieving a 36-hour turnaround, thereby strengthening customer loyalty.
- Improvement in customer service by maintaining high service levels during peak demand cycles where demand increases from an average of 30,000 products to more than 80,000 in a single month.
- Reduction in the time required to bring products to market, improvements in efficiency, and reductions in total costs.

## Supply Chain Management Systems

Global competition has forced companies to deemphasize the management of physical inventory and to focus on information about the supply chain. This problem is compounded when there are hundreds of items in various locations organized by different identifiers, such as serial numbers, container or bin numbers, and unique product codes. Various SCM systems have been developed to integrate data on inventory quantity, location, status of WIP, expectation of delivery from suppliers, promises of delivery to customers, costs incurred, likely sales price, forecasting of future demand, and other functions. See Exhibit 7.3 for a representative listing of SCM capabilities.

The complexity of these analyses forces companies to use SCM systems provided by specialized software vendors. The demand for these products has created an $8.5 billion a year business, with leading vendors of these systems including SAP, Oracle, JDA Software, and Manhattan Associates.[6] For a listing,

**EXHIBIT 7.3**  Typical SCM Functions

- ▪ Inventory Management
  - ▪ Inventory manifest preparation
  - ▪ Order alert and target stock levels for multiple warehouses
  - ▪ Reporting for items below reorder alert levels and target stock levels
  - ▪ Lot and serial numbers assignment to inventory
  - ▪ Inbound stock reservation for customer back orders
  - ▪ Assignment of and stock transfer of inventory to multiple warehouses
  - ▪ Inventory tracking in multiple picking locations
  - ▪ Inventory valuation reports by alternative costing methods (e.g., FIFO, LIFO, average cost)
  - ▪ Order management modules
- ▪ Order Management
  - ▪ Inventory information during order entry
  - ▪ Estimated time of arrival for inbound vendor orders
  - ▪ Order status by due date
  - ▪ Notification to customers on order status
  - ▪ Billing and shipping addresses editing during order entry
  - ▪ Customer payment information
  - ▪ Bill of lading and packing slip printing
  - ▪ Integration with common carriers (e.g., FedEx, UPS, USPS)
  - ▪ Assignment of freight to calculate landed costs
- ▪ Manufacturing
  - ▪ Bill of materials tracking
  - ▪ Work order item assemblies
  - ▪ Customized item assemblies work orders
  - ▪ Reporting of material requirements and cost tracking

see Exhibit 7.4; the largest companies have grown significantly, while those below the top three have experienced a decline in revenues.

There are versions of these systems now available for nearly any size company. Although specific quantitative savings vary, reported benefits include reductions in working capital requirements, increased customer satisfaction, and improved integration with corporate strategic initiatives.

 **ABF: INVENTORY FINANCING**

Asset-based financing, discussed in Chapter 6 regarding accounts receivable, is used for working capital with a company's inventory functioning as

**EXHIBIT 7.4**   SCM Software Vendors

| Rank | Company Name | 2012 Revenue | Website |
|------|--------------|--------------|---------|
| 1 | SAP | $1.721 billion | www.sap.com |
| 2 | Oracle | $1.453 billion | www.oracle.com |
| 3 | JDA Software | $ 426 million | www.jda.com |
| 4 | Manhattan Associates | $ 160 million | www.manh.com |
| 5 | Epicor | $ 138 million | www.epicor.com |
| 6 | IBM | $ 112 million | www.ibm.com |
| 7 | Infor Global Solutions | $ 111 million | www.infor.com |

the collateral for the loan. Lenders typically use a conservative valuation of inventory and a loan somewhat less than the valuation figure, with the key factor being marketability of that collateral. Interest rates charged on inventory financing are similar to those for receivables lending. The interest cost is typically the prime rate plus 2 percent.

Typical lender discounting allows a loan of 60 to 80 percent of the value of a retail inventory. A manufacturer's inventory, consisting of parts and other unfinished materials, might be only 40 percent. Inventory that is financed through ABF programs typically is industrial and consumer durables that can be readily identified by a serial number or other tag. Some lenders specialize by line of business. For example, Textron Financial lends to aviation and golf course customers, while ORIX lends on technology purchases. Selected industries that could consider ABF are noted in Exhibit 7.5.

## Asset-Based Lenders: Inventory

Working with ABF lenders that accept inventory as collateral requires different skills from borrowing from a bank through a line of credit. For a list of inventory lenders, see Exhibit 7.6.

Companies considering using inventory as collateral in an arrangement with an asset-based lender should consider the following:

■ Typically, the business experiences rapid growth, is highly leveraged, and is undercapitalized.
■ Inventory turns several times a year, and there is some seasonality.
■ Borrowing requirements are substantial (above $500,000) to justify the lender's cost to monitor the loan.

**EXHIBIT 7.5**    Industries That Use Inventory as Collateral in ABF

Agricultural equipment
Electronics and appliances
Food service and equipment
Home furnishings
Hearth
HVAC (heating, ventilating, and air conditioning) equipment
Technology products
Trailers
Lawn and garden
Manufactured housing
Marine industry
Motorsport vehicles and equipment
Musical instruments
Pool and spa
Office products
Recreational vehicles
Sewing and vacuum equipment

**EXHIBIT 7.6**    Selected Inventory Lenders

- Bank of America
- CIT Group
- Citibank
- First Commercial Credit
- GE Commercial Finance
- Ally Financial
- ORIX USA Corporation
- Textron Financial
- Wells Fargo

- A good inventory tracking system is required, with tags, labels, bar codes, or other unique identifiers.
- Daily communications between borrowing companies and lenders on the sale of specific inventory items.
- Lenders designate a bank account for deposits of collections.
- Companies can use other banking services of the lender if available; e.g., for disbursements to other vendors and for payroll.
- Strict loan covenants are limited on other borrowing arrangements, and on the payment of salaries and dividends.

- Periodic visits by the lender to ascertain adherence to the loan agreement.
- Lender expectation that stale inventory will be periodically purged.

These restrictions may be onerous, so any ABF decision should be carefully considered.

## SUMMARY

The two aspects of inventory management are (1) purchasing of materials and components and (2) management of those materials and components as they are retrieved and used to produce goods for sale (work-in-process). Several economic and financial factors are relevant in managing inventory, including price, volume purchasing, pricing concessions, and the timing of delivery of material prior to the beginning of manufacturing. The integration of these concepts through supply chain management involves economic order quantity (EOQ) and just-in-time (JIT) delivery. As with receivables, asset-based financing using inventory has become an important source of working capital financing.

## NOTES

1. A **hedge** is a position established in one market in an attempt to offset exposure to price fluctuations in an opposite position with the goal of minimizing exposure to unwanted risk.
2. Numerous excellent SCM references are available, including Michael H. Hugos, *Essentials of Supply Chain Management*, 2nd ed. (Hoboken, NJ: John Wiley & Sons, 2006); and Thomas Schoenfeldt, *A Practical Application of Supply Chain Management Principles* (Milwaukee, WI: ASQ Quality Press, 2008).
3. For a discussion of the methodology used in these calculations, see James Sagner, *Financial and Process Metrics for the New Economy* (New York: AMACOM, 2001).
4. **Carrying cost** is the cost of holding inventory, and includes warehousing costs such as rent, utilities and salaries, financial costs, and inventory costs related to perishability, shrinkage, and insurance.
5. According to Brian H. Maskell, less than 5 percent of production time is actually used for manufacturing activities. See *Performance Measurement for World Class Manufacturing* (Portland, OR: Productivity Press, 1991), 124.
6. Bob Trebilcock, "2013: Top 20 SCM Software Suppliers," *Modern Materials Handling*, July 1, 2013, reporting on research by AMR Research, at www.mmh .com/article/top_20_scm_software_suppliers_2013.

# CHAPTER EIGHT

# Payables and Working Capital Issues

This chapter covers these topics:

- Consideration of appropriate policies and organizing for payables management.
- Understanding how ratios and other metrics assist in payables management.
- Learning about active versus passive management of payables.
- Evaluation of internal processes and outsourcing alternatives in managing payables.
- Review of methods of disbursing payroll, including direct deposit and paycards.

THE CURRENT LIABILITY WITH THE MOST working capital significance is accounts payable, which involves payments to vendors for inventory, supplies, and services. There can be little dispute as to the need to pay bills as they come due. However, decisions on payment dates and practices are often turned over to payables clerks who have limited knowledge of the float consequences of their actions.

As a result, companies make poor choices on when to pay, whether to take cash discounts, and how to manage the payables portion of the working capital timeline. In addition, current liabilities involve the payment of salaries and wages, and techniques for managing this activity are included in this chapter.

 **ELEMENTS OF PAYABLES MANAGEMENT**

There are important elements in establishing a program to manage payables, including establishing policies, organizing for policy implementation, and monitoring results.

### Developing Payables Policies

Policies formalize decisions on the disbursement of company funds for payables. In addition to the inventory rules listed in Chapter 7, guidelines should be thoughtfully developed on several issues, including the following:

- Should we pay our vendors on or after established terms, e.g., if the terms are net 30, should we pay on day 30 or a specified number of days after day 30 (which is the practice in many companies)?
- If cash discounts are offered, should we take the discount?
- Should we attempt to negotiate prorated discounts (**dynamic discounting**) for any payment made before the net period ends?
- How should we handle situations when documentation is missing from a bill, such as a PO, a receiving report, an authorization (whether by signature or voucher), and/or budget codes?
- If a vendor requests special treatment (such as an occasional early payment), should we comply?
- Should we allow vendors to buy lunches, drinks, or similar entertainment for our payables staff? If this is allowed, what limits are appropriate?
- Should we operate our own payables cycle, or should we outsource payment activities to a bank or other provider?

Policies establish required practice for all parties that cannot be modified except by senior management. This is important when vendor representatives approach payables clerks with early payment requests or offers of entertainment. Any violation should trigger appropriate responses by management.

## Organizing for Payables Management

Many companies have an accounts payable manager responsible for the payment of bills from vendors. There are large float and cost implications of payables, and inappropriate decisions or inefficient procedures can add significant costs, adversely impacting working capital. Because of these considerations, the payables manager should meet frequently with finance and other relevant functions.

 **PAYABLES CYCLE MONITORING: RATIOS**

We calculated various working capital ratios in Chapter 2; however, there is no standard accounts payable ratio. RMA publishes supplemental ratios including payables turnover, defined as cost of goods sold (cost of sales) divided by payables. For plastics manufacturing, the result is 21, 11, and 8 turns, and 17, 32, and 47 days. The Rengas Company has $100 million in cost of goods sold and $15 million in payables, resulting in 6.7 turns and 54 days.

These results are slightly above the interquartile range, meaning that any lengthening of the payables cycle—that is, paying more slowly—would likely affect vendor relationships. The common-size balance sheet data we noted in the previous chapter can also be used to analyze payables. Our company had 12.0 percent (of total liabilities and net worth) in payables, while the industry results showed 16.2 percent. This is somewhat of a variation from the industry.

## Payables Metrics

Various metrics can be used to measure a company's performance in managing payables.

- **Issuance of accounts payable disbursements.** Payables practice may be at variance with predetermined target dates. Such targets can be the discount date, the due date, or an established number of days after the due date. It is useful to determine industry practice by referring to industry ratios or statistics provided by trade associations, or at least to establish the parameters for payment so that the decision is not left to the discretion of payables clerks. For example, if our competitors pay an average of 10 days after the due date, when should we pay?

■ **Cash discounts taken/not taken.** Although only about 10 percent of vendors offer discounts, any such opportunities should be individually evaluated and either explicitly taken or passed. Many companies either take all or none of the discounts offered, which is suboptimal practice. In addition, it may be possible to negotiate *dynamic discounting* with vendors offering prorated discounts based on days paid prior to the due date.

■ **Use of bank disbursement products.** Although many companies prefer to use check disbursement systems to pay vendors to either extend float or have a paper trail proving the payment, there are attractive and cost-effective bank products that should be considered. A metric logging the review and use of these alternatives to traditional disbursing should be developed.

■ **Positive pay and account reconcilement.** Certain bank services are primarily used for control to assure that payments are not altered and fraudulently diverted; see Chapter 3. Logs should be maintained to indicate company compliance with appropriate audit controls.

## THE ACCOUNTS PAYABLE FUNCTION

Although accounts payable in the typical company is not accorded much visibility, the job is vital: to review POs and receiving reports against bills from vendors; to find discrepancies; to approve or request clarification or additional documentation; and to request that a disbursement be issued. The actual check printing and mailing function is often split between finance, information technology (to actually print the checks and remittance advices[1]), and the mailroom.

### Active versus Passive Payables Management

Companies often do not actively manage the payables function and merely pay bills as presented if the necessary authorizations and accounting codes are provided and supporting documentation is attached. In these situations, there is little concern for the appropriateness of the expense, for the value of float, or for variances among vendors as to their need for timely payment. In fact, a vendor payment may be made before the due date if a formal diarying system does not exist. Each vendor must be individually examined to determine optimal practice.

## Float Costs of Mismanaged Payables

Here's a situation involving mismanaged payables. The business of The World of Animals is to stock zoos and circuses. Working capital was a continuing problem, and a study of payable practices seemed appropriate. Disbursements were made by check, with two major payables runs on the 5th and 20th of each month. The results for its largest vendors are displayed as follows, showing an annual value of float costing nearly $30,000. Investigation into two of the vendors that were paid early determined the following:

- Charlie's was paid early because his sister-in-law worked at the company and saw no harm in issuing payments once the payables cycle was completed.
- Claire's was paid early because its salesperson had once asked for an early check to make her monthly sales goal. The payables clerk embedded the check release date as an ongoing system instruction.

The company immediately researched other vendor transactions, and found similar problems. The total cost to The World of Animals from all vendors in lost payables float was determined to be about $40,000 a year (see Exhibit 8.1).

Other companies actively manage payables to maximize float while maintaining good vendor relations. Decisions are made regarding the importance of each supplier, and markers in the payables system indicate whether cash discounts should be taken or if an invoice should be paid on or after the due date. These "pay fast/pay slow" alternatives require accounts payable managers to emerge from their clerical function of paying invoices as presented, and manage the process against such constraints as vendor sensitivity and the time value of money.

Regardless of the payables approach chosen by companies, many now use integrated purchasing/payables systems. These products offer various analytics, including controls on purchasing and payment decisions, limits on access to lists of approved vendors, file maintenance of all relevant vendor data, and interfaces with disbursement systems. Later generations of purchasing/payables (known as enterprise resource planning or ERP systems) are integrated with various business applications.[2] We'll discuss ERP systems in Chapter 10.

**EXHIBIT 8.1** The World of Animals: Billing Activity of Largest Vendors (all invoices are received on the first or second of the month)

| Vendors and Accompanying Notes | Terms | Usual Payment Date | Days Paid Early vs. Net Terms | Discounts Offered | Amount of Annual Purchases (most recent year) | Value of Forgone Float (at 10%) |
|---|---|---|---|---|---|---|
| Amy's Alligators (1) | 1/10, n/30 | 5th | 25 | 1/10 discount | $3,800,000 | N/A |
| Ben's Bobcats (2) | net 20 | 20th | 0 | | $2,200,000 | $ 0 |
| Charlie's Cassowaries (3) | net 30 | 20th | 10 | | $2,000,000 | $ 5,550 |
| Claire's Cobras (4) | net 30 | 20th | 10 | | $1,500,000 | $ 4,170 |
| Denali's Deer (5) | 2/10, n/30 | 5th | | 2/10 discount | $ 925,000 | N/A |
| Owen's Ostriches (6) | net 30 | 20th | 10 | | $ 830,000 | $ 2,300 |
| Robert-Paul's Ravens (7) | 2/20, n/90 | 20th | 70 | 2/20 discount | $ 740,000 | $14,390 |
| Sarah's Sea Lions (8) | net 30 | 5th | 25 | | $ 635,000 | $ 880 |
| Stephen's Scorpions (9) | 1/20, n/30 | 20th | 10 | 1/20 discount | $ 700,000 | N/A |
| Tessa's Tigers (10) | net 45 | 5th | *10 | | $ 670,000 | $ 1,860 |
| Annual Cost of Float Forgone | | | | | | $29,150 |

*Paid on the 5th of the 2nd month with the final due date of the 15th of that month

N/A = not applicable

Notes:

(1) Amy's cash discount was valued at 18% (30 – 10 = 20; 360 ÷ 20 = 18 × 1%) and worth taking.

(2) Ben's was paid on the due date.

(3) Charlie's was paid 10 days early, valued as ($2,000,000 ÷ 360 × 10 × 10%).

(4) Claire's was paid 10 days early, valued as ($1,500,000 ÷ 360 × 10 × 10%).

(5) Denali's cash discount was valued at 36% (30 – 10 = 20; 360 ÷ 20 = 18 × 2%) and worth taking.

(6) Owen's was paid 10 days early, valued as ($830,000 ÷ 360 × 10 × 10%).

(7) Robert-Paul's was paid 70 days early versus the due date, valued as ($740,000 ÷ 360 × 70 × 10%). The cash discount was valued as 10.3% (90 – 20 = 70; 360/70 = 5.15 × 2 = 10.3%), and not worth taking.

(8) Sarah's was paid 5 days early, valued as ($635,000 ÷ 360 × 5 × 10%).

(9) Stephen's cash discount was valued at 36% (30 – 20 = 10; 360 ÷ 10 = 36 × 1%) and worth taking.

(10) Tessa's was paid 10 days early, valued as ($670,000 ÷ 360 × 10 × 10%).

## PAYABLES USING INTERNAL PROCESSES

Businesses that complete the payables cycle through company functions have the option of disbursing through checks, ACH or Fedwire, or through procurement cards. In these situations, the entire process is handled internally, although banks allow companies to stop disputed payments before the transaction is complete.

### Checks, ACH, and Fedwire

Checks, ACH, and Fedwire are the most usual methods of disbursement for payables. A regular bank checking account receives activity during normal business hours, which means that any holder of a check can request funds from the account (or "cash" the check) at any time. The account owner must either leave balances or transfer funds into the account to cover such activity, or risk the embarrassment and expense of checks returned to depositors (such as vendors) for non-sufficient funds (NSF).

A better alternative is a controlled disbursement account, which is funded once during the business day to cover daily check presentments, eliminating the need for companies to leave balances to cover clearing items. Early notification of that day's clearings allows funding of the account and helps the finance manager determine the company's cash position. The funding is by intrabank transfer, through an interbank ACH, or by Fedwire.

The company completes the payables activity by releasing the payment in satisfaction of an outstanding invoice. However, the bank will require resolution of any mismatches of issued file data compared to clearing data if positive pay is used. When the payment is by ACH, the rules of the clearinghouse (NACHA) require that a prenotification ACH be satisfactorily completed before the ACH can be completed. Due to their cost, Fedwires are infrequently used for disbursements and are final once released.

### Costs of Check Issuance

Companies that issue disbursements for payables should carefully examine the all-in cost, not just the bank check clearing charge. Exhibit 8.2 lists a company's charges for 3,000 vendor checks a month, with the cost of nearly $7 per payment totaling almost $250,000 a year. Using another disbursement method would result in significant savings: per item bank charges range from about 15 cents for ACH to about 75 cents for comprehensive payables. If the latter were used, avoidable costs are about two-thirds of the charges in *italics* and all of the charges in CAPITAL LETTERS (see Exhibit 8.2). The potential savings are almost $140,000 ($247,500 less $108,967).

**EXHIBIT 8.2** Illustrative Savings from Comprehensive Payables

| Labor | Hours Per Month | Cost Per Hour | Monthly Cost | Proposed Monthly Cost |
|---|---|---|---|---|
| | Current Paper-Based Check Disbursement System | | | Comprehensive Payables |
| *Computer processing* | 50 | $50 | $ 2,500 | $ 833 |
| COMPUTER PRINTER | 30 | 40 | 1,200 | 0 |
| BURSTING AND SIGNING | 30 | 20 | 600 | 0 |
| Disbursement Management | 30 | 30 | 900 | 900 |
| FOLDING AND STUFFING | 75 | 20 | 1,500 | 0 |
| MAIL OPERATIONS | 15 | 20 | 300 | 0 |
| RECONCILIATION | 20 | 30 | 600 | 0 |
| Report Preparation | 10 | 35 | 350 | 117 |
| Total Labor | | | $ 7,950 | $ 1,849 |

| Supplies and Banking | Volume Per Month | Cost Per Item | Monthly Cost | Proposed Monthly Cost |
|---|---|---|---|---|
| CHECK STOCK | 3,000 | $0.05 | $ 150 | $ 0 |
| REMITTANCE ADVICES | 3,000 | 0.10 | 300 | 0 |
| ENVELOPES | 3,000 | 0.05 | 150 | 0 |
| PRINTER SUPPLIES | | | 75 | 0 |
| BANK CHARGES (all services) | 3,000 | 0.50 | 1,500 | 0 |
| Postage | 3,000 | 0.45 | 1,350 | $ 1,350 |
| Total Materials | | | $3,525 | $ 1,350 |

| Fixed Costs | Equipment Used | Cost of Equipment | Monthly Cost | Proposed Monthly Cost |
|---|---|---|---|---|
| PRINTER | 3 | $350 | $ 1,050 | $ 0 |
| FOLDING AND STUFFING EQUIPMENT | 2 | 300 | 600 | 0 |
| Software Support | | | 2,000 | 666 |
| POSTAGE METERS | 2 | 100 | 200 | 0 |
| Computer | | | 2,000 | 666 |
| Rent Allocation | | | 1,500 | 500 |
| Senior Management | | | 1,800 | 1,800 |
| Total Fixed Costs | | | $ 9,150 | $ 3,632 |
| Total Monthly Costs | | | $ 20,625 | $ 6,831 |
| Total Annual Costs | | | $247,500 | $ 81,972 |
| Cost per Disbursement | | | $ 6,875 | $ 2.277 |
| Annual Costs of Comprehensive Payables | | | | |
| Disbursement Costs | | | $247,500 | $ 81,967 |
| Banking Costs | | | | $ 27,000 |
| Total Costs | | | | $108,967 |

See the preceding text for an explanation of the use of CAPITAL and *italicized* letters.

## Procurement Cards

Procurement cards (also known as purchasing cards) are corporate cards issued to designated employees to make local purchases on behalf of the company. These cards differ from credit cards in the following respects:

- The company (rather than the employee) receives the bill and is responsible for payment.
- Codes are embedded in the card to restrict purchases to eligible types of products and services, and to limit the total amount spent.
- Automated data capture enables the company to receive next-day summaries of purchasing activities for company review and the determination of appropriateness and accuracy.

Purchasing can be simplified through the use of the cards for routine items. A major procurement card benefit is the elimination of the paperwork inherent in creating a PO and other documentation. In addition, volume discounts may be arranged with vendors frequently used, and employees can be encouraged or instructed to use those suppliers. Many national and regional banks now have procurement card programs.

Savings arising from procurement card programs can be 80 percent to 90 percent of the cost of the traditional PO cycle. Opposition to card programs has been primarily from purchasing departments that see these cards as a threat to their position in the company. However, widespread card usage has minimized this problem, particularly as management is generally pleased with the savings typically achieved. Furthermore, the use of cards for small items allows purchasing managers to concentrate on major buying decisions and to negotiate with vendors for volume discounts when cards are presented.

 **PAYABLES OUTSOURCING**

Electronic disbursements, outsourcing of payment issuance, payroll, and freight bills may be effective strategies for companies.

### Electronic Disbursements

In an actual situation, a large hospital and medical center received a high percentage of invoices in paper form requiring extensive manual handling including validation, review, and approval. A vendor-maintained electronic settlement process allowed the hospital to involve all of its suppliers, including medical, pharmaceutical, office supplies, food service, and construction; such other vendors as legal services and printing companies were later added. As a result, savings were developed throughout the payables cycle:

- Comprehensive payables grew to three-fourths of all disbursements.
- The cycle to complete payables was compressed from 80 to 20 days.
- Exceptions and adjustments were reduced by one-sixth.
- The percent of cash discounts increased to three times the amount offered to the typical buying company.

## Freight Bills

Numerous organizations offer comprehensive freight and logistics services, including the auditing and payment of bills from transportation carriers.[3] Freight invoices are reviewed for excessive charges such as misclassifications, incorrect discount levels, incorrect mileage calculations, extension mistakes, and other errors. Overcharge claims can be filed and tracked to request refunds of fees overpaid.

Other services offered include verification of shipper liability, rate negotiation, review of contracts, classification and routing assistance, customized transportation and distribution systems, carrier selection, and contract negotiations. These freight payment services audit both large freight movements and small parcel services such as UPS, FedEx, and DHL. A particular concern is on-time performance and the filing of claims for refunds if delivery does not occur within the time guarantee.

Here's the typical data flow: based on company instructions, carriers submit freight invoices to the designated freight payment provider. The firm will verify the freight movement by reviewing bills of lading[4] and signed proof of delivery, and accuracy of the invoice will be determined by examination of freight rates, freight discounts, misapplied charges, and other sources of potential errors. In addition, recommendations are made regarding carriers used, transportation and logistics systems used, packaging and container labels, and payment alternatives.

## Comprehensive Payables Concepts

Several banks offer a complete disbursement outsourcing service generically referred to as **comprehensive payables.** The company authorizing payments transmits a file in any of several formats containing the following payment data:

- Due date of payment (as payments can be warehoused by the bank)
- Dollar amount

- Payee and payee's address
- Mechanism (i.e., check, Fedwire, or ACH)
- Accompanying remittance detail

The bank creates payments as instructed and issues them on a specified date. Some banks determine the appropriate payment mechanism based on company-determined parameters. Electronic payments are issued as requested by the company, and transaction fees are based on the bank's standard pricing.

 ## CHECK PAYMENTS IN A COMPREHENSIVE PAYABLES ENVIRONMENT

When a check is the preferred method of payment, the disbursement is prepared for mailing, including any desired remittance detail. Data provided typically include invoice or item numbers being paid and adjustments to the billed amount, including discounts taken or credits for damaged merchandise. Certain industries require lengthy descriptions of payments, such as the "explanation of benefits" (EOB) statements provided by insurance companies to insured individuals and healthcare providers.

Most comprehensive payables banks can process all of these activities, including stuffing envelopes and applying postage. Banks can also print company logos, signature lines, and promotional statements, such as, "Ask us about direct deposit." Inexpensive desktop technology allows the issuance of emergency checks and the transmission of a supplemental issued file to the bank.

The bank will attempt to gain the highest postal discount offered by the USPS for quantity mailings. The amount of the discount varies by the quantity of items to each receiving zip code and other criteria.[5] As the checks clear, the bank performs the usual positive pay service, and funds the resulting daily debit based on instructions from the company. In addition, account reconciliation and check storage are provided.

### Benefits of Comprehensive Payables

There are significant benefits to companies using comprehensive payables:

- Consolidation of the payments function. Instead of having to maintain different systems for various types of payments, companies can use a single system for all disbursements.

- Outsourcing the entire disbursement function, including check printing, mailing, and the reconciliation process. Several internal company responsibilities can be entirely eliminated, and the risk of internal fraud is significantly diminished with the process managed by a bank.[6]
- Cost savings. Studies indicate that the all-in cost of creating and sending a payment is approximately $5, although fees vary by issuer. Banks are currently bidding the comprehensive payables service for about 75 cents for paper disbursements. Electronic disbursements are charged at the bank's price for ACH or Fedwire with an additional charge for managing the disbursement process. The company continues to have some expenses for general bank contact, including overall supervision and the daily "pay" or "no pay" positive pay decision. An estimate of the total cost of using a bank for outsourced payments is $1 per transaction plus postage.
- Vendor access to payment status. As the process is on a hosted web-based platform, vendors can log onto the system at any time and view the status of their invoices and payments pending. Some banks (e.g., Bank of America) allow vendors to factor these receivables to accelerate cash flow.

 ## PAYROLL DISBURSEMENTS

ACH direct deposit is the principal method now used by companies for payroll, although checks are still issued when requested by employees. The widespread acceptance of this payroll mechanism has been a fairly recent phenomenon, assisted by active promotion by banks and employers, and by the obvious advantages of convenience and day of pay access to the funds.

### Mechanics of Direct Deposit

The employee provides a voided check to his or her employer at the time of employment or later enrollment. The transit routing and bank account data from the bottom of the check are used to build a file record. Depending on the arrangement with the disbursement bank, the ACH transfer is made one or two days before the pay date, assuring that good funds will be in the employee's account on the pay date. Alternatively, an outside payroll service calculates the amount of net pay and the various deductions (including tax and employee-paid benefits), and transmits a file of these data to the bank that is used.

The leading payroll services are ADP, Paychex, Administaff, and Trinet Group. The primary advantages of direct deposit are:

- Low cost to the employer, as the cost of an ACH is about 15 cents (vs. about $5 to issue and reconcile a payroll check).
- Reduced employee absence, as there is no reason to leave company premises to deposit or cash the payroll check.
- Convenience for the employee, as the pay is in the bank regardless of weather, vacation, business travel, or the loss of the payroll envelope.
- The funds are credited to the employee's account, the earnings on which, depending on the type of depository account, may or may not pay interest for his or her benefit. However, earnings on deposit accounts are fairly nominal, so this should be a minor consideration.
- Fraud prevention, as there is no need to verify the identification of an employee attempting to cash a payroll check.

Disadvantages include the following:

- The employer loses all use of the funds deposited for the payroll—the float—on pay date. Studies of payroll check clearing show that the average delay in check clearing is about three business days.
- The employer must manage a dual payroll system—check and direct deposit—unless all of payroll is converted to electronic. This is not a major concern for companies that use an outsource service.

## Promoting Payroll Direct Deposit

Employees who resist direct deposit may want to hide pay from a spouse or significant other, may not have a bank account, or are simply uninformed about the mechanics of the program. Companies can require direct deposit as a condition of employment (but not after), but must allow employees to select the financial institution to which their pay is sent.

Consider involving the bank in providing an educational program to assist in overcoming resistance. Companies find that their financial institution will market their services to employees, and promotions often used are a year's free checking, a discounted mortgage or home loan program, free credit card programs, or other promotions. The current banking environment may be an excellent time to offer these services.

Sufficient employment at a single site may justify the bank installing an ATM for employee banking (which may have to be subsidized by the company). Corporate benefits include eliminating any petty cash maintained to accommodate check cashing and travel or expense reimbursement, and not having employees leave the premises during work hours to conduct banking activities. In addition to the management and replenishment of these funds, the company avoids the risk of theft.

## Paycards

Employees may choose not to receive a direct deposit or a check for various reasons. Many banks and payroll services offer paycards, which are ATM cards specifically used for payroll. The employee need not have an account at the payroll bank. Instead, an ATM card is issued along with a PIN number, allowing access through any ATM machine or at merchants that accept the card family (e.g., Visa or MasterCard). The employee receives a monthly statement detailing withdrawals, payroll credits, and purchases.

Paycard is a convenient way of paying seasonal workers and other employees who may only be at a job for a short period of time. Other employer paycard advantages include:

- Elimination of stop-payment fees for lost or stolen paychecks.
- Minimizing exposure to paycheck fraud.
- No need for employer encashment of payroll checks.

Advantages for employees include:

- No time wasted waiting in lines at banks or check-cashing stores.
- No fees for check cashing (which can be a significant cost).
- No requirement for multiple forms of identification to cash checks.
- Access to funds anytime and virtually anywhere.

 **SUMMARY**

Decisions on accounts payable dates and practices are made by disbursement clerks in many companies, who have limited knowledge of the float consequences of their actions. As a result, suboptimal choices are often made on when to pay, whether to take cash discounts, and how to manage the payables portion of the working capital timeline. There are various processes that should be considered in disbursing funds, including the traditional mechanisms noted in Chapter 2; procurement cards; such outsourcing methods as freight and logistics services and comprehensive payables; and direct deposit and paycard for payroll.

 ## NOTES

1. A **remittance advice** is normally attached to a check indicating which bills are being paid and whether items are in dispute.
2. **Enterprise resource planning** (**ERP**) is an integrated system that manages internal and external resources of a company including tangible assets, financial resources, and materials purchasing. ERP systems are based on a centralized computing platform, consolidating all significant business operations into a uniform environment. The larger vendors of SCM software in Exhibit 7.4 also provide ERP systems.
3. See, for example, www.cassinfo.com, which is the website of Cass Information Systems. Other prominent global companies include C.H. Robinson Worldwide (www.chrobinson.com), CEVA Group Plc (www.cevalogistics.com), and DB Schenker (www.dbschenker.com).
4. A **bill of lading** is a document issued by a carrier to a shipping company that specified goods have been received on board as cargo for transporting to a named place to a recipient (usually the purchaser).
5. For further information, see bulkmail.info/fcrates.html or www.usps.gov.
6. A chronic source of fraud is inadequately supervised blank-check stock. On more than one occasion, blank checks have been stolen from unlocked file drawers, issued to phony businesses, and cashed. A suggested fix is printing the entire check face on blank paper at the time that the check is prepared; for one vendor's solution, see www.troygroup.com.

CHAPTER NINE

# International Working Capital

This chapter covers these topics:

- Consideration of the working capital opportunities in international business.
- Awareness of the financing of international transactions
- Appreciation for the basic concepts of foreign exchange.
- Evaluation of country risk and other issues in international working capital.
- Understanding global corporate behavior and cultural differences.

U NTIL ABOUT 30 YEARS AGO, some finance texts would not have included a section on international working capital. Large companies have been active in world trade beginning at about the end of World War I. However, IBM, General Motors, Coca-Cola, and other businesses that found global opportunities raised capital at home; owned and controlled their foreign operations; and often paid their vendors in the strongest currency in the world, the U.S. dollar.

Starting at about the time of the 1973–1974 OPEC oil embargo, the U.S. Department of Commerce realized that American business had to substantially increase exports in order to pay for oil and other imports, and developed initiatives to improve participation in global trade. In the ensuing time, the U.S. dollar steadily declined in value (with brief periods of appreciation against other currencies). Companies make and receive payments in local currencies; capital is raised wherever the cost is lowest; and companies actively seek foreign joint venture partners.

##  CAPITALISM GOES GLOBAL

American companies originally demanded ownership over foreign operations. The primary motives were to keep all of the profits and to absolutely control activities thousands of miles away on the theory that "the home office knows best." It took years of business mistakes and some hostile governments and/or local agitation for multinational corporations to learn their lesson.

Regardless of political orientation, nearly all international markets operate on capitalistic principles. This is an advantage for participants, permitting the following:

- **Global sourcing of capital for borrowers and investors.** This opportunity is particularly important in developing economies where the financial markets may not be as sophisticated as in the United States, Western Europe, or Japan.
- **Reduced risk for providers of capital.** The nearly unlimited investment alternatives in global markets allow lenders and investors to spread their risk exposures and to achieve portfolio diversification of business assets.
- **Private enterprise.** The privatization movement that British Prime Minister Margaret Thatcher began in the 1970s has spread to nearly every country. Government-owned enterprises that were inefficient and stodgy are now owned by investors who seek profits through improved customer satisfaction and innovation.
- **Deregulation.** Beginning at about that same time, the financial markets moved toward deregulation. This development has increased competition, reduced fees and interest rate charges, encouraged the use of technology, and allowed the development of international policies to prevent financial crises.

## Elements of International Working Capital

Practices vary significantly in the management of international working capital; globalization is an intriguing concept but will require decades to accomplish. The "point" person in many large companies is the global treasury manager with responsibilities to manage banking relations, foreign exchange, and other cash-related activities.

Other elements of working capital are often overlooked, and practice may decline to levels far below that of equivalent domestic activity. For example, collecting payments on outstanding invoices may require 40 days in the United States; in some countries, the typical receivables period can be more than twice that time.

Many developed country business services firms have made significant profits by locating in developing economies near major corporations. Do not expect to find support for working capital initiatives from local vendors; for example, companies are unlikely to find counterparties for JIT, factoring, or electronic payment systems in many countries.

## Corporate Governance

An important global development has been the recent demand for transparency and ethical behavior. The 2008–2009 global credit crisis increased the expectation of responsible corporate behavior with the position of international finance (including working capital) elevated to be advisory to senior management.

The United States began this initiative with the Sarbanes-Oxley Act of 2002 (SOX), which was enacted as a reaction to a number of major corporate and accounting scandals. These losses cost investors billions of dollars when the share prices of affected companies collapsed, shaking public confidence in the securities markets. Two relevant sections of SOX deal with corporate governance:

1. **Corporate responsibility.** Title III mandates that senior executives take responsibility for the accuracy and completeness of corporate financial reports. It enumerates specific limits on the behaviors of corporate officers and describes forfeitures of benefits and civil penalties for noncompliance.

2. **Enhanced financial disclosures.** Title IV requires enhanced reporting requirements for financial transactions, including off–balance sheet transactions, pro forma figures, and stock transactions of corporate officers. It specifies internal controls for assuring the accuracy of financial reports and disclosures, and mandates both audits and reports on those controls.

The international manager will find widely varying attitudes toward corporate governance. Certain countries such as Great Britain have followed the U.S. lead; others permit situations of questionable transparency and ethical behavior to occur.

 ## THE FINANCING OF INTERNATIONAL TRANSACTIONS

With domestic transactions, financial managers attempt to optimize liquidity and efficiency. In contrast, global finance focuses on risk (to be discussed in Chapter 11), particularly the impact of foreign exchange and other exposures. **Foreign exchange** (FX) is the conversion of one currency to another currency. The most important form of financing—which will be discussed later in this section—is the letter of credit, which mitigates the risk of selling to customers in foreign markets we don't know.

### Global Financial Risks

A company doing business internationally is typically exposed to any or all of the following types of risk:

- **Transaction exposure** is due to a movement in FX rates between the time a transaction is booked and the time it settles, potentially impacting the value of the deal. For example, if the euro weakens over the next month, the value of a euro receivable due in 30 days will be worth less in U.S. dollars when paid than the value today.
- **Translation exposure** is the balance sheet exposure that results when a company consolidates its financial statements and then reports the change in the net value of its foreign currency assets. The exposure results from fluctuations in FX, which change the rate at which the net assets are valued.
- **Economic exposure** refers to the impact of fluctuating exchange rates on the value of future cash flows from long-term contracts. The longer the term of the contract, the greater the exposure.

### Letter of Credit Concepts

As already noted, the principal method to mitigate credit risk in international transactions is the **letter of credit** (LC). The buyer requests an LC from an international bank that guarantees that the bank will pay the seller (or exporter) when the conditions of the LC are fulfilled. The bank requires that the buyer is known to the bank, or that an equivalent value of collateral is deposited to ensure that the bank will be fully compensated for the amount it finances. In essence, the bank substitutes its credit for that of the buyer.

Most LCs are irrevocable, meaning terms can be modified only if both the buyer and seller approve. Banks providing LCs are compensated by a fee (usually in the hundreds of dollars) paid by the buyer. However, the extensive document management involved in an LC often costs the bank as much as the fee received. This burden has been alleviated in recent years as banks have placed the LC forms on a secure website, requiring the participating companies to do most of the necessary paperwork.[1]

### Letter of Credit Documentation

Following the issuance of the LC, the buyer's bank informs the seller's bank that the goods may be shipped. The seller must deliver a set of documents to its bank as required by the LC, which usually includes the following:

- An invoice
- Any required governmental documents approving the transaction such as an export license
- A packing list
- An inspection certificate
- Proof of insurance
- A **bill of lading**, which is a contract for shipment indicating that the goods are in transport to the buyer and proof of ownership

When the seller's bank is satisfied that the documents meet the terms of the LC, the seller receives payment; see Exhibit 9.1. The buyer's bank approves of the contents of these documents, and pays the seller's bank. At that point, the buyer's bank expects reimbursement from the buyer.

Some transactions do occur on open credit where the buyer (or importer) is known to the seller or where credit reports are available.[2] Where the buyer is not known, selling companies may demand a substantial portion or all of the payment in advance ("cash in advance").

 ## THE FOREIGN EXCHANGE MARKETS

So far we have been assuming that the buyer and seller in an international transaction are operating in a currency acceptable to both buyer and seller, be it a major world currency—the US$ (dollar), the € (euro), the British £ (pound)

**EXHIBIT 9.1** Letter of Credit Documentation Flow

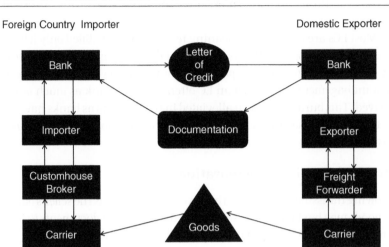

These steps in normal chronological order are as follows:

1. The exporter (seller) and the importer (buyer) agree on the conditions of sale.
2. The importer requests its bank to open a letter of credit.
3. The importer's bank prepares a letter of credit (LC) and sends it to the exporter's bank.
4. The importer's bank confirms the LC and transmits it to the exporter (its customer).
5. The exporter reviews the LC and arranges to deliver the goods to the importer through a freight forwarder.
6. The carrier prepares a bill of lading; other documents are prepared by the insurance company, the exporter (the invoice), and the appropriate government official (perhaps a certificate of origin). All documents are accumulated by the exporter.
7. The exporter presents the documents to its bank.
8. The exporter's bank reviews the documents and if in order, credits the exporter's bank account.
9. The exporter's bank couriers or e-mails the documents to the importer's bank, which presents them to the importer and debits the importer's bank account.
10. The importer presents the documents to the customhouse broker and receives the goods.

or the Japanese ¥ (yen)—or any of the other currencies used throughout the world. However, transactions may be in a currency that is not readily available to the buyer or infrequently received by the seller, and either party may decide to convert those funds into its "home" currency.

FX involves the largest and most liquid markets in the world, operating on a nearly continuous basis. FX mechanisms allow buyers and sellers to **hedge**— that is, to engage in transactions that mitigate exposure to a risk by taking a position opposite to the initial position.

## FX Mechanisms

FX allows the conversion of one currency to another through any of several mechanisms designed to meet the needs of a company engaged in international business:

- **Spot rates** are FX for delivery in two business days. (*Cash rates* are for same-day FX delivery.) The spot rate is the FX that is most often quoted in the financial newspapers; for example, the rates for March 2014 are shown in Exhibit 9.2. Spot rates are used to settle business transactions; retail transactions are in much smaller quantities and are not as favorable as spot rates.
- **Forward rates** are hedging instruments used for the delivery of the FX on a specified later date, and are used by businesses to "lock in" a rate when it is likely that an international transaction will settle in, say, 30 or 60 days. Forwards are available from international banks and the largest FX dealers, and are written for specific amounts and dates negotiated between the company and the bank. A company—the FX buyer—would consider using a forward contract when there is concern that the home currency may lose value in the coming period (FX risk) and that waiting to buy spot FX may cost more at the time that payment must be made.

  Here's an example: A company owes 100,000£ in three months, and it is concerned that the home currency, the US$, will decrease in value. A recent quote on a forward contract was $1.6736, which allows a company to lock in the £ at a slightly different rate than spot FX. In addition, the FX dealer will charge a small commission. (Note: The recent spot rate was $1.6747.)
- **Futures contracts** are available through U.S. commodities exchanges. Futures are similar to forwards in that the FX is for delivery at a later date. However, these contracts are based on standard-sized contracts rather than tailored to a company's specific requirement and are written for delivery on specified dates. For example, the standard size contract for the UK£ is 62,500 £s, which were trading at $1.674 for one-month delivery. The contract sizes for other major currencies are CD$100,000 (Canada), €125,000, ¥12.5 million, and 500,000 Mexican pesos. These contracts are listed on the Chicago Mercantile Exchange and are traded on a company's behalf by a commodities broker.

**EXHIBIT 9.2** Selected FX Rates (for March 2014)

| | Foreign Currency in US$ | US$ in Foreign Currency* |
|---|---|---|
| Australia (dollar) | 0.903 | 1.07 |
| Canada (dollar) | 0.910 | 1.10 |
| China (renminbi) | 0.165 | *6.07* |
| Europe (euro) | 1.369 | 0.73 |
| India (rupee) | 0.016 | *61.83* |
| Japan (yen) | 0.010 | *101.80* |
| ---- 1 month forward | 0.010 | *101.79* |
| ---- 3 months forward | 0.010 | *101.75* |
| ---- 6 months forward | 0.010 | *101.70* |
| Mexico (peso) | 0.076 | *13.24* |
| Russia (ruble) | 0.028 | *35.10* |
| Switzerland (franc) | 1.120 | 0.893 |
| UK (pound) | 1.675 | 0.597 |
| ---- 1 month forward | 1.674 | 0.597 |
| ---- 3 months forward | 1.674 | 0.598 |
| ---- 6 months forward | 1.672 | 0.598 |

*Where the convention is to state the US$ in the quantity of the foreign currency, this is indicated in an italicized FX quote.
Note: These are currency trades in amounts of $1 million or more as quoted by various sources. There are several published sources of FX rates, including the *Wall Street Journal*, the *New York Times*, and *Barron's* (in the "Market Week" section and at www.barrons.com/data).

The forward or future FX rate differs slightly from the spot rate due to market expectations regarding the specific currency. Forwards (or futures) may be greater or less than the spot rate; for example, £ forwards sell at a slight discount from the spot rate, possibly in anticipation of an interest rate cut by the Bank of England.

## Continuous Link Settlement versus Spot FX

Foreign exchange markets have traditionally settled on a *spot* basis—that is, two business days ahead. The specialist financial institution CLS Group (for continuous link settlement) enables banks to settle foreign exchange for themselves (and their customers and other third parties). CLS has become the market standard for foreign exchange settlement between major banks.

The motivation behind CLS was to eliminate the risk associated with cross-currency transactions, specifically referred to as Herstatt risk, named after the German bank that almost caused the collapse of the banking system in 1974. Herstatt's Luxembourg Branch declared bankruptcy and failed to settle its foreign exchange contracts.

The currencies that settle through CLS include:

Australian dollar
British pound
Canadian dollar
Danish krone
European Union euro
Hong Kong dollar
Israeli new shekel
Japanese yen
Mexican peso
New Zealand dollar
Norwegian krone
Singapore dollar
South African rand
South Korean won
Swedish krona
Swiss franc
U.S. dollar

## Factors Influencing FX Rates

With few exceptions, the FX markets float without intervention by central banks or other government agencies. This situation has existed since the early 1970s when the U.S. dollar was taken off of the gold standard that had been established in 1944 at the Bretton Woods (NH) conference. At that time, the US$ was deemed convertible at 1/35th ounce of gold on demand. However, the diminishing reserves of American gold forced the Nixon administration to stop redeeming dollars for gold on demand from foreign holders of dollars.

There are various influences on FX rates, and at any given time, one or another drives rates higher or lower against other rates. The most important influences are the following:

▪ **Inflation.** Differences in purchasing power due to inflationary pressures are an important influence on FX.

- **Interest rates.** High interest rates tend to make a currency attractive as investors seek higher returns; lower rates, as the United States experienced since 2008, caused the US$ to decline against other major currencies.[3]
- **Balance of payments.** The calculation of trade and other government transfers constitutes a country's balance of payments; chronic deficits usually cause a currency to decline relative to other FX.
- **Government spending and taxation.** The FX markets react positively to a country's efforts to maintain stability between revenues and spending.

These factors operate over a long cycle and are not reliable for short-term FX forecasts that most international transactions require. However, it is instructive to note that the US$ had declined rather markedly in the period before the Great Recession. The recent improvements in the pound and the euro do not reflect the somewhat weakened economic conditions in those areas and appear to be market responses to less accommodative central bank policies.

Even more startling, the US$ had declined about 40 percent against the major currencies since the beginning of the twenty-first century (as of the beginning of the current credit crisis). The deteriorating position of the US economy during that time was directly reflected in the value of its currency.

## Multicurrency Accounts

FX can be managed using a single international bank account with the capability to receive deposits and withdrawals of several major currencies; this facility is often called a **multicurrency account**. These centralized currency accounts are easy to establish and maintain. There is one set of account-opening documentation, low maintenance fees, and a single point of contact for customer service.

The disadvantage of such arrangements is that a currency handled in a country other than that of its domicile (e.g., the pound in France) may be subject to availability delays upon deposit and up to two days' delay on transfer. Regular cross-border currency transfers are usually done on a spot basis.

## Electronic Payments

Many developed economies have made significant progress toward electronic payment instruments.[4] The United Kingdom recently announced that it had set a target date of October 2018 to stop the central clearing of checks, which have declined in use by about two-thirds from the peak in 1990. The abolition of checking in Britain would produce annual savings of nearly £1 billion and prevent the destruction of nearly 50,000 trees.[5] The UK lead on this issue and the rise of the "green movement" could spread to other economies, particularly other European Union (EU) countries.

In a related initiative, the Single Euro Payments Area (SEPA) will enable making cashless euro payments to any party located in the euro area using a single bank account and set of payment instruments. All retail payments will become "domestic" as there will no longer be any differentiation between national and cross-border payments within the euro area. The implementation of SEPA is ongoing, with milestone events currently in progress.[6]

 ## COUNTRY RISK ANALYSIS

Country (or sovereign) risk is the possibility that a foreign government will interfere with normal business transactions between counterparties due to an economic or political crisis. Examples of such actions include the debt moratoria declared by the Brazilian and Mexican governments in the early 1980s, and the financial problems of various Asian countries in the late 1990s. Country stability can be monitored through evaluation models published by *The Economist, Euromoney, Business Monitor International,* and other sources.

**Country risk assessment** (CRA) quantifies the possibility that transactions with international counterparties may be interrupted by the interference of the foreign government or due to local conditions through the analysis of political and economic risks. Disruptions may take the form of prohibitions or limitations on currency flows due to economic problems or for political reasons. There were several examples of such outcomes in the 1980s and 1990s in parts of South America, in Mexico, in Russia, and in several Far Eastern countries. Countries with recent problems include Greece, Spain, and Portugal.

### Country Risk Experience

As an illustration of a specific situation, several Asian nations, following Japan's lead, pursued economic practices contrary to those of free market nations. This included overinvesting in factories making products that could not be sold at a profit; oversaving, which dampened the extremely important economic stimulus of consumer spending; overregulating, which distorted the discipline provided by global competition; and (at least in Japan) the cultural tradition of *giri-ninjo*, or the retention of inefficient business practices because of feelings of commitment and empathy toward workers and the community.

In contrast, Western economies have generally encouraged investment but have never assumed that production surpluses could be managed through exporting and planned trade surpluses; have undersaved according to many economists, certainly as reflected in the trillions of dollars of outstanding U.S. debt; and have moved decisively toward deregulation. This is a significant consideration because of the promotion of international business through the World Trade Organization (WTO). The emergence of China has energized the Western economies to seek global opportunities with seemingly huge potential.

Country risk exists when doing business in any sovereign nation, in that rules and laws could change or be unenforceable in a dispute. China and other countries may appear attractive, but working capital managers must be knowledgeable about the country risk. Political, economic, or social instability could disrupt business operations in developing countries, particularly in times of recession or mediocre economic growth.

##  OTHER SIGNIFICANT ISSUES IN INTERNATIONAL WORKING CAPITAL

We noted that the traditional model in organizing for international finance was to direct activities on a centralized basis from the home office. Inefficiencies and delays in accessing markets and in responding to changing conditions have refocused finance to various forms of regional management.

### Structures to Manage FX

Two popular FX management structures are tax-advantaged centers and reinvoicing centers:

1. **Tax-advantaged centers.** Several countries offer low corporate taxes and other benefits to attract multinationals, anticipating that they will establish offices for the management of their various business functions, including finance. In return, the local economy receives economic activity and employment.

   Among these centers are the International Financial Services Company (IFSC) in Ireland, the Belgian Coordination Center (BCC), Swiss and Luxembourg Holding Companies, and Singapore's Operational Headquarters (OHQ). The search for continued efficiencies has led to India, the Philippines, and the Czech Republic becoming increasingly popular locations for these centers.

2. **Reinvoicing centers.** These are centralized financial subsidiaries used by multinational companies to reduce transaction exposure. All home country exports are billed in the home country currency and reinvoiced to each operating affiliate in that affiliate's local currency. Business units do not deal directly with one another but place their orders through the center.

Although title passes to the center,[7] the goods are shipped directly to the purchasing subsidiary. The center gives the multinational enhanced control over international flows while providing both quantitative and qualitative benefits. These include management of FX exposure and improved global working capital management.

## EU Tax-Advantaged Centers

Tax-advantaged centers may eventually be eliminated in the European Union as efforts toward tax harmonization proceed. (**Harmonization** is the enactment of laws in different jurisdictions, such as neighboring countries, that are consistent with one another.) The European Union has discussed such action, but tax rates and practices vary significantly across member countries.

Although no action is likely to occur until the world economy is clearly in recovery, these centers face pressure to be eliminated in favor of standardization and the harmonization of tax regimes. Companies seeking tax benefits may be forced to consider locations outside of the European Union.

## Cross-Border Clearing and Settlement

Delays are nearly always involved in cross-border transactions, primarily because currencies must eventually settle in their country of origin. There are various examples where a foreign currency (usually the U.S. dollar) is widely used in a local economy, and arrangements have been made to clear locally drawn and payable items offshore.

The UK Currency Clearing system clears checks drawn and payable in the City of London in U.S. dollars, Canadian dollars, Australian dollars, Japanese yen, and Swiss francs. Singapore, Hong Kong, the Philippines, and Canada all clear electronic payments and checks in U.S. dollars. Ultimately, the currencies will settle across correspondent accounts in their country of domicile; for example, British pounds will settle in the United Kingdom.

Trade transactions are covered by a well-established, internationally recognized body of rules and regulations issued by the International Chamber of Commerce (ICC). Although the United Nations and the European Community

(EC) are currently attempting to establish limited international guidelines, cross-border movements of cash at present are not subject to any internationally accepted codes of performance.

 ## CULTURAL AND CORPORATE PRACTICES AFFECTING WORKING CAPITAL

Western businesspeople generally do not have enough exposure to international cultures and corporate practices to easily transfer their business activities to foreign countries, particularly where English is not the primary language. A major source of past mistakes has been the arrogance of U.S. executives who were certain that their successes would be repeated in European, Asian, or other societies. Following are some other complexities that need to be considered.[8]

### Cultural Differences

Cultural differences between countries that can affect business relationships include:

- Different holidays, weekends, and religious practices that can significantly limit common business days and delay cross-border transfers.
- Payment preferences may vary; many countries prefer to use electronic payment methods and paper transactions are unusual.
- Payment terms differ. For example, Scandinavian countries usually have credit terms of 15 to 30 days; other countries, such as Italy and Spain, stretch terms out to 90 to 120 days.
- "Getting right down to business" is not always appreciated and may even be regarded as offensive; business discussions may need to be prefaced with an obligatory "small talk" or entertainment session.

### Banking Practices

Banking practices differ between countries in several ways:

- Banking systems of the world vary in structure and have limited cross-border connectivity. Countries have different rules as to who may open accounts and can be authorized signers.
- Bank compensation often varies from U.S. practice; in particular, **value dating**—a determination of a future date on which payment will be

credited in a bank—may be used.[9] Other practices include turnover fees, with some countries charging fees based on a percentage of the value of the activity (debit or credit) in the account; ad valorem charges, based on a percentage of the value of the transaction; and fixed annual charges for access to a high value payment system.

- **Pooling** is offered by many banks. In this arrangement, debit and credit balances of a company's separate accounts are offset daily to calculate a net balance with the bank paying or charging interest on the net debit or credit.
- **Netting** is a process that allows entities to offset their total receivables against their total payables, with each entity either receiving or paying the net amount to the netting center in their local currency.

## Communications Infrastructure

The differences in communications infrastructure include the following:

- Certain developing countries are not able to support the level of technology used in the United States and other developed countries.
- Data lines may not be available or robust for long-distance transmissions.
- A continuous flow of electricity cannot be assumed in certain locations.

## Legal and Tax Issues

Legal and tax issues can also vary:

- Some countries have exchange controls that prohibit the free flow of funds outside the country, or laborious paperwork is required to document a transfer of funds.
- Taxes will likely be due on revenues generated in the local country; the extent to which they are deductible against income on the consolidated financials will depend on whether there is a double taxation treaty.[10]

## Time Zones and Language Barriers

Time zone and language barriers can also complicate business dealings:

- Time zones can have a considerable impact on how working capital is managed. Most companies prefer to organize on a regional basis, ensuring local expertise and a reasonable time span in which to operate.

- Instructions may not be correctly interpreted, problem resolution can be difficult, and account-opening forms can be difficult to understand and complete.
- Although much of the international business world speaks some English, cultural biases and colloquial nuances may result in a different interpretation of a conversation, even between English-speaking people.

 ## SUMMARY

Global working capital management emphasizes risk rather than efficiency (as is the focus in domestic finance), particularly the impact of foreign exchange. The major risks that must be managed are transaction, translation, and economic exposures, and various methods are discussed that allow financial managers to reduce these concerns. International finance is conducted in a cultural and corporate environment that is often at variance from domestic practice, and several of these issues were reviewed.

The chapter also discussed letters of credit and other mechanisms available to reduce the risk of selling to international customers whose creditworthiness is uncertain. Country risk assessment was reviewed, which allows managers to understand concerns in doing business in specific countries. The management of global working capital involves cultural and corporate values that require modifications to domestic practice, as noted toward the end of the chapter.

 ## NOTES

1. To view the LCs of international banks, see www.key.com/pdf/sampleloc .pdf or www.jpmorgan.com/cm/cs?pagename = JPM/DirectDoc&urlname = bd_loc_standby_app.pdf.
2. Credit reporting was discussed in Chapter 6. The firms noted have extended their services throughout North America, Western Europe, and parts of Asia.
3. Money tends to seek the highest possible returns regardless of the global location (except for the issue of risk). As the result, low interest rates in a country will cause investors to execute transactions in a higher-yield currency.
4. For a discussion of international electronic payment mechanisms, see Michele Allman-Ward and James Sagner, *Essentials of Managing Corporate Cash* (Hoboken, NJ: John Wiley & Sons, 2003), 137–170.
5. See "The Demise of the Cheque," House of Commons, document dated Feb. 10, 2010, at www.parliament.uk/business/publications/research/briefing-papers/SN05318/the-demise-of-the-cheque.

6. For further information, see the European Central Bank website, www.ecb
.int/paym/sepa/html/index.en.html.
7. The concept of **title** refers to the ownership of an asset; in this case, the goods
being sold.
8. This listing of international complexities is based on Allman-Ward and Sagner,
Chapter 9, note 4.
9. **Value dating** is a bank practice of taking days of value as a form of compensation. Forward value dating is when the receiving bank provides available
funds on an incoming credit one or two business days forward. With back
value dating, the originating bank will back-value the debit to the account by
one or two business days.
10. A **double taxation treaty** stipulates the rates at which taxes will be levied
between two countries and whether taxes paid in one can be offset against
taxes due in the other.

# Information and Working Capital

This chapter covers these topics:

- Consideration for the ending of the "special" status of information technology and the development of a rational business perspective.
- Understanding how working capital information products are used to communicate between information providers and their business clients.
- Reviewing the features, benefits, and disadvantages of Internet-based bank technology.
- Analyzing enterprise resource planning (ERP) as a more comprehensive approach to developing working capital information.
- Development of a strategy for the selection of a working capital information system.

A S WE HAVE REPORTED THROUGHOUT this book, the management of working capital is complex, involving many different tasks, organizational functions, and sources of information. Fortunately, developments in computer technologies and communications make these activities relatively user-friendly and efficient, with banks and vendors offering integrated platforms requiring secure access to business users. We will first review standard bank technology, discuss ERP systems, and then note customary phases of the selection process.

 ## INFORMATION TECHNOLOGY

Technology is not magic! Systems that support working capital functionality are like all sources of information: successful applications require good management. For any technology to succeed, it must work in harmony with the people and the processes in its organizational function. While many information systems may use a fair amount of their output (volume) capacity, most only use a fraction of their features (functionality).

Far too often, technology can be employed as a remedy for intellectual laziness, in which an organization hands its unresolved problems over to a software vendor with the hope of a miraculous and inexpensive remedy. Technology can also create its own self-serving universe within certain circles and take on a life—complete with insider language and culture—of its own. This can distract attention away from the purpose of the application to the intricacies of the tool.

### The Special Status of IT

Until the recent credit crisis, a significant issue in managing a business was the special status of the information technology function, in that when new hardware or software is requested, it is usually approved. Few companies subjected these acquisitions to rigorous evaluation, and information products were approved based on little more than faith. This situation is changing due to the need to carefully manage capital and the trend toward the outsourcing of technological applications.

Working capital issues to consider in any information technology decision include:

- **Does the project meet the company's requirements?** Large sums have been spent on systems that were never properly scoped and designed, and inevitably more money and time became necessary for even partial implementation. SCM (Chapter 7) systems have been particular problems, as are applications that purport to analyze risk management (to be discussed in Chapter 11).
- **Does the project have internal support, or is a vendor the major proponent?** Internal support is often referred to as having a *champion*.

Technology vendors are talented at developing interest in a project that no one ever considered before, particularly as their compensation is often based on sales commissions. The internal supporter should be willing to stake his or her budget, credibility, time, and even career on a technology success.

■ **Have all costs been considered?** External solutions can appear to be reasonably inexpensive; after all, the vendor may have priced the technology at only $3,000 or $5,000 a month. However, there are many other costs to consider, including parallel testing, implementation, training, staffing, special facilities requirements, documentation, security, additional computing and communications equipment, establishing second sites in the event of a disaster, and other expenditures. The investment only begins with the acquisition of the system. Some costs will directly affect working capital, while others will be depreciated over the expected life of the technology.

■ **Has our company considered outsourcing the project to an application service provider (ASP)?** An **ASP** is a business that sells access to software applications through central servers over a communications network. ASP providers include IBM, Oracle, and hundreds of other companies, some of which focus on the computing requirements of specific industries. Major advantages include the following:

  ■ The ASP's core competency is to support the technology requirements of its clients for a reasonable monthly fee.
  ■ Costs are significantly lower than developing, owning, supporting, creating a backup site, and upgrading a complete system.

Significant disadvantages of ASPs are:

  ■ Specific client requirements cannot be supported except at substantial cost.
  ■ Clients may rely on the ASP to provide a critical business function that limits their control of that function.
  ■ The ASP could decide to limit or terminate the service.
  ■ There could be a change in management support, ownership, or even failure of the ASP.

 ## BANK INFORMATION TECHNOLOGY

Bank information products allow companies to electronically access a full range of financial services and to execute many types of transactions, activities previously available only by personal contact or through separate and costly computer systems. The menu of possible actions is fairly extensive; listed in the following section are modules providing standard and advanced services.

## Development of Bank Systems

Data on daily bank activity were first electronically transmitted on dumb terminals. Little customization was required for clients to receive this transmission, and the banks could provide a useful product, recover their costs, and capture their customers in a semi-permanent relationship. Once a demand for online reporting had been confirmed by customer acceptance, newer versions of the product were developed. A few of the deficiencies included the requirement for repetitive keying to other systems, the need to create company-specific spreadsheets, and the lack of analytical tools.

The result was ill-advised investments in treasury information system (TIS) products with various modules and interfaces. These products were supposed to do everything, be user-friendly, and be easy to install, but not cost a lot more than the early versions of the product, because, after all, banks did not charge much for noncredit services. The problem was that enhancements required enormous development and implementation costs, along with systems professionals to maintain the product.

As banks abandoned these products given the inevitable losses, nonbank vendors jumped into the market with sophisticated, multifunctional products. Traditional pricing has totally changed with such companies as SAP, People-Soft, and SunGard charging well into the hundreds of thousands of dollars, far beyond the equivalent fees received by the banks.

These vendors provide consulting services to assist companies in the analysis of requirements, integration with legacy systems, general ledger interface, implementation, and training. Another approach to TIS today is delivery through the Internet. Vendors create and maintain these systems, usually under the name of the client bank.

## Basic Transactional Functionality

At the most basic level, bank systems are used to optimize and expedite the transactions required to conduct business. In other words, these systems promote information flow, providing the side benefit of convenience, without losing accuracy or compromising security, privacy, or regulatory compliance. Since most commercial software provides the basic transactional functionality, any automated differentiation must be realized by setting system parameters. This is an important requirement in a search if the plan is to offer a unique product or service supported by technology.

Many bank systems are accessible internally and externally using Internet technology. This immediate and seamless delivery of information has improved efficiency and offered banks, and their customers, great gains in service. This exponential growth in functionality makes the basic management of working capital fairly routine. However, the technology used by the bank is important to the customer because access will be through firewalls, security restrictions, and other safeguards.

## Modules for Standard Services

The following modules provide the standard reporting services required by many companies. The term *reporting* refers to information summaries and details of bank account activity.

- **Balance and activity.** The ledger and available balances of yesterday and today are listed in balance and activity reports, including details of debits and credits, float by day (zero, one and two business days), and other transactions. Companies use these data to begin the periodic (often daily) process of developing a cash budget. Banks run their DDA systems (from which much of this information is derived) at night, with previous-day activity available the next morning. As same-day reporting requires feeds from separate systems and is more costly to provide, there is usually a premium charge for this service. DDAs and cash budgets were discussed in Chapter 4.
- **Multibank polling and parsing.** Account data can be retrieved by *polling* banks electronically and then downloading or *parsing* information into reports based on a script developed at the time of installation. Important features include the following:
  - Automatic dialing of banks
  - Electronic responses through scripts
  - Selection of appropriate data
  - Formatting into reports
  - Exception reports of banks for whom information was unavailable
- **Wire transfer.** As discussed in Chapter 3, Fedwire transfers are same-day, final transfers used primarily for large-dollar transactions. Appropriate practice for control and security strongly encourages that these transactions be initiated, approved, and released through a bank's software (rather than by telephone or fax), using keys and passwords unique to the sender and receiver. In fact, the few recent cases of fraudulent wire transactions involved manual wires, and some banks charge as much as $100 per manual wire to discourage such activity.
- **ACH.** Many banks now offer terminal-based ACH, allowing debit and credit transfers to be initiated by finance rather than through the mainframe computer system. This permits flexibility in sending and receiving payments for a low fee, and allows the initiation of ACHs or intrabank transfers to cover the daily clearing amount in controlled disbursement accounts.

- **Controlled disbursement.** TIS modules offer various electronic reporting options, including stop payments (for checks issued in error), the transmission of checks issued files (for positive pay review and monthly reconciliation), the review of positive pay mismatches, and account reconciliation data.
- **Bank relationship management.** This module includes information on bank relationships and contacts including:
  - Name, address, telephone, and fax numbers
  - Names of senior managers, calling officers, and customer service staff
  - History of the relationship and calling efforts
  - Listing of services used, persistent problems, and unique capabilities
  - Credit facilities available and used, as well as fees, restrictions, and other covenants

## Modules for Advanced Services

Larger banks offer additional modules designed to meet the needs of companies doing business globally:

- **Foreign exchange (FX).** Modules to expedite the process of purchasing or selling FX, primarily in the major currencies used in international transactions. Other FX may be available based on the market presence of each bank and the requirements of its corporate customers. In addition to automating FX transactions, these modules offer lower transaction charges and better rates than by manually contacting financial institutions.
- **Letters of credit.** Export and import financing often requires bank letters of credit (LCs) to ensure payment once all documentation and other requirements have been completed; see Chapter 9. LC modules enable automated processing of the LC and supporting documentation.
- **International money transfer.** Funds movement between global banks involves linking various different international money transfer systems, usually using SWIFT formats.[1] In addition, extensive cross-border payment capabilities help companies manage payments globally through a single message to the bank.
- **Investment management.** Portfolios of investments can be managed by listing short- and long-term holdings, including trades, market-to-market pricing, and the tracking of dividends, interest, and other income. Larger financial institutions offer a full array of products, including:
  - Automated sweep services
  - Fixed income securities

- Money market funds
- Tax-advantaged investments
- Managed account solutions
- **Debt management.** Debt modules report credit line activity, commercial paper outstanding, fixed and floating rate instruments, and intercompany loans. Global capabilities may include pooling, a technique used by in-house banks (often located in treasury centers) to offset the deficits in the accounts of certain subsidiaries with excess cash in the accounts of other subsidiaries; and netting, involving the reduction in the number of intracompany payments through the consolidation and aggregation of individual transactions. These techniques were noted in Chapter 9.

 ## INTERNET BANK TECHNOLOGY

The widespread use of the Internet has evolved to the current situation where banks have backed away from product support. This development has occurred due both to the cost of the expertise and equipment and to the difficulty of keeping products current with rapidly evolving customer demands. A number of banks use systems provided by ACI Worldwide, Fiserv, and other ASP vendors.[2] See Exhibit 10.1 for selected working capital functionalities provided by ASPs.

**EXHIBIT 10.1**  Working Capital Internet Technology Features

Business intelligence

Compliance

Cross-selling capability and client support

Document management and imaging

End-to-end bank platforms

Image technology

Integrated risk management

Multichannel customer sales and service

New account setup

Online banking

Relational databases

Secure online banking channels and transactions

Straight-through processing

Teller, mobile, and Internet banking

Entry to bank Internet-based systems is through a standard Web browser, allowing the menu of financial services to be accessible at any time and in all locations. As a result, the finance manager is no longer tied to a specific PC loaded with the bank's proprietary software. This allows distant computing in situations when staff is traveling, when other personnel must review a transaction, or if a disaster were to prevent entry to the usual office location.

## Responsibilities in Banking Decisions

The appropriate organizational responsibility must be involved in banking decisions. While finance manages banking, relevant information often resides in another area of the company. As an example, check mismatches (where the issued and clearing check numbers and/or amounts due not match) occur due to errors by company or bank personnel, or because the recipient or a thief has altered the check.

Banks provide positive pay to find these situations and report them to the issuing company, with a time limit on whether or not to honor the check; see Chapter 3. The issuing function (e.g., accounts payable) can review positive pay files directly to determine if check mismatches should be honored or rejected.

Before Web-based platforms became standard practice, this process was handled by finance staff that was often uninformed as to the purpose or validity of a particular disbursement. The result was a series of telephone calls, e-mails, or faxes, and any delay meant that the period for review (usually only about four hours) might expire. In that situation, the bank decision reverts to the preset "accept" or "reject" rule made by the company at the time the account was established, and that default is almost always "accept."

Other functions in a company similarly require data from banks that can be viewed using the Internet. For example, sales managers want to ship but experience slow-paying customers that present a risk to the collection of receivables. With access to lockbox receipts, they can quickly determine whether payments have been received and if it is appropriate to ship against pending orders.

## Benefits of Internet Bank Technology

There are various advantages to the use of Web-based technology services:

- **Cost.** A full range of modules is available to users at nominal cost. Automating bank transactions greatly reduces costs for personnel, technology, and customer service, and presents a suite of technology services previously unavailable to many medium-sized and smaller companies.

- **Secure single-platform access.** Access through a single platform allows the corporate user to move easily from one product to another. Security is provided through transport layer security (TLS) protocols,[3] multiple levels of user IDs, monitoring by the bank, and various other controls.
- **Ease of implementation and upgrading.** New modules can be installed with minimal setup, delivery effort, and cost. User-friendly menus enable users to quickly learn and adopt new technology, and banks provide online tutorials to allow on-demand training and unlimited repetitions. There is no requirement for physical installation of software, as the information modules reside on the bank's server.
- **Disaster recovery.** Banks have multiple backup sites for their computer services, and these locations are widely dispersed to avoid the risk of a catastrophe affecting more than one data center. These facilities are stress tested frequently for reactions to emergency situations.
- **File exporting.** Working capital management is simplified through file exporting in various formats to support accounting, receivables, payables, and inventory management. However, the working capital file interfaces are generally not integrated in a common platform, as are ERP systems.
- **Reports.** Companies can receive summary and detailed reports on every service, each user, by product and by bank account. Control is enhanced through this reporting and the archiving of activity; see Chapter 8 for a comment on the control requirements of the Sarbanes-Oxley Act.

## Disadvantages of Internet Bank Technology

Disadvantages include the following:

- **Noncore competency.** Many banks would prefer not to allocate the required capital or expertise to the design and maintenance of an Internet-based product. For this reason, ASPs have become the primarily providers of bank technology. As a result, the bank does not "own" the product; the ASP does.
- **Service coverage.** The scope of functions offered by even the largest banks is limited to standard financial products.[4] As a result, information is not provided on the other working capital functions as listed in Exhibit 10.2.

**EXHIBIT 10.2** Working Capital Lines of Business Features (for Typical ERP Systems)

**Finance**
■ Accelerate closing of financial statements.
■ Optimize working capital.
■ Integrate and support functions for treasury and cash management.

**Asset management**
■ Improve visibility of company assets.
■ Enhance access to management of intellectual property.
■ Increase asset safety and compliance.

**Human resources**
■ Improve management of employees.
■ Control HR management costs.

**Environment, health, and safety**
■ Increase the ability to identify and mitigate environmental, health, and safety risks.
■ Streamline environmental, health, and safety processes.
■ Manage and report compliance for corporate safety policies.

**Manufacturing**
■ Synchronize global manufacturing fulfillment.
■ Increase efficiency in logistics and fulfillment processes.
■ Manage configured products and service parts better.
■ Control the global network of suppliers.

**Marketing**
■ Optimize sales and marketing efforts.
■ Leverage insight to align marketing and sales activities.
■ Retain profitable customers.

**Procurement**
■ Streamline and centralize procure-to-payables processes.
■ Enforce comprehensive contract compliance.
■ Improve visibility into supplier performance.
■ Increase visibility of purchasing activities.

**Product development**
■ Accelerate delivery of innovative products to market.
■ Collaborate with partners in the delivery of safe products.

**Sales**
- Implement sales strategies that promote growth.
- Increase the efficiency of sales teams.
- Accelerate sales cycles.

**Service**
- Deliver superior customer service.
- Quickly resolve customer problems.
- Optimize the use of resources available for service.
- Increase cross-selling and up-selling to existing customers.

**Supply chain management**
- Respond to global supply and demand dynamics.
- Synchronize supply and demand.
- Leverage technologies to uniquely identify inventory.
- Deal effectively with supply chain incidents like recalls.

**Information technology**
- Use information technology to increase enterprise competitiveness.
- Lower total cost of ownership of technology.
- Increase user satisfaction with installed software.

*Source:* Derived from descriptions of SAP ERP systems, at www.sap.com, Oracle ERP systems, at www .oracle.com, and Sungard ERP systems, at www.sungard.com.

## ERP: AN ALTERNATIVE APPROACH

We briefly mentioned the topic of ERP in Chapter 8, defining the concept as an integrated approach to managing a company's resources. The coverage of an ERP installation is much broader than bank Internet technology, involving many of the working capital accounts discussed throughout this book. Furthermore, the extension of these applications into so many business activities goes far beyond traditional accounting system data, which focus on ledger entries in response to fairly rigid regulatory requirements, providing assistance to management in its decision-making activities.

### Why ERP?

ERP responded to manager demands for information that would provide in-depth information on many working capital issues and help answer "what if"–type questions. Why are sales declining in a particular market? Why is this customer less profitable than that customer? What has been the sales outcome when prices rose or advertising expenditures fell?

In order to accomplish this goal without creating individual systems for each company, ERP was organized around standard modules, requiring that existing business processes be mapped using a thorough business process analysis before selecting an ERP vendor and beginning implementation.

This analysis should document current operations, enabling selection of an ERP vendor whose standard modules are most closely aligned with the established organization. Furthermore, ERP systems can extend beyond a single organization to support comprehensive business activities that cross a company's organizational, departmental, and geographic boundaries, including customers, suppliers, and partners.

## Advantages from ERP

There are various advantages to the use of ERP:

- **Common interface.** A typical problem that companies face is the lack of a common interface between the various systems they use. For example, most accounting software does not interact with bank technology, while supply chain management involves yet another entirely different platform and data entry protocols. As we noted, files can only be interfaced through exporting protocols. ERP can end these "silos" and allow functional components of a business to communicate rather than be separate and focused on their own objectives.
- **Best practices.** Vendors use generally accepted "best practices" to design the modules that support ERP. These procedures assist inefficient companies in adapting effective approaches to specific business activities through the necessary redesign and reengineering that allows ERP to function.
- **Control of sensitive data.** ERP systems reduce the risk of the loss of sensitive data by combining multiple access permissions and security models into a single structure. Security features protect against outsider crime, such as industrial espionage, and insider crime, such as embezzlement.

## Disadvantages of ERP

ERP systems are typically complex and usually impose significant changes on staff work practices. Implementing the process is typically too complicated for internal personnel, forcing companies to hire outside assistance to implement these systems. As the result of these complexities, there are three issues to consider, particularly when compared to competitive bank technology as supported by internal systems:

1. **Modules require standardization.** ERP systems inherently require modular components based on standard business processes. Companies desiring to implement ERP must reconfigure existing activities to meet the system's requirements, and it is precisely the unique approach of a business that may have led to marketplace success. While there is nothing wrong with reengineering an established set of procedures,[5] the effort should provide clear added value.
2. **Time, cost, and other implementation issues.** The length of time to implement ERP is often greater than one year, and involves both internal staff and consultants. The cost of an ERP can be $1 million or more considering software and consultant fees.[6] Any estimate of time and cost depends on the size of the business, the number of modules, the extent of customization, the scope of the business change, and the willingness of the company to take ownership for the project.
3. **Training.** Other than implementation, a considerable problem with ERP results from an inadequate effort in ongoing training. With bank systems, the training is focused on the user (and not on the information technology function) through Internet downloads and tutorials. This avoids reengineering entire business processes, purchasing new generations of hardware and software, and other potential delays.

## CHOOSING WORKING CAPITAL INFORMATION SYSTEMS

The implementation of a working capital system should be constructed as a multiphase effort, with each phase logically following from the conclusions reached in the previous step. It is appropriate to remind readers that many information projects fail, and the culprit is poor management, not flawed technology.

The Standish Group, which has performed extensive research on project management for the last several decades, estimates that about two-thirds of these efforts fail because they do not meet at least one of the following three criteria: estimated completion date, anticipated cost, or promised features. In fact, most projects miss more than one of the criteria, and all too often dates and costs are "met" by significantly overestimating the initial projection.[7]

## Information System Problems? It's Easier to Unplug Than Sue

In considering a working capital information system, remember that bank products are "plug and play"—that is, there is little implementation other than to comply with relatively simple bank protocols. Furthermore, these modules reside on bank computers (or on those of the third-party provider that actually sells and supports the system). If a company is unhappy or dissatisfied with the product, it can "unplug" and inform the bank to stop invoicing.

ERP systems are major capital investments that cannot easily be abandoned. According to *CIO Magazine*, the recent history of this software "is packed with tales of vendor mud-slinging, outrageous hype and epic failures."[8] A partial listing of dissatisfied companies includes Hershey Foods, Nike, Hewlett-Packard, and Select Comfort. These situations resulted in losses in the hundreds of millions of dollars, unhappy customers, lawsuits, and other unfortunate outcomes.

### Phase 1: Determine Requirements

The decision on working capital technology begins with an analysis of a company's requirements, particularly considering how data are currently used and whether there are any perceived deficiencies. Management should focus on situations where information is clearly inadequate to support decision making. For example, which products are profitable, by customer and by market? Would this information assist us in making better decisions, or is it interesting but not particularly critical? And, can it be developed from existing data sources?

A useful approach is to establish an ad hoc project team to compile a list of unanswered questions that are important to the business. This committee should represent functions likely to be affected by any decision on a new system. The list should drive the decision on whether to proceed to step two. Here are a few concerns noted by companies in recent technology reviews:

- **What time of day does the company typically know its cash position?** Is this timing adequate to allow finance to make optimal investing or borrowing decisions?
- **Are interfaces to other systems primarily manual?** That is, do interfaces with accounting, financial, and other systems involve internal company communications and the rekeying of data? Does this situation cause difficulties in managing our business or an unacceptable error rate, or is it merely an inconvenience?

- **Does the company use JIT (see Chapter 8)?** Is there sufficient knowledge about the financial health of vendors? What would happen if there were a bankruptcy or a serious shipping delay?
- **What is the customer retention history?** Does the company attempt to sell "up" to more profitable customers, or is marketing primarily reactive to incoming opportunities?
- **Do employees understand the strategy for expanding business?** Would better training, selection practices, and/or compensation improve the ability to deliver quality products or services to the marketplace?
- **Would a function-specific application be adequate for the company's requirements?** For example, would an FX and investment quotation system (e.g., Bloomberg) be adequate, or a system that supports specific assets or liabilities (such as have been discussed throughout this book), or a risk management system (see Chapter 11)?

## Phase 2: Conduct Vendor Search

Venues that provide competitive information on bank and ERP products include the following:

- **Bank technology conferences.** The most important exhibition for banks and affiliated vendors is the Association of Financial Professionals (AFP) annual conference, which meets every autumn in a major U.S. city. The number of exhibitors at this event is about 200, perhaps one-third of which offer some form of working capital technology. In addition, local treasury associations hold regular meetings. For further information, see www.afponline.org.
- **ERP conferences and seminars.** As with most systems products, conferences and seminars tend to be either sponsored by the vendor (i.e., Microsoft) or by a vendor's user group, or for a specific industry (i.e., retailing). For a partial listing of webinars, see panorama-consulting.com. Some universities offer courses on ERP; for example, the Missouri University of Science and Technology offers programs in conjunction with SAP covering various ERP topics.[9]
- **Websites and bank contacts.** See Appendix II for a listing of websites. Bankers and ERP salespeople can arrange for product demonstrations.

### Technology Demonstrations—Travel or Stay Home?

The cost of attendance at a national conference that offers opportunities for bank demonstrations of Internet systems can be $4,000 or more, including registration fees, hotel, meals, and transportation. The opportunity to see and compare systems in one central venue was cost-effective until the credit crisis that began in 2008. The resulting reduction in staff at many companies, restrictions on travel, and advances in teleconferencing and website demonstrations now make the in-office review and analysis of competing systems quite feasible.[10]

Banks and vendors should be contacted for detailed information on technology offerings, including modules, hardware requirements, implementation support, and typical pricing. The responses should be reviewed for compatibility with business requirements, and a ranking should be developed to focus on no more than three or four candidate systems. An early recommended step is to request and contact references of companies that are comparable in size and industry coverage. See the appendix to Chapter 5 for more information on the process of reviewing bank and vendor proposals.

### Phase 3: Provide Justification to Senior Management

Companies' requirements should be matched against the technology specifications provided by bidders. However, traditional economic analysis will not be of much assistance in making the decision on working capital information software. There are three important benefits from such a system that are difficult to subject to traditional capital budgeting analysis:

1. **The quality of the information.** Rather than receiving (or searching for) raw data, working capital managers had the opportunity to view a variety of data organized through logical analysis and reporting.
2. **The opportunity for rationalization of documents and processes.** Bank technology and ERP systems organize existing files from various sources, making it possible to quickly locate actionable information leading to the choice of appropriate business tactics.
3. **The general business process efficiencies gained through the improvement of existing practices.** The reengineering of established but somewhat out-of-date procedures is a major benefit from the decision to implement new working capital technology.

If the decision is based solely on economics, the likelihood is that bank technology will be chosen. In most situations, ERP can only be justified if the time and cost to implement supports the long-term strategy of the company. Whatever decision is made, the following issues should be addressed in the justification statement:

▪ Which provider will service and maintain the product: the bank, the vendor, the ASP, or internally (probably through the information technology function)? Will the service be available 24/7 or only during normal business hours? Is the product supported by technology experts or by customer service staff who respond to questions?

■ What happens in the event of a system failure or disaster? Does the service provider have adequate, secure backup facilities?

■ Is there concern for compatibility with other financial and accounting systems?

■ Is the product user-friendly, or will extensive training be required?

■ What is the commitment of the bank or vendor to the business? How long is the provider likely to continue to offer, support, and improve the product?

## Information Principles

When considering information changes in support of working capital management, consider seven basic principles to guide decision making:

1. Remember that technology is not magic, nor is it an end; it is a means (a tool) to the end.
2. Define the purpose of the working capital function.
3. Determine the functions and proper use of people, process, and technology.
4. Use a disciplined methodology to create and reengineer the workplace.
5. Learn how to exploit the functionalities of bank or ERP systems.
6. Analyze the costs and benefits of information systems as rigorously as any capital budgeting decision.
7. Ensure that there is security, privacy, and regulatory compliance.

 **SUMMARY**

Information technology decisions require the analysis of several issues: Are our requirements likely to be met; is there adequate internal support; do we fully understand the necessary investment; and have we considered using an outsourcing vendor (such as an ASP)? The two primary choices are bank information technology and enterprise resource planning (ERP) systems, and decision factors include cost, ease of access, comprehensiveness of the module offerings, the opportunity to redesign internal processes, and the extent of future internal commitment to manage these resources. A three-step process is recommended to resolve these issues: (1) determine requirements, (2) conduct a vendor search, and (3) provide justification to senior management.

**NOTES**

1. SWIFT messages allow a "host" electronic banking platform to act as the conduit to transmit wire transfer messages to other banks. SWIFT is an acronym for Society for Worldwide Interbank Financial Telecommunications. For further information, see www.swift.com.
2. For additional information, see Fiserv at www.fiserv.com or ACI at www.aciworldwide.com. The consulting firm Booz•Allen & Hamilton has a useful explanation of ASP capabilities at www.boozallen.com/media/file/ASP_Whitepaper.pdf.
3. Transport Layer Security (TLS) and its predecessor SSL are cryptographic procedures that provide security for communications over the Internet and other networks.
4. Regulation Y (12 CFR 225.21) issued by the Federal Reserve prohibits banks from engaging in businesses that are beyond the scope of traditional banking activities. For this reason, it is unlikely (at least for the foreseeable future) that banks will offer information services that go beyond the standard concept of "cash."
5. Indeed, the author's first book was entitled *Cashflow Reengineering* (New York: AMACOM, 1997).
6. "The Total Cost of ERP Ownership," Aberdeen Group, October 17, 2006, reported at www.oracle.com/corporate/analyst/reports/corporate/cp/es101306.pdf.
7. See "CHAOS Summary 2009" (April 23, 2009), www.slideshare.net/AccelerateManagement/chaos-summary-2009-the-standish-group. This conclusion was supported by academic research reported in H. Liang, N. Saraf, Q. Hu, and Y. Xue, "Assimilation of Enterprise Systems: The Effect of Institutional Pressures and the Mediating Role of Top Management," *MIS Quarterly* 31 (2007): 59–87.
8. See Thomas Wailgum, "10 Famous ERP Disasters, Dustups and Disappointments," *CIO Magazine* (March 24, 2009), at www.cio.com/article/486284/10_Famous_ERP_Disasters_Dustups_and_Disappointments.
9. See the Missouri University of Science and Technology's website at www.mst.edu.
10. For example, visit JPMorgan Chase at www.jpmorgan.com (Treasury Services tab) to register for a demonstration and explanation of their electronic banking products. Other bank websites with similar capabilities are listed in Appendix II.

# CHAPTER ELEVEN

# Managing the Working Capital Cycle

This chapter covers these topics:

- Understanding risk management issues in working capital, including ERM.
- Appreciation for the measurement of working capital efficiency.
- Determination of the process of liquidity management.
- Consideration of how traditional and modern attitudes have changed the management of working capital.
- Review of working capital ideas and implementation procedures.

THROUGHOUT THIS BOOK WE HAVE discussed the accounts on the balance sheet that drive working capital, including current assets and liabilities. In addition, we devoted chapters to international and information systems issues. There are three concerns in managing the working capital cycle that encompass essential topics in managing any business: risk management, efficiency, and liquidity. Each will be discussed in this chapter.

**RISK AND WORKING CAPITAL**

**Risk** is in the possibility of loss or injury. The measurement of risk has traditionally been through the frequency of human or property loss in specific categories, such as death or disability by age, sex and occupation, or the frequency of fire damage to specific types of construction at various locations. In the past, we managed risk using established hedging mechanisms, including insurance, futures, and options.

With **insurance**, the policyholder accepts a small certain loss—the premium expense—rather than the possibility of a large catastrophic loss. Futures and options are types of derivative contracts traded on exchanges that guarantee a price at a specified later time. The buyer of the contract is under no obligation to take delivery and may terminate the contract by selling (closing) the position.[1]

### Risks Inherent in Working Capital

Markets now recognize that there are types of working capital risk that require management action even though there are no established hedges to mitigate these events:

- **Operational risk** is normal to business, as it arises from problems with technology, employees, or operations. These risks are often managed by the establishment of policies and procedures to govern the conduct of ongoing activities. Realistically, behaviors cannot be regulated by proclamation. However, assigning specific duties states the company's position on responsibilities, sets a charter for acceptable corporate and employee behavior, and assesses penalties should violations occur.
- **Credit risk** concerns the failure of customers to pay amounts owed and due in a timely manner. We manage these types of risk through credit reports and debt management services provided by credit reporting companies; see Chapter 6 for a discussion.
- **Liquidity risk** is a company's inability to pay obligations as they come due, resulting in financial embarrassment, a negative impact on the company's credit rating, and vendor relations and potential bankruptcy. This risk is managed by arranging for lines of credit and access to other "safety" financing.
- **Information reporting risk** is the receipt of inaccurate information from a financial institution or vendor, most usually in the daily transmission of bank account entries, balances, or transactions. These errors can result from formatting errors or from misunderstandings as to the meaning of specific data fields. This risk is managed by carefully matching book

(ledger) entries to bank or vendor entries, and immediately reconciling any variances by communications with the reporter of the information.

## TRADITIONAL RISK MANAGEMENT

In the past, the management of risk has been through separate business functions, the responsibilities for which reside with various organizational units. When risks are treated separately, internal specialists have managed risks as independent activities. For example:

- Lawyers and compliance officers treat regulatory and political risks.
- Insurance buyers acquire coverage for various types of life, health, and property and casualty risks.
- Security specialists, occupational safety and health advisors, environmental engineers, and contingency and crisis management planners all work individually toward a safe and secure work environment.
- Financial staff manages derivative, liquidity, foreign exchange, interest rate, and financial institution risks.
- Credit and collection or accounts receivable monitors credit risk.

Using this approach, the interdependencies and interrelationships of business risks can be overlooked, resulting in potentially inadequate safeguards for the assets of the enterprise.

## ENTERPRISE RISK MANAGEMENT

**Enterprise risk management** (ERM) attempts to identify, prioritize, and quantify the risks from all sources that threaten the working capital and strategic objectives of the corporation. The ERM approach views risk as pervasive in a company and considers a coordinated approach through a formal organizational function to be essential.

ERM reduces the volatility inherent in business activities and helps to achieve consistent earnings and manage costs. Adverse business and financial incidents have occurred in various industries, such as the Exxon *Valdez* oil spill (in 1989),[2] the Ford/Bridgestone-Firestone tire recall crisis (in 2000),[3] and the BP Gulf of Mexico oil spill (in 2010).[4]

One popular approach to ERM has been **value-at-risk (VaR)**. VaR is an approach to determining the risk exposure in a portfolio of assets. Although certain risks (e.g., financial instruments, credit, commodity prices) can be forced into the VaR model, it is a process that is heavily dependent on historical patterns. Other risks are not subject to the same statistical calculations and may be inadequately considered. Some companies using VaR supplement their analysis by stress-testing to determine likely performance in various worst-case scenarios.

VaR calculates the amount of risk inherent in a financial portfolio with a predefined confidence level (usually 95 percent), including risk covariance.[5] Computer model simulations typically cannot anticipate the "perfect storm" (or worst-case) scenario, when all factors are adverse at the same time. The latter can occur when markets are illiquid (as in 2008–2009).

 ## THE ERM PROCESS

ERM involves three separate steps that should be supported by a continuous monitoring process:

1. **Identify risk.** The first step is to scan or recognize the elements of a company's working capital risks. Although various types of risk were noted earlier, every organization faces a unique set of variables that must be specified and enumerated.
2. **Measure and prioritize risk.** Not all risks can be proactively managed, and managers should prioritize and act on those with potential significance to the security of the business. High-priority working capital risks could include the following:

   ▪ A marketing decision that could impact a product or a customer relationship
   ▪ Significant problems with critical information systems
   ▪ Substantial increases in cost factors
   ▪ Sudden cash outflows due to unexpected expenses
   ▪ Suppliers and/or customer defaults

   Medium-priority risks would include any action that could impact the goals in the business plan but does not threaten the company. Examples could include problems with noncritical information systems and the loss of a significant customer or of a contract.
3. **Manage enterprise risk.** The company must determine the likely occurrence of each risk not yet subject to traditional risk management techniques, the application of outcome probabilities, the determination of the covariance of risk dependencies, and the development of appropriate actions.

# EFFICIENCY AND WORKING CAPITAL

The ratios developed in earlier chapters are insufficient to absolutely determine evidence of good or poor working capital management. Using Troy's metrics that were referenced in Chapter 2, it can be seen that the Rengas Company we examined is producing superior profitability compared to its industry (plastics manufacturing); see Exhibit 11.1. Additional evidence in Exhibit 11.2 implies that Rengas is doing an excellent job in managing cash and other working capital components. Let's look a little deeper.

## Management Differences in Current Asset Accounts

As we discussed in Chapter 1 (in the traditional and modern views of working capital), excessive working capital constitutes a hindrance to performance.

**EXHIBIT 11.1**  Financial Ratios

|  | Industry Mean | Rengas Company |
|---|---|---|
| Current ratio | 1.5 times | 2.9 times |
| Quick ratio | 0.8 times | 2.2 times |
| Receivables turnover | 7.4 times | 5.5 times |
| Inventory turnover | 7.2 times | 6.7 times |
| Profits-to-sales | 1.5% | 9.1% |
| Return-on-equity | 7.9% | 21.8% |

*Sources:* Industry ratios are based on Leo Troy, *Almanac of Business and Industrial Financial Ratios* (Riverwoods, IL: Commerce Clearing House, 2006 and 2009); company ratios are derived from the Exhibits 1.1 and 2.1 financial statements.

**EXHIBIT 11.2**  Supplemental Ratios

| (times) | Industry Mean | Rengas Company |
|---|---|---|
| Net sales to WC | 10.0 | 3.5 |
| Current assets to WC | 3.0 | 1.5 |
| Current liabilities to WC | 2.0 | 0.5 |
| Total receipts to cash flow* | 9.1 | 30.0 |
| CGS to cash flow* | 6.6 | 20.0 |

WC = working capital
*Troy defines cash flow as the difference between cash receipts and cash disbursements. For purposes of this analysis, the net cash position in Exhibit 1.1 is used in Exhibit 11.2.
*Sources:* Industry ratios are based on Leo Troy, *Almanac of Business and Industrial Financial Ratios* (Riverwoods, IL: Commerce Clearing House, 2006 and 2009); company ratios are derived from the Exhibits 1.1 and 2.1 financial statements.

Emphasis should be on reducing these requirements so that current liabilities can be funded from the ongoing operations of a business. Close examination of our illustrative company shows that both current assets and current liabilities are excessive compared to working capital, and that both receivables and inventory are underperforming versus the industry.

These findings are summarized in the current and quick ratios, both of which are superior in the traditional view but mediocre in the modern view of working capital. More aggressive management of accounts receivable to the industry average would reduce that current account to about $20 million (from $27.5 million), and of inventory would reduce that account to about $14 million (from $15 million). The total savings would be about $8.5 million, valued at $850,000 at a 10 percent cost of capital.

It is somewhat ironic that the cash portion of the working capital cycle in our example shows superior performance but the receivables and inventory portions are underperforming. The urgency of access to cash has led to various banking products that have improved cash management, while focus on other working capital elements has lagged.

Banks began to develop these services in the 1970s when short-term interest rates rose to nearly 20 percent. Companies gradually became educated in their use and advantages, and financial institutions found that attractive returns and corporate client "capture" resulted from aggressive promotion of suites of cash products.

There has not been a similar effort in inventory, receivables, or payables management, and in fact, materials suppliers and customers demonstrate behaviors that often lead to poor management. For example, if a company has acquired unsalable inventory or materials that have decayed, the natural response is to buy replacements and scrap or warehouse the unusable portion. In effect, the problem continues and may even become worse, and only gets attention the one time a year that a physical inventory is taken for purposes of financial reporting. Similarly, slow- and no-paying customers are carried beyond any reasonable time, because it is easier to sell to existing customers than find new buyers.

### The Required Teamwork

Opportunities to reduce total working capital cycle time must be investigated by the appropriate disciplines:

- The materials element requires input from the purchasing function.
- Production managers should examine the work-in-process element.

▪ Invoice preparation needs attention from production, invoicing, and information technology managers.

▪ Receipt of funds includes elements of receivables management, finance, and credit and collection, and it requires input from these areas.

The development of data from these various functions demands more teamwork than is customary in many traditional line-and-staff organizations; recall our earlier comments regarding organizing for each working capital element. Lack of cooperation is often the cause of failure when results are below industry averages. The required application of modern business processes is difficult as the priority of employees and managers is accomplishing day-to-day work assignments. Our recommended integrative approach can be used both to plan the pricing and profitability of products and services, and to determine the cause of failure to meet profitability targets.[6]

 ## WORKING CAPITAL AND LIQUIDITY

The examination of recent data on liquidity shows that the current ratio of American businesses has barely changed in the past three years, while the cash required to support sales activity has declined in every observation selected from a sample representing 20 percent of U.S. industries; see Exhibit 11.3.[7] Stability in the current ratio and the resulting minimal information content reflect the realignment of working capital by companies to changing economic conditions.

### How to Measure and Manage Liquidity

A much more useful measure of liquidity is total receipts (revenues for most companies) divided by cash flow (TR/CF). Between 2005 and 2008, TR/CF declined from 9.8 times to 6.8 times.[8] Applying these revenue data to the ratio of receipts to cash flow, we calculate that cash rose from 10.2 percent to 15.4 percent of the balance sheets of the companies in this sample, an increase of more than one-third in only three years. This reflects the rapidly declining reliance of businesses on short-term credit lines from banks and other sources, and the hoarding of cash to meet transactional and precautionary needs.

These data support our previous conclusion that many businesses have become knowledgeable and aggressive in managing their cash positions:

▪ **Adjustment by business.** Companies adjusted remarkably well to the 2008–2010 contraction of credit and liquidity, and to weakened economic

**EXHIBIT 11.3**   Changes in Liquidity Ratios in U.S. Industry Groups (2006–2009)[a]

| Industry Groups | NAICS Series[b] | Change in Current Ratio | Change in Total Receipts to Cash Flow |
|---|---|---|---|
| Agriculture | 11 | 0.17 | −0.23 |
| Mining | 21 | −0.25 | −0.40 |
| Construction | 23 | 0.08 | −0.29 |
| Manufacturing | 31–33 | 0.01 | −0.41 |
| Wholesaling | 42 | 0.00 | −0.29 |
| Retailing | 44–45 | −0.03 | −0.15 |
| Transportation and Warehousing | 48–49 | 0.13 | −0.20 |
| Information | 51 | −0.02 | −0.38 |
| Other | 62 & 72 | 0.11 | −0.12 |
| Unweighted Change[c] | | *0.02* | *−0.30* |

[a] The period representing the top of the economic cycle to the present time.
[b] For a complete listing of all North American Industry Classification System (NAICS) codes, see www.naics.com.
[c] Calculated based on the individual changes in 25 industries.
*Sources:* Based on calculations by the author from a sample of Current Ratios (#30) and ratios of Total Receipts to Total Cash Flow (#42) for 25 industries (of about 135 industries); Leo Troy, *Almanac of Business and Industrial Ratios* (Riverwoods, IL: Commerce Clearing House, 2006 and 2009). Table 1: Companies with and without Net Income. Excluded from the sample were public utilities (as revenues are regulated by public service commissions), financial companies, and professional service organizations.

conditions. Certainly there have been companies that failed to adequately cope with these unprecedented conditions (at least since the Great Depression), and the result has been bankruptcy. However, many businesses have taken the necessary steps to survive, such as terminating marginal employees, negotiating with vendors and landlords, and working harder and smarter.

▪ **Need for new liquidity measurements.** The traditional tools for measuring liquidity are not helpful in the current situation. The underlying assumptions in using these techniques are predictable revenues and costs, and available credit at a fair price to worthy borrowers. As businesspeople know only too well, revenues have not been predictable and credit remains tight in recent times.

Instead, liquidity needs must be calculated from longer-term results, by industry, using data from Troy on TR/CF. Banks are taking note of this situation, and future loan covenants may stress TR/CF over the less useful standard liquidity ratios as protection against providing credit in deteriorating business conditions.

■ **Liquidity is more than cash.** Cash is only a portion of the liquidity requirements of any business. The typical U.S. company may carry about 10 percent of its balance sheet as cash in normal times, assuming that an additional 5 percent of liquidity will be from bank credit lines. In times of economic distress such as 2008–2009, cash holdings rise to about 15 percent of the balance sheet. Inevitably, higher cash holdings results in lessened expenditures for current assets and capital project investments, stifling growth and profitability.[9] However, the priority in a credit crisis must be survival rather than long-term strategic concerns.

■ **Business needs an integrated approach to managing other working capital accounts.** Cash is only one portion of a comprehensive working capital effort; receivables, inventory, and payables are collectively more significant and deserve equivalent attention.

## SUGGESTED ACTIONS

Following are 50 action steps that companies should be taking to ensure survival and eventual growth. Measuring and understanding working capital requirements are essential components of any company's financial plan.

### General Ideas

1. Calculate the cost of capital to value the savings that may be available in reducing working capital.
2. Determine the amount of working capital float and consider alternative processes to improve float management.
3. Use ratio analysis to compare working capital performance against industry averages.
4. Understand that cash is found in three forms—bank cash, line of credit cash and cash invested short-term—and each must be individually managed for optimal results.
5. Forecast short-term business activity; consider the distribution method or another statistical technique.
6. Develop a cash budget capability and maintain updates at appropriate frequencies.
7. Review risk management techniques for elements of working capital.

## Banking Ideas

8. Examine bank products for possible application to the management of float and prevention of fraud.
9. Determine the appropriateness of company's bank account structure. What is the cost and purpose of each account, and who are the authorized signers?
10. Review procedures used to mobilize funds in depository (collection) account(s) for transfer to the principal bank account(s) and disbursement account(s).
11. Arrange for a bank line of credit to cover temporary cash deficiencies.
12. Consider financing working capital through an asset-based lending facility.
13. Drain any excess funds from bank accounts where only a minimal earnings credit rate is received.
14. Invest temporary excess cash through an appropriate short-term instrument.
15. Write policies for short-term investments.
16. Develop long-term bank relationship(s) including credit and non-credit services.
17. Consider using a request-for-proposal to bid (or rebid) banking services.

## Receivables Ideas

18. Develop appropriate policies, and focus on the management of receivables.
19. Review and take appropriate action on the receivables aging schedule.
20. Consider using sales financing to assist customers in purchasing company products. If sales financing is currently used, review the terms of these credit deals to ascertain that the company is receiving a fair return.
21. Use a credit reporting service to assist in decisions on accepting or rejecting new customers.
22. Review terms of sale, possibly adding or changing any cash or other discounts offered.
23. Analyze the entire process of generating invoices, including design and timing.
24. Use a debt collection agency to pursue slow- and no-paying customers.

## Inventory Ideas

25. Develop appropriate policies and focus on the management of inventory.
26. Examine the purchasing cycle and determine if it is in compliance with appropriate procedures.

27. Determine if there are specific purchasing problem areas such as high prices paid, or lack of compliance with PO and receiving report requirements.
28. Calculate EOQ for each significant purchase and determine optimal procedures.
29. Consider whether JIT is appropriate and any possible risks.
30. Examine supply chain management systems for adaptation to the company.

## Payables Ideas

31. Develop appropriate policies and focus on the management of payables.
32. Actively manage accounts payable and determine when to release payments.
33. Review the terms of sale offered by vendors, possibly taking any cash or other discounts offered.
34. Consider alternatives to check disbursements for vendors, such as procurement cards, freight and logistics services, and comprehensive payables.
35. Evaluate alternatives to payroll checks, including direct deposit and paycard.

## International Ideas

36. Establish an international working capital committee to monitor current asset and liability activities and to provide input to local managers on appropriate policy.
37. Review policies on corporate governance and work toward transparency and reporting on the behavior of the company in global markets.
38. Manage foreign exchange transaction exposure using forward contracts.
39. Request letters of credit to manage credit risks from international sales. Review LC activity and consider using banks with electronic LC services.
40. Consider establishing multicurrency accounts to manage FX.
41. Begin moving international transactions to any of several electronic mechanisms in order to eliminate paper checks.
42. Review business risk in international markets using country risk assessment services.
43. Consider the potential advantages of tax-advantaged or reinvoicing centers to manage regional activity in global markets.
44. Be aware of different cultural and corporate practices in international working capital.

## Information Technology Ideas

45. Review existing and/or proposed information technology to determine that current and future requirements are addressed. Ascertain if a comprehensive approach (e.g., ERP) is better than limited improvements to existing systems as supplemented by bank technology.
46. Determine if an information project has an internal champion or whether the idea came from senior management or a vendor who has possibly lost interest.
47. Fully analyze all acquisition and implementation expenses to determine the project's economic viability, and consider whether an ASP might be more cost effective solution.

## Ideas on Managing the Working Capital Cycle

48. Analyze the business risks facing the company. Determine if ERM may be appropriate as a comprehensive risk management program.
49. Review the efficiency with which working capital is managed. Efforts to reduce the total working capital cycle time require a cooperative effort by appropriate business disciplines.
50. Manage the liquidity requirements to meet current and potential demands for access to cash regardless of the business environment. Once the current economic crisis has passed, prepare to reduce cash and to resume aggressive actions to minimize the investment in working capital.

## Changes to Working Capital Management— How to Get Started

Any attempt at a comprehensive working capital effort will seem daunting when management is faced with the variety and quantity of issues developed in this book. The task of improving working capital management could be organized by working capital account, that is, assign cash or receivables, or inventory or international initiatives, or information or risk management to managers with relevant expertise. The choice could be to use a different allocation of assignments, such as by the oldest or newest information system affected by the idea, or by the extent of the effort necessary to effectuate change (from heroic through minor).

The next step is to determine current practice—the "baseline" case. Documentation of that status assists in deciding whether change is necessary and feasible, and eventually how much the change will cost. Each committee or task force should issue a report showing: a brief description of the working capital change, how the system currently works, which functions are responsible, whether information technology or vendor interfaces will be affected, the cost and benefits from the change, any additional data that are required, and the time required for implementation. Senior management can then prioritize company working capital change efforts.

## DEVELOPMENTS IN WORKING CAPITAL MANAGEMENT

There have been important changes to the economic structure of entire industries in the past few decades as business has become global, technology has affected decision making and communications, and finance has offered new challenges and opportunities.

### Twentieth- and Twenty-First-Century Business Models

Traditional business strategies required holding current as well as fixed assets on the balance sheet to create differentiated manufacturing, technology, and marketing processes. Few competitors could match an established company's blend of product offerings and distribution channels, and this special market position generated oligopolistic profits.[10] Industries could continue in their protected status for years, confident that any disruptions could be fixed and that a challenge by an upstart could be met.

The vertically integrated twentieth-century manufacturing company often dominated an entire economic sector. Businesses like General Motors owned sources of raw materials, converted that inventory to finished goods, controlled distribution channels, and only dealt with vendors when special products were required for a continuous manufacturing flow, for example, automobile and truck tires. Vendors, auto dealers, and even customers were their captives, and the accumulation of current and fixed assets was critical to the perpetuation of this position.

Best Buy (discussed in Chapter 1) and other twenty-first-century companies have introduced a different business model—one where results are based on minimum working capital, tight control over costs, low profits per transaction, very high sales turnover, and fewer owned assets. An important element is the development of strategic relationships between businesses and their vendors.

## The Cost of a Transaction

The aggregated time in a working capital cycle may require weeks or months, with each segment having a financial value or cost, identified as float, as measured by the transaction dollars being managed times the cost of capital times the time period (measured as the percentage of a year). Recall the example in "Calculating Receivables Float" in Chapter 6, where the float cost was 22 days, equivalent to over $3 million.

To optimize the working capital timeline, financial managers must encourage their staffs to adopt a consultative attitude, seeking areas within the company for application of financial knowledge. Cash and information are the critical elements, because each step in the operation of a business involves decisions that impact both resources.

 ## THE GIZMO DEAL: HOW DELAYS TURN PROFITS INTO LOSSES

In a typical situation, profits are planned so that returns exceed costs; in capital budgeting terms, the internal rate of return (IRR) exceeds financing costs. Fine—the threshold requirement has been met. Or has it? While the expectation is a small ledger profit, the company may really be receiving a minimal return when adjusted for the cost of capital (in other words, the float).

Let's take a "live" example. A customer wants 200 gross gizmos on which the target is a 10 percent margin (profit). However, the customer wants some concessions:

- A 4 percent price discount—a sales issue.
- Delivery to particular quality standards—a manufacturing or engineering issue.
- Billing 30 days after delivery—a credit or accounts receivable issue.
- An advertising rebate—a marketing issue.
- A check that will take two days to clear that will be sent 40 days after invoicing—a treasury issue.

Why do we bother to cite the functions responsible? These decisions take time and cooperation among various internal organizations, which was acceptable in the twentieth century but not in the competitive business climate of the twenty-first century.

## Accept or Decline the Deal?

Should we accept or decline the gizmo deal? In the past, there were weeks to decide. In that time, management could ponder the situation; consult accountants or old records; talk to a priest, rabbi, or bartender; or negotiate a better deal with the customer. Competitive pressures today provide only hours or possibly minutes to decide. Many bad decisions will be made unless the number of days is calculated that are required to perform each element in the working capital cycle. In fact, there is a strong likelihood of large, established, mostly traditional companies facing a potentially disastrous series of transaction losses.

Here are summarized financial calculations. The target margin per gross is $500. The ledger actual margin is $67, due to a sales discount on the standard price and various additional cost elements. However, when float is considered, the return is actually –$17. This is primarily due to delays in receiving payment for the sale, alleviated to a very slight extent by delays in paying for the costs associated with the sale.

All of the elements of the working capital timeline affect profitability. In the gizmo deal, 10 of 25 analyzed manufacturing elements contributed and all of the administrative elements analyzed contributed to the profitability problem, with no single element responsible.

Here are our choices:

- Negotiate with our customer.
- Improve our internal operations.
- Decline the deal.

## How These Situations Can Occur

In 30 years of dealing with global Fortune 1000 companies, we have seen countless situations of inefficiencies and inappropriate financial practices in these "nonfinancial" business functions. Many organizations permit managers, supervisors, and even clerks to have some financial "authority" without either the specific delegated responsibility or an understanding of important financial concepts.

Such decisions often occur on the spur of the moment in order to move a transaction along to its completion. However, success for the function—such as closing a sale—may actually be a mediocre result for the organization if the financial component of the deal is a nominal gain or a loss. Estimates of financial inefficiencies in U.S. business are in the billions of dollars annually. Clearly, the profession must actively pursue opportunities to improve business processes and restore competitive performance.

## Interconnectivity in the Twenty-First Century

Companies in the twenty-first century will continue to focus on business activity groupings that optimize the only resources that cross all organizational functions: cash and information. And financial managers must begin to accept the idea—regardless of functional domicile—that they are their enterprise's experts for managing its working capital and other financial assets. Furthermore, this focus must transcend the company's boundaries and optimize operations with suppliers and customers.

■ Suppliers will become partners in managing working capital, because they will hold inventory until just prior to its use and will provide a level of quality that allows materials to immediately enter into a production process.
■ Customers will be partners, as they will be expected to pay for goods and services at a time nearer to when they place orders (which is the business model used by Dell Computer) or when the merchandise is purchased (which is the Best Buy model).

If suppliers and customers cannot accept these conditions, then a hard choice must be made as to whether they should be in the relationship. But note: This must be a partnership and not an ongoing conflict between adversaries. What a revolutionary idea!

 **SUMMARY**

The three enterprise concerns in managing the working capital cycle are risk management, efficiency, and liquidity. Working capital analyses of risks, including operational, credit, liquidity and information reporting, and enterprise risk management (ERM) systems, attempt to provide comprehensive risk solutions. Efficiency and liquidity issues relate to the interrelationship of working capital timeline elements and the need to focus greater management emphasis on receivables, inventory, and payables.

 **NOTES**

1. A forward is similar to a futures contract, but differs in that it is a private agreement in which no exchange or clearinghouse participates. Forwards are almost entirely used for foreign exchange transactions. We discussed forwards in Chapter 9.

2. A tanker belonging to the Exxon Corporation—the Exxon *Valdez*—ran aground in Prince William Sound in Alaska, spilling millions of gallons of crude oil into the water. As a result, thousands of fish, fowl, and sea otters died; miles of coastline were polluted; salmon spawning runs were disrupted; and groups of fishermen, especially Native Americans, lost their livelihoods.

3. Bridgestone/Firestone recalled 6.5 million tires in response to claims that their 15-inch Wilderness AT, radial ATX, and ATX II tire treads were separating from the tire core, leading to a series of deadly crashes. These tires were mostly used on the Ford Explorer, the world's top-selling sport utility vehicle (SUV).

4. Gulf residents and cleanup workers continue to suffer serious health problems from the 2010 disaster; see the Smithsonian Institution's analysis at www.ocean.si.edu/gulf-oil-spill.

5. **Covariance** is the measure of how much two random variables vary together; that is, if an independent event were to occur (such as a fire in one location), what is the likelihood that another independent event will occur (such as a flood in a different location)?

6. For a complete discussion of these concepts, see James Sagner, *Financial and Process Metrics for the New Economy* (New York: AMACOM, 2001).

7. This section is based on James Sagner, "How to Measure and Manage Liquidity Today," *Journal of Corporate Accounting and Finance* (Nov./Dec. 2009): 47–50. Recent unpublished analysis by the author extends this analysis with the same result.

8. Based on calculations by the author from a sample of Current Ratios (#30) and ratios of Total Receipts to Total Cash Flow (#42) for 25 industries (of about 135 industries); Leo Troy, *Almanac of Business and Industrial Ratios* (CCH, 2006, 2008, and 2009, as updated for 2012), Table 1 data.

9. A 2010 study by Thomson Reuters concluded that the top 50 companies in the U.S. held nearly $500 billion in cash. Reported by Michael J. de la Merced, "Flush and Looking to Spend," *New York Times* (April 1, 2010), p. F2. By late 2013, the estimate was $1.5 trillion! See Matthew Philips, "Corporations Are Swimming in Cheap Cash. So Why Aren't They Investing," *BloombergBusinessweek* (October 14, 2013), www.businessweek.com/articles/2013-10-14/corporations-are-swimming-in-cheap-cash-dot-so-why-arent-they-investing.

10. An **oligopoly** is a form of industrial concentration where there are several large companies, any one of which can affect the price and product features offered.

# CHAPTER TWELVE

# Introduction to Working Capital Cases

T HE CASES IN THIS BOOK attempt to highlight specific working capital issues. The material includes a narrative that describes the company's situation along with financial data. It is not the intention of these cases to detail every working capital concern. Rather, the concept is to illustrate methods to gain further insight into a company and to think of ways to improve the financial efficiency and managerial insight.

 ## SEQUENCE OF THE CASES

This chapter contains a comprehensive case: Widget Manufacturing, a consumer electronics manufacturing company. It is presented in three sections with questions; suggested solutions are at the conclusion to introduce the process of case analysis. In the next part of the book, cases for analysis are presented as a series of questions, with readers developing answers based on the facts presented and on external research. Suggested solutions are available on the instructor's website at www.wiley.com. They appear in the following order:

- Dinner Bell Hotel (a seasonal resort): cash budgeting and alternative actions
- Koala Fun (computer games and electronic arts): basic working capital issues for a small company
- Miller Building Supplies (building materials for contractors): general working capital concerns for a seasonal business
- Office Smart (communications and computer service): a small business that is considering a new banking relationship
- Quacker Cracker (specialty foods manufacturing): financial planning in a medium-sized family-controlled company
- Young Brands (athletic clothing and equipment manufacturing): financial planning for significant future growth

 ## THE CONCEPT OF THE WORKING CAPITAL CASE

You could be a financial manager (perhaps the CFO or treasurer) at a company or an interested outside observer such as a banker, an investment analyst, an external auditor, or a consultant. Your assignment is to integrate the external environment with the company's situation. In other words, one cannot evaluate a case as if it were only in finance, or marketing, or manufacturing, or other business discipline.

Merely calculating the significant ratios, or developing a cash flow analysis, or determining the optimal cost of capital, is only a part of the puzzle. You must consider whether internal company functions are doing a reasonable job and if the organization is responding in an appropriate manner to known and likely changes in the global marketplace. In this regard, it is extremely important to consider the effects of inefficient or problematical working capital practices on the full range of company operations.

Too often financial concepts are learned mechanically; that is, a capital budgeting decision (which is not covered in this book) involves the comparison of a mathematical calculation of internal rate of return (IRR) to the company's weighted average cost of capital (WACC). The result may be theoretically pleasing—accept the project—but unrealistic in terms of the capacity of the business to accept additional debt or equity. Similarly, a working capital decision must be realistic, that is, in the context of what customers, vendors, banks and other constituents can accept.

## Case Analysis: Defining the Problem

A logical sequential process to analyze working capital cases is presented as follows:

1. **What are the company's goals?** How will senior management develop strategies that are consistent with these objectives? Is the firm pursuing goals in a logical and consistent manner? In developing your analysis, consideration must be given to whether objectives are attainable, are logical, and are consistent with the resources and competence of the company. For example, the goal of becoming a global company in five years may be realistic for a publicly held national firm (see Young Brands), but beyond the reach of a regional business whose customers are primarily in four or five states.

2. **What will happen if nothing is done?** That is, assume that the company does not take your advice. Will it manage to survive and prosper, albeit at a rate of growth that is lower than if it had access to and use of the requested financing? Or will the company's current problems conceivably topple the organization if allowed to continue uncorrected? In other words, are we advising a healthy or an ailing business?

3. **Which facts bear on the problem?** A case can overwhelm the reader with the quantity of facts, particularly when Internet and library research is used to supplement the case data. Remember, data are not information; they are knowledge elements that may or may not be relevant to the problem. The correct definition of the problem will drive the research to develop useful facts and approaches.

   For example, if you suspect that there is an inappropriate policy on inventory (the critical problem), you could compare the company's inventory turnover ratio to its competitors and to results of earlier years. In addition, you can investigate whether modern inventory management techniques are being used, such as economic order quantity (EOQ) or just-in-time (JIT).

4. **Does your analysis support your recommendation?** Your listing of possible actions should be exhaustive, exploring possibilities that may not be on the mind of the company. The more realistic alternatives should then be tested for likely impacts on the situation and a decision reached. Evidence should be provided from industry practice, financial calculations, and other evidence.

##  CASE: WIDGET MANUFACTURING

It was beautiful and sunny just before the Memorial Day holiday when Arnold Parks left a difficult meeting with his banker, Uriah R. (U. R.) Clueless of Second National Bank of Chicago. Arnold and his father, Arnold Sr., who had established Widget Manufacturing, have banked with Second Chicago for almost 30 years. U. R. had just informed Arnold that the bank will not extend its line of credit beyond the current amount.

In addition, the overdue portion of notes payable must be paid within three months, by Labor Day. Although Arnold was irritated by the lender's demand, the note was over 30 days past due, and Arnold did not see how any more than a token payment could be made during the next 60 days.

### Company History

Arnold's father founded Widget Manufacturing in 1946 shortly after he had completed his military service in World War II. The company originally focused on radio components and eventually branched out into various types of consumer electronics products. Shortly after 1950, the first salesmen were hired to call on stores in the Midwest. During the next decade, the business continued to grow, and by 1976, when Arnold took over as president, annual sales had risen to $75 million.

The current product line supplements nationally advertised merchandise in many stores using the retailer's own private brand. The private brands offer a cheaper price to consumers than such name brands as Hewlett-Packard (HP) and Samsung. For stores that do not have a private brand, the Widget brand name—Diode Circuitry—is used.

### The Cash Cycle

Although some stray checks are received in the Chicago headquarters (about 10 percent of the total billed), Widget's manufacturing facilities are individually responsible for their own billing and collections activities. Customers are instructed to mail their remittances to the address of the plant responsible for the merchandise; the plants are located in the following cities:

| | |
|---|---|
| Televisions and radios | St. Louis, MO |
| Wireless telephones and related equipment | Decatur, IL |
| Laptop computers and related equipment | South Haven, MI |

The mail is delivered by U.S. Postal System local route mail carriers to each of the plants between 11:00 a.m. and 2:00 p.m. daily.

On the first business day of the month, the plant manager at each location reviews the prior month's ending balance at the local bank and determines if cash is above or below the target balance level. He or she deposits excess cash to the principal bank (Second National) by mailing a check drawn on the local bank, or draws down cash to cover shortfalls by depositing a Second National Bank check at the local bank. The plant managers also prepare forecasts of cash requirements for the current month. They fax their month-end cash positions, transfers by check, and cash forecasts to the corporate treasurer, Ernie Paydoff, by the second business day of the month.

Ernie gets daily balance reports on his computer from Second National, which has a target balance of $1 million in the master account, and estimates his cash position by 1:00 p.m. When there is excess cash, it is invested in overnight repos in increments of $50,000. Shortfalls are covered by borrowing against a revolving line of credit at the bank for which the company is currently charged prime +3 percent (although this is likely to increase the next time credit is negotiated).

## Bank Relationships

A monthly cash forecast is compiled, and Ernie reviews the balances and transfers cash to or from Second National to maintain the local account target balances that he has established. Ernie does not monitor the local bank balances because they are usually stable during the month once all the plant managers have made their deposits and withdrawals.

If one of the business units requires an emergency infusion of cash during the month, the plant manager calls Ernie to report that he or she is writing a check against the principal account. As long as there is an adequate amount in that account, Ernie does not worry about funding it until the normal month-end cycle.

Widget maintains relationships with several banks around the country, primarily because of the decentralized nature of the organization, the autonomy granted to plant managers, and the concern for access to borrowing should Second National pull its credit line. Though none of the business units negotiate individual credit facilities with its banks, each maintains its own noncredit services.

The plants and the home office maintain a general operating account at a local bank. This account is used for deposit of all remittances and payment of all expenses except payroll. Payroll accounts are maintained at separate banks, primarily because each of the plant managers wants to deal with more than one local bank.

**EXHIBIT 12.1**  Significant Industry Ratios

|  | Industry |
|---|---|
| Current ratio | 2.75 |
| Quick ratio | 1.63 |
| Receivables turnover | 7.72 |
| Average collection period (in days) | 47.48 |
| Asset turnover | 1.96 |
| Inventory turnover | 7.02 |
| Return on equity (%) | 25.95 |

# I.M. Cash Is Promoted

In the past, Arnold had only dealt with his high school friend, golfing buddy, and banker Ira M. (I. M.) Cash, and after talking about their favorite rounds of golf and their twelfth-grade antics, an increase in the line of credit had always been granted without I. M. even looking at the financial results. However, three months ago, I. M. had been promoted to senior vice president in the bank, and Arnold's first meeting with U. R. Clueless had been depressing.

U. R. had asked to see an up-to-date set of financial statements at their first meeting. After reviewing these reports (see Exhibits 12.1 through 12.3), U. R. had talked about cash problems and even noted the possibility of a financial emergency. There had been no backslapping, no reminiscing about the time they tied the vice principal to the flagpole, and no golf stories.

**EXHIBIT 12.2**  Income Statement (in $ millions)

|  | Widget $ | Widget % |
|---|---|---|
| Net sales | $931.6 | 100.0 |
| Cost of goods | 683.9 | 73.4 |
| Gross profit | 247.7 | 26.6 |
| General and administrative expenses | 179.1 | 19.2 |
| Depreciation expense | 16.8 | 1.8 |
| Interest expense | 30.2 | 3.2 |
| Earnings before taxes | 21.6 | 2.3 |
| Income taxes | 7.3 | 0.8 |
| Net income | $14.3 | 1.5 |

**EXHIBIT 12.3**   Balance Sheet ($ millions) (% to total assets and to total liabilities and equity)

|  | Widget $ | Widget % |
|---|---|---|
| Cash | $   8.0 | 0.97 |
| Inventories | 285.2 | 34.14 |
| Accounts receivable | 217.8 | 26.07 |
| Total current assets | $ 511.0 | 61.18 |
| Net fixed assets | 324.3 | 38.82 |
| Total assets | $835.3 | 100.00 |
| Accounts payable | $  98.2 | 11.76 |
| Notes payable | 112.1 | 13.42 |
| Other current liabilities | 8.6 | 1.03 |
| Total current liabilities | $ 218.9 | 26.21 |
| Long-term debt | 289.3 | 34.63 |
| Total liabilities | $508.2 | 60.84 |
| Stockholders' equity | 327.1 | 39.16 |
| Total liabilities and equity | $835.3 | 100.00 |

## Questions

1. Calculate the most important financial ratios and compare Widget's results with industry averages. What do these ratios indicate?
2. What changes do you recommend to the cash cycle of the Widget Company?

## Arnold's Reaction

Arnold could not believe that U. R. had the gall to tell him he needed to drastically reduce the company's receivables and to strongly suggest a clearance sale to reduce inventory. Since the founding of Widget Manufacturing (previously described), no inventory sales had ever been held, although there was a period during the late 1970s recession when the price of televisions had to be reduced to move merchandise.

The growth of the business is causing Arnold to consider opening a fourth production site, with both Texas and Tennessee under consideration. However, ongoing cash problems have put this idea on hold. There are 10,000 total employees, 5,000 in St. Louis and 2,000 each in Decatur and South Haven, and 1,000 in the home office in Chicago. Each site maintains local vendors and

**EXHIBIT 12.4** Bank Account Fees and Balances

| Business Unit (Segment) and Site | Purpose | Average Balance | Bank | Monthly Fees |
|---|---|---|---|---|
| Televisions and radios, St. Louis, MO | Payroll | $1,000,000 | Last National Bank of St. Louis | $ 6,000 |
| Televisions and radios, St. Louis, MO | Payables; local collections | $ 900,000 | Next-to-Last National Bank | $ 6,000 |
| Wireless telephones, Decatur, IL | Payroll | $1,200,000 | Almost Last National Bank | $ 5,000 |
| Wireless telephones, Decatur, IL | Payables; local collections | $ 1,100,000 | Mediocre National Bank | $ 6,000 |
| Laptop computers, South Haven, MI | Payroll | $ 800,000 | Inept National Bank of Michigan | $ 7,000 |
| Laptop computers, South Haven, MI | Payables; local collections | $ 800,000 | Epter National Bank of Michigan | $ 7,000 |
| Corporate Home Office, Chicago, IL | Central payroll | $ 600,000 | Second National Bank of Chicago– Account A | $ 6,000 |
| Corporate Home Office, Chicago, IL | Payables; local collections | $ 600,000 | Second National Bank of Chicago– Account B | $ 5,000 |
| Corporate Home Office, Chicago, IL | Master Account | $1,000,000 | Second National Bank of Chicago –Account C | $ 7,000 |
| Total | | $8,000,000 | | $55,000 |

bank relationships for trade payables, payroll, and collections; see Exhibit 12.4 for a listing of these accounts.

## Collection Activities

The mailroom personnel at each site sort the mail and deliver it to accounts receivable, where envelopes are opened manually and contents are processed. After cash has been applied against customer accounts, the receivables clerks at each location hand deliver the checks to the receivables manager. He or she endorses the checks, prepares a deposit slip, and takes the bundle home for the night to be able to drop the deposit at the bank first thing in the morning, on the way to work.

Arnold had slowly increased the amount of inventory with the belief that many sales were lost because an item was not in stock when a customer

**EXHIBIT 12.5**  Inventory to Sales ($ millions)

| Year | Inventories | Net Sales |
| --- | --- | --- |
| 2005 | 224.2 | 829.5 |
| 2006 | 246.7 | 863.4 |
| 2007 | 264.6 | 894.5 |
| 2008 | 285.2 | 931.6 |

requested it. Sales did grow steadily each year, which bolstered Arnold's idea that sales were directly related to larger inventories and lenient credit. In fact, sales had increased by 1½ times in the last 10 years, but inventory had doubled over that same time period. See Exhibit 12.5 for recent inventory and sales data.

## Disbursement Activities

As previously noted, Widget maintains payables and payroll activities at each site. Selection of vendors is by the local plant manager, with advice from his or her supervisors. Maintenance of local vendor relations is considered important. All payables disbursements are by check, using a variety of accounting software systems, with two major payables runs on the 10th and 25th of each month. The clerk handling payables at each site is also responsible for maintaining payroll records and preparing all checks. That clerk signs payables checks unless they exceed $2,500, in which case the plant manager must also sign.

Central disbursement accounts are maintained at the home office for executive and staff payroll, payables, and miscellaneous expenses. The latter category includes expenses not directly related to the company's business activities, such as interest costs on loans, credit line charges, sales and marketing expenses, corporate airline tickets, and the like.

The weekly payroll is by check drawn on local banks, with the payroll envelopes distributed on Fridays just before lunch. The payables clerk maintains cash in a strongbox for employees wishing to cash their payroll checks. An average of $25,000 is maintained at each site and at the home office for this purpose, which is replenished by a check cashed by that clerk at the bank.

These cash funds are occasionally used by executives and salesmen to pay for travel and entertainment expenses. A voucher is prepared to show the withdrawal of funds for such needs, signed by both the plant manager and the payables clerk.

Widget's disbursement system produces a total of 27,500 checks a month, 20,000 for the semimonthly payroll and 7,500 for payables. The all-in cost of the payables checks is $5.00 each. Various ideas have been suggested by the company's bankers and outside auditors to make the disbursement system more efficient, including analyzing computer requirements to reduce computer time and support; renegotiating bank disbursement costs following competitive bidding; and outsourcing most disbursement activities to a bank and/or vendor.

## U. R. Clueless Gives Advice

The growth of inventory had seriously depleted the company's cash flow in the past few years. The cash crunch had been managed through increases in the line of credit at the bank, by not taking vendor cash discounts, and by Arnold's reducing his salary and bonus and forgoing his annual vacation. About 40 percent of purchases by Widget were on terms of 1½/10, net 40, and until this year the cash discount had always been taken. Now payables are almost 50 days past due, and vendors are demanding payment. This situation had forced Arnold to visit his bank to seek additional financing.

U. R. suggested that Arnold request the help of an advisor who could help him establish better controls over his working capital. In addition, the present credit line would be extended only if payment were made of the overdue note amount within 90 days. U. R. also noted that Arnold should reduce his inventories and accounts receivable to be in line with the industry. U. R. and Arnold argued over possible remedial actions, with U. R. insisting that cash be raised as the first priority and Arnold wanting to continue his current management style.

Attacking past-due receivables was a particularly difficult point with Arnold, for he realized that he had no stomach for aggressive actions against his customers. Arnold feared that he would offend them if he demanded payment on these past-dues. Widget sold about 60 percent of its sales on terms of net 30, but several customers took advantage of Arnold's good nature; see Exhibit 12.6. As he walked the four blocks between the bank and his office,

**EXHIBIT 12.6** Accounts Receivable Aging Schedule

| Days Past Due | Amount ($ millions) | Percent Past Due |
|---|---|---|
| 0–29 | $ 69.5 | 31.9 |
| 30–59 | 47.5 | 21.8 |
| 60–89 | 47.5 | 21.8 |
| Over 90 | 53.3 | 24.4 |
| | $217.8 | 100.0 |

**EXHIBIT 12.7** Monthly Forecast of Sales and Expenses ($ millions)

|  | Sales | Expenses |
|---|---|---|
| April | $ 60.0 | $ 64.0 |
| May | $ 80.0 | $ 70.0 |
| June | $100.0 | $ 86.0 |
| July | $120.0 | $104.0 |
| August | $100.0 | $ 86.0 |
| September | $ 80.0 | $ 70.0 |
| October | $ 60.0 | $ 60.0 |
| November | $ 60.0 | $ 56.0 |

Note: In preparing a cash budget, you will need the following information. All sales are credit sales, with 20 percent collected in the month of the sale, 60 percent collected in the following month, and the remainder collected in the second following month. All expenses are paid during the month they are incurred; in addition, tax payments of $10 million are due in July and in September. From Exhibit 12.3, the beginning cash balance on June 1st was given as $8 million.

Arnold began to realize that the business was in serious trouble and wondered if things could ever be fixed.

## Questions

3. What changes do you recommend to the inventory management systems? What are the estimated benefits?
4. What is Widget's cost of not taking the vendor discounts?
5. What changes do you recommend to the collections and disbursement systems?
6. Based on the information in Exhibit 12.7, prepare a cash budget for June through August.
7. The company's minimum allowable cash balance is $5 million. Using the cash budget you prepared in question 6, prepare a surplus—deficit cash projection for those three months (June to August). Show cumulative borrowing activity beginning in June. What do you conclude?
8. What should Arnold Parks do?

## The Mexican Option

Once Arnold began to implement various working capital changes, the position of Widget Manufacturing significantly improved. In fact, U. R. Clueless was impressed by Widget's willingness to take the necessary steps to collect overdue receivables and sell excess inventory, and responded by extending the company's credit line. As noted, there was even consideration of a new production site, but the original idea of locating in the United States began to refocus on Mexico.

Considering Mexico or any other international site had been totally out of Arnold's mind-set. However, as U. R. introduced Arnold to various international experts at Second National, the idea of moving into a global market began to have significant appeal. The bankers noted the extensive manufacturing experience that several Mexican companies had in consumer electronics, the significantly lower labor cost, the incentives provided by the Mexican government for new businesses, the free trade between NAFTA countries, and the potential gateway to Latin American retailers and their customers.

Large store retailers like Walmart have been extremely successful in Mexico; in 2013, that organization had about 2,200 stores in Mexico (see corporate.walmart.com/our-story/locations/mexico). However, Mexico's economic growth has been severely impacted by the recent global crisis, with real growth at −6.5 percent in 2009 (as compared to an average of +2.3 percent for the two preceding years and between 3.5 and 4 percent in 2013); see www .cia.gov/library/publications/the-world-factbook/index.html.

Arnold is concerned about foreign exchange (FX) issues. His corporate treasurer, Ernie Paydoff, has no international experience; in fact Ernie hated to travel outside of the United States, although he had once been to Toronto. U. R. assured Arnold that the FX issue could be managed through forward contracts written by the bank to convert Mexican peso receipts into U.S. dollars. Furthermore, expenses such as payroll, local purchasing, and lease costs for the site would be paid in pesos and not U.S. dollars, so the extent of the FX conversion would be limited.

## Widget's Information Gap

In discussing the Mexican option with Ernie, Arnold asked about the quality and usefulness of the information received from Second National and other banks, and about the general nature of the bank relationships that Ernie saw in his work as corporate treasurer. Arnold believed that many things that had happened were due somewhat to the poor advice and inadequate information he had been given.

Ernie became somewhat defensive, claiming that he had done his job. While Arnold couldn't completely argue with this, he was concerned that Ernie was thinking of the treasurer's role as it was in 1980 and not the central focus of working capital management that it had become in many twenty-first-century companies.

Based on comments from his banker, U. R. Clueless, and other Second National officers, Arnold was beginning to consider the need for a major study of his information technology needs, particularly whether Internet-based bank technology would be the solution, as his bankers claimed, or if an enterprise resource planning (ERP) package should be considered.

## Questions

9. Is Arnold correct in his concerns? Will the cost of FX transaction exposure management offset the potential profits from this opportunity?
10. Are there other working capital issues Arnold should consider in deciding on a Mexican operation?
11. Should Arnold seriously consider either the Second National Bank technology (called "Second Cash") or an ERP program, such as those offered by SAP and Oracle? What are the initial steps in deciding on an appropriate course of action?

 **SUGGESTED SOLUTIONS**

**Solution 1.** The first step in helping Arnold is to calculate the ratios that will be important in identifying the problems at Widget.

| | Widget | Industry |
|---|---|---|
| **Liquidity Ratios** | | |
| Current ratio | 2.33 | 2.75 |
| Quick ratio | 1.03 | 1.63 |
| Receivables turnover | 4.28 | 7.72 |
| Average collection period (days) | 84.16 | 47.48 |
| **Other Ratios** | | |
| Asset turnover | 1.12 | 1.96 |
| Inventory turnover | 2.40 | 7.02 |
| Return on equity | 0.04 | 25.95 |

The results clearly show that Widget is below all of the industry's averages, and has not been managing working capital in the modern (vs. the traditional) manner. There really are no exceptions, with Widget now forced to come to terms with problems throughout the business. It is astonishing that Arnold was able to convince I. M. Cash to go along with him on providing financing over the years; he and I. M. must have pulled some interesting pranks in high school! However, I. M. did not do Arnold any favors; he was the person who should have warned Arnold about poor management decisions years ago.

**Solution 2.** Arnold should be looking for the correct level of net working capital and how he will finance it.

- Inventories are turning about three times slower than the industry average, indicating that the firm probably has either excess or stale inventory. Regardless of the cause, Widget has too much capital tied up in inventory that is not earning a reasonable return per dollar invested.
- Accounts receivable are similarly out of line, turning at just under twice the industry's rate. Although Widget's terms are the same as those of the industry, receivables are much higher, indicating that the company could tighten its collection policy without hurting sales.

Month-end reporting of local balances by plant controllers is inadequate for maintaining tight control over cash balances. Although computerized balance reporting systems may not be cost justified for the smaller banks, daily or weekly telephone calls may be appropriate. Excess or deficit cash positions should be handled via ACH or Fedwire funds transfers rather than paper checks. Balance management would become much more controllable if collections are moved to lockboxes at a single site and disbursements are done through that bank.

More timely and improved cash forecasting processes would permit aggressive short-term investment management, yielding better returns than those available through overnight repos late in the day. It could also minimize the need to borrow from the line of credit at the prime rate +3 percent (a total of 6¼ percent as of April 2013).

**Solution 3.** Without a physical inspection by a qualified expert, it is difficult to judge the condition of the inventory. There is a real possibility that a significant portion is stale and will bring only a small amount of the carrying cost, particularly given the fast obsolescence in the consumer electronics industry. In any event, Arnold's objectives should be to raise cash by attracting buyers to Widget's low prices and to get inventories in line with what is reasonable based on average industry results.

**Solution 4.** The value of vendors' cash discount is 360 ÷ 30 (derived from 40 "net" days less 10 "discount" days) or 12, × 1½ percent = 18 percent. This is not sufficiently attractive to be worth taking, although likely higher than Widget's cost of capital. Furthermore, if Widget pays all of these invoices in 50 days rather 40 days, the value becomes only 13½ percent. Note: We cannot calculate the cost of capital from the data in the case. However, it could very well be higher than the 10 percent used throughout the book as Widget has numerous operational problems that any good banker (like U. R. Clueless) is certain to spot.

**Solution 5.** Widget is currently receiving remittances at three plant sites. Without centralizing the processing of receivables, each business unit must maintain a receivables capability. There is no reason these sites couldn't be located at only one location, possibly a bank lockbox. While we cannot determine the optimal site without further analysis, it is nearly certain that a Chicago lockbox bank—generally acknowledged as the first or second fastest mail city in the United States (along with Atlanta)—would be a reasonable choice. The first step is to centralize collections and close local bank accounts. The potential savings are calculated below.

The four accounts for payables (discussed in the next section) and collections that can be eliminated are as follows (from Exhibit 12.4):

| | Average Balance | Monthly Fees |
|---|---|---|
| Next-to-Last National Bank | $ 900,000 | $ 6,000 |
| Mediocre National Bank | $ 1,100,000 | $ 6,000 |
| Epter National Bank of Michigan | $ 800,000 | $ 7,000 |
| Second National Bank of Chicago–Account B | $ 600,000 | $ 5,000 |
| Totals | $3,400,000 | $24,000 |

The gross savings from eliminating balances would be $340,000 (calculated as $3.4 million × the 10 percent cost of capital), and from bank fees of nearly $290,000 a year ($24,000 × 12 months). In addition, there would be float savings of probably 2 days through the use of a Chicago lockbox. The savings are equivalent to about $745,000 a year (calculated as 2 days × Daily sales of $3.73 million [$931.6 million ÷ 250 business days] × 10 percent).

Assuming an average payment of $20,000, the lockbox cost would be $50,000 (calculated as about 50,000 payments × $1 per lockbox transaction). Note: Calculations were developed on the float or cost for a full year and are based on 250 business days.

There would also be savings by eliminating the labor-intensive function of receiving and depositing collections. The result would be a total savings of perhaps $1.25 million a year (assuming most payments are converted to lockbox). In addition, control would be improved in that Widget employees would not be touching any live checks. The lockbox and other fees paid to Second National would greatly enhance the Widget banking relationship.

The next step is to develop or outsource a centralized invoicing system. This action would have the additional advantage of eliminating redundant receivables clerks, would place all of the data about receivables aging by account in one location, and would improve control over the entire process. The aging schedule (Exhibit 12.6) shows 20 percent of receivables are past due ($931.6 million ÷ $217.8 million), with more than 5 percent over 90 days late! This is simply an intolerable situation, and these customers should be told to pay or find another vendor and face legal action.

Local payroll and payables activities create too many bank accounts, too many funding activities, and too expensive a disbursement banking system. The costs of the current payroll system are as follows:

|  | Average Balance | Monthly Fees |
|---|---|---|
| Last National Bank of St. Louis | $1,000,000 | $ 6,000 |
| Almost Last National Bank | 1,200,000 | 5,000 |
| Inept National Bank of Michigan | 800,000 | 7,000 |
| Second National Bank of Chicago – Account A | 600,000 | 6,000 |
| Totals | $3,600,000 | $24,000 |

The float value and fees for these accounts is $650,000 ($3.6 million × 10 percent + about $290,000), with net savings of about $600,000 after the cost of direct depositing. Paying the payroll by check off local banks misses the opportunity to direct deposit pay, which would save the cost of managing that portion of the disbursement accounts. If checks are the preferred method of payment, a single account should be used for all payrolls to maximize float and to simplify account management. Many of these costs can be reduced by eliminating accounts and using an outsourcing payroll vendor.

Local payables management could cause some early payment of invoices, some missed cash discounts, and failure to negotiate quantity purchase discounts. Because the same clerk is handling both cash and accounting functions, there is a control issue at each company site. The second signature requirement is not an adequate safeguard against fraud as the clerk could issue checks to a phony vendor for any amount under $2,500.

Widget issues 7,500 checks a month for payables at a cost of $5 each. The total cost of this activity is $450,000. If a comprehensive payables bank were used for these payments, the savings would be $360,000 ($450,000 – $90,000, assuming $1 per disbursement). In addition, there would be no control issues with regard to check or electronic payment issuance.

Maintaining an encashment facility at each site not only invites theft but also costs the company in lost float. As there are three plant sites plus the home office handling cash, the total amount of cash is as much as $100,000 at any given time, worth $10,000. An additional cost may be incurred by banks charging for coin and currency services, perhaps another $5,000. The use of this fund for travel and entertainment advances is a control issue in that there may not be adequate documentation provided for each advance. Widget should consider a procurement card for designated managers for such expenses and for small purchases.

In summary, net savings that we calculated are as follows:

| | |
|---|---:|
| Lockboxing/collection system | $ 1,250,000 |
| Payroll | 600,000 |
| Comprehensive payables | 360,000 |
| Encashment | 15,000 |
| Total | $ 2,225,000 |

Furthermore, there are savings opportunities from various other changes, as well as improved control and reduced possibility of fraud.

**Solution 6.** As discussed in Chapter 4, the sales and expense amounts are accrual accounting estimates and must be converted to cash accounting based on when cash is spent or received. The net cash is added or subtracted from the cash at the beginning of the period and the minimum cash required is deducted from the result. This shows the borrowing required for the period.

The cash budget beginning in June would be as follows:

| ($ millions) | June | July | August | September | October |
|---|---|---|---|---|---|
| Sales | 100 | 120 | 100 | 80 | 60 |
| Collections | | | | | |
| That month (20%) | 20 | 24 | 20 | 16 | 12 |
| Month after (60%) | 48 | 60 | 72 | 60 | 48 |
| 2 months after (20%) | 12 | 16 | 20 | 24 | 20 |
| Total cash in | 80 | 100 | 112 | 100 | 80 |
| Payments | | | | | |
| Expenses | 86 | 104 | 86 | 70 | 60 |
| Taxes | 0 | 10 | 0 | 10 | 0 |
| Total cash out | 86 | 114 | 86 | 80 | 60 |
| Net cash in/out | −6 | −14 | 26 | 20 | 20 |
| Beginning cash | 8 | 2 | −12 | 14 | 34 |
| Ending cash | 2 | −12 | 14 | 34 | 54 |
| Minimum cash required | 5 | 5 | 5 | 5 | 5 |
| Surplus/deficit* | −3 | −17 | 9 | 29 | 49 |
| Cumulative borrowings** | 3 | 20 | 11 | Repay 18 | Repay 49 |

*Deficit cash is a negative and shows required borrowings for any given month.
**For this problem, these borrowings are assumed to begin in June (although we know from the case that Widget had been previously borrowing against its line of credit). "Repay" indicates that these amounts are available to repay earlier borrowings as discussed in the case.

**Solution 7.** Based on the calculations in Solution 6, we would borrow $3 million in June and $17 million in July. We would then pay down these borrowings in August in the amount of $9 million and $11 million in September. Although it was not asked in the case, October is shown to indicate that the trend of loan repayment is continuing and positive. Arnold will have to defend these forecasts with names of retailers likely to make purchases and the possible amounts, specific expense data, and other projections.

**Solution 8.** There are so many problems at Widget that it is hard to know where to start. To save the business, Arnold should begin as many of the following changes as possible:

- Have an expert examine inventory and eliminate whatever can be sold, particularly stale inventory.
- Aggressively pursue overdue receivables, even if some customers become offended. They are likely only marginally profitable and are not helping Widget's profits. The aging schedule and the average collection period indicate that Widget really needs to be more aggressive.
- Determine if other assets can be sold and then possibly leased back if essential to Widget's business mission.
- Ignore vendor cash discounts as this would not be a good use of Widget's limited liquidity.
- Advise U. R. Clueless that payments against existing loans can be made in September, later than demanded but certainly substantial in amount. This should give the business a fighting chance to receive an interim loan and to begin to restore the rapport with Second Chicago.
- Work with U. R. to improve Widget's situation at Second Chicago. Periodic meetings would be useful in improving the relationship.
- Consider raising equity capital. While a sale through the securities markets is unlikely until financial results improve, it might be possible to attract private equity or other sources of funding.
- Begin to work at these changes, and continue to postpone your vacation!
- Consider an outright future sale of the business.

**Solution 9.** Arnold has ample reason to be concerned, as neither he nor Ernie has experience in international transactions. Although peso receipts can be hedged using forwards, there is a cost to these transactions and limited competition in foreign exchange outside of the four major currencies (US$, £, ¥, and €). Furthermore, forwards require a firm transaction date in the future, whereas Mexican and other businesses outside of the United States that may buy from Widget have been known to delay payments for weeks.

There is no FX forwards market for currencies from Central and South America should Widget expand into Latin America. Arnold could demand a letter of credit for each transaction, but Mexican buyers may choose to do business with a "friendlier" company that has no such requirements.

In addition, Arnold (or Ernie) will have to establish local banking relationships for Mexican peso collections and disbursements. Some receipts will be in pesos and nearly all expenses will be in pesos, including local purchases, payroll, taxes, and payments on leased space. Inevitably, mistakes will be made. The complexity of international working capital requires hiring a local treasurer or working capital expert, which will certainly affect the profitability of the planned expansion.

**Solution 10:** The important working capital issues that Arnold should consider are receivables practices, particularly expectations of when invoices will be paid; inventory management issues in a foreign country, including delivery of essential components; and country risk assessment given the somewhat volatile nature of the Mexican economy. Although the concept of a joint venture[1] (with a Mexican partner) goes beyond the coverage of this book, such an approach may be viable for a fledgling international business.

**Solution 11:** The resolution of these questions is fairly open ended. Widget Manufacturing is clearly in need of a major overhaul of its business functions and staffing. For example, is Ernie the right person to lead the finance function over the next 10 years? Transitioning in a new treasurer could provide an opportunity to consider an ERP system. However, such a radical transformation may be very disruptive to the company and interfere with the many incremental changes so obviously required. For these reasons, and because of the significantly lower cost, bank technology from Second National Bank ("Second Cash") may be the prudent choice for now.

The initial step in deciding on a course of action is described in Chapter 10, "Determine Requirements." An analysis must be made of the company's needs for access to files and records, particularly in consideration of whether there are any glaring deficiencies. The focus should be on situations where information is clearly inadequate to support decision making. Bring the skills and experience of all managers to outline these requirements and to determine whether Second Cash (or another product) can begin to formulate an answer.

**NOTE**

1 **Joint ventures** are organized in various formats and ownership shares, with the most common form of structure currently being an international company that partners with a local owner(s). International companies have come to prefer this form of ownership because of the complexity of the culture and the language, the difficulty for foreigners in obtaining approvals and business contacts, the need to keep good managers through an equity incentive, and the tax benefits extended to companies with local participation. However, the loss of control must be considered in any plan to joint venture.

# Cases on Working Capital Management

# Dinner Bell Hotel

"MY INTERNAL 'FARMER'S ALMANAC' warns me that there could be cash flow problems soon," said Sarah Clare, the manager of Dinner Bell Hotel (DBH), a Michigan resort. (The *Farmer's Almanac* is a periodical famous for its long-range weather predictions and astronomical data, as well as humor, trivia, and personal advice.) Sarah continued: "We need to know *now* what the likely situation will be. I think I'd better redo the forecast."

 ## CASH FLOW ISSUES

Two months ago (in early January 2011), Sarah and her financial staff had prepared a cash flow forecast for the period July 2011 to March 2012. July through early November are the busiest times for the hotel. Summer and fall guests enjoy the atmosphere of an old-fashioned resort with large meals, farm animals, a petting zoo, nature walks, bicycling and hiking trails, fishing, tennis courts, a lake for swimming and boating, and a nine-hole golf course.

The phrase "dinner bell" dates back about two centuries, when people who lived and worked on vast tracts of land as ranchers or farmers needed a way to be called to dinner. The hotel continues that tradition by ringing a bell to announce mealtime. The weather gets too cold by early November for most outdoor activities, so the hotel built an indoor pool and developed long theme weekends like classic movies, card tournaments, and supervised child and teen amusements.

It is not unusual for the hotel to run cash deficits during most, if not all, of the months between November and April, and about break-even in May and June. However, the cash surplus generated during the peak period, from July through November, is typically sufficient to meet the shortfall. This is what Sarah had predicted would occur when she had made the cash budget projection for July onward. But now, in early March, she is having second thoughts about the forecast due to several concerns:

- The hotel requires major renovations to continue to be attractive to five-day to weeklong guests, which is the typical reservation. The work planned for January needs to be more extensive than originally thought. Sarah, her engineers, and the contractors had estimated the cost to be $250,000, but it appears $300,000 of work is necessary.
- The resort's longtime group sales and convention manager left unexpectedly in February, and her replacement is not as effective in obtaining business from regional businesses and organizations.
- The Great Recession has affected much of the area, and sales at the hotel are definitely sensitive to the regional economy. Fewer offsite meetings have been scheduled, as companies prefer to stay in a location where attendees can commute from their homes to avoid the costs of rooms, some food, most recreational charges, and transportation.

These concerns make recent forecasts—thought to be the "most likely" case—too optimistic. "I can see indications of this now," she tells the monthly meeting of the hotel's senior managers and board of directors. "Revenue was off 15 percent for January and February, and our advance bookings through the fall months are also down. I'm sure we won't hit the levels we predicted." Sarah has always been an advocate of cash budget forecasts and constantly revises an estimate in light of new information. There is no doubt a new projection is necessary.

**ALTERNATIVE ACTIONS**

Some thoughts from the monthly meeting follow, along with Sarah's responses. As she explained, there are problems with most of these alternatives.

*"Can any of the renovations be postponed?" (a comment from the construction engineer)*
    If the renovations are not made in January, sales will likely suffer in future months. The resort is showing signs of wear, and it is important to improve the hotel's appearance periodically. And, of course, the renovations are best made during an off-peak month like January.

*"Should we increase the advertising budget?" (a comment from the new sales and convention manager)*
    Advertising is expensive, and there is no evidence that print or broadcast marketing has very much effect on our potential guests. They repeatedly state that their visits are due to the wide variety of facilities and the meals, and to referrals from other guests. Very few guests mention that an advertisement affected their vacation plans.

*"Should we reduce the planned spending on food, such as offering fewer entrée choices?" (a comment from the catering manager)*
    Worst idea of all—our guests come for the food! You might as well change our name to the "Fast-Food Hotel"!

*"Should we delay disbursements for accounts payable?" (a comment from the accounting manager)*
    We could be completely open with the suppliers about the hotel's financial situation and ask for a deferment of some payments until August. In return, we will promise to pay COD (cash on delivery) when business picks up. "They just might agree to this. We've been a good customer, and it is in their interest to help us out. After all, it's not like we're in danger of bankruptcy."

*"Should we arrange for a bank loan?" (a comment from a board member)*
    The prospect of a loan is not particularly appealing. The bank, even assuming it would grant a loan, is likely to impose severe restrictions on the operation of the resort through covenants in the loan agreement. That would be an unwelcome interference.

*"So . . . what will you do in the event of a cash shortfall?" (a comment from a board member)*
    The good news is that reservations for next summer are extremely strong, and we should be rolling in cash by September. We've got to do

another cash flow forecast to know how bad the situation is. Why don't we meet again tomorrow morning? By then, the senior managers and I can prepare a new cash budget.

Sarah asks the managers to return with relevant reports and records so that a new plan can be considered.

 ## THE "RAW" DATA

Sales in December were $228,500 and in January were $157,500. Typically, 65 percent of the resort's sales are paid in cash; that is, by cash, debit, or credit card. The other 35 percent is paid as a hotel charge and collected in the month following the sale, and is permitted for group meetings and conferences. Assume that there are no uncollectible receivables.

The hotel incurs the following monthly expenses: mortgage, $30,000; utilities and maintenance, $25,000; and rental and miscellaneous expenses, $22,500. Property taxes of $75,000 are due in February, income taxes of $10,000 are due in November and in May, and the renovations will be paid for in February. Estimated payroll and supplier expenses are attached. Supplier expenses in November were $85,000 and in December were $45,000. One-third of the supplier expenses are paid one month after they are incurred and two-thirds in two months. The required minimum cash balance at its bank is $50,000, and the expected balance at the beginning of February is $400,000.

 ## QUESTIONS

1. Prepare a cash budget for the period February through August. See Exhibit C1.1 for necessary data.
2. Is there any advantage to extending the forecast through September, October, and November? Explain.
3. Let's assume the hotel's cash flow would not be sufficient to cover any shortfall occurring during the cash budget period. What proportion of payables must be deferred to get the resort through this period?
4. Sarah, in essence, may be asking the firm's vendors for a loan if she requests a deferral on payables. From the hotel's point of view, the size of the loan is your answer to question 3. From the suppliers' point of view,

however, the size of their investment in the loan is actually less than that amount. Explain why.

5. Do the suppliers have an incentive to cooperate? Explain.
6. The suppliers may be unable to cooperate. Why?
7. As a follow-up to question 6, if the suppliers are unable (or unwilling) to cooperate, how do you think Sarah should proceed?
8. Do you think that a cash budget is a more important financial tool for a small operation such as Dinner Bell Hotel or a large firm such as Exxon? Explain.

**EXHIBIT C1.1**   Forecasts for the Dinner Bell Hotel Cash Budget ($000s) (in the month incurred)

|                   | Sales   | Payroll | Suppliers |
| ----------------- | ------- | ------- | --------- |
| January (actual)  | $157.5  | $65.0   | $45.0     |
| February          | 180.0   | 65.0    | 50.0      |
| March             | 255.0   | 65.0    | 70.0      |
| April             | 275.0   | 90.0    | 80.0      |
| May               | 275.0   | 100.0   | 100.0     |
| June              | 380.0   | 175.0   | 120.0     |
| July              | 550.0   | 200.0   | 135.0     |
| August            | 650.0   | 225.0   | 150.0     |

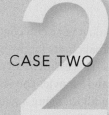

# Koala Fun

ILLION-DOLLAR COMPUTER GAME companies such as Activision, Blizzard, and Zynga are unusual in the electronic arts industry, which consists primarily of small developers. One such firm is Koala Fun (KF), located in Baltimore, MD. KF was started seven years ago by Owen Charles and Tessa Benjamin, who between them had over 15 years of experience with various computer systems design companies.

The partnership initially blended very well. Owen, reserved and introspective, is creative with a flair for designing games and spotting trends. Mainly as a result of his genius, the KF brand is synonymous with intriguing electronics with high graphic appeal. Tessa, more outgoing with a strong marketing focus, has assumed the role of the firm's chief operating officer.

## THE PARTNERS' FIRST SUCCESS

The first successful product the two partners developed was a game called Koala Fun, which they used as the company name. The game uses a cute image of a koala bear cub chasing treasure and villains around coastal Australia—the koala homeland—while helping "rescue" heroes and animals. The game was so successful that various spinoff products were licensed, including stuffed toys and a movie. The Chinese even picked up on the idea and joint-ventured games with KF using a giant panda as the theme.

Tessa was particularly good at marketing opportunities like the panda deal and working with resellers like the retailers GameStop and Target, the online merchandiser Amazon, and other large companies. She also sold to smaller resellers who provided national and some global distribution. However, the Great Recession and the resulting reduction in consumer discretionary spending affected KF. In addition, competition from free or low-cost Internet games made it more difficult to sell the tens of thousands of games and other products required for an assured, constant revenue flow.

A problem with this industry is that it experiences cyclicality, as players (usually children and teens) move on to other activities. The company enjoyed initial success, showing profits by its second year. Owen and Tessa preferred to work on designing new games and the development of marketing strategies over the administrative aspects of the business. As the result, new games and products were in development and production costs escalated, but sales were somewhat slow to be realized.

 **FINANCIAL CONCERNS**

Owen and Tessa loved their company but were inexperienced in business matters. Owen asked his mother, Amy, an accountant, for assistance. After studying the ledgers and other records, she reported that there was a significant working capital problem with declining cash, unsold inventory (mostly old Koala Fun games), and vendors who had not been paid.

Tessa had been handling this side of the company, but that had mostly involved writing checks to employees and for payables while waiting around airports. Files were misplaced, documents were missing, and some money was unaccounted for. The problems appeared to be more related to failing to prioritize financial matters rather than any deliberate mistakes.

Owen's first reaction was to consider the sale of his half interest in KF. Though he has enjoyed the creative side of the business, he was upset by his mother's report and by Tessa's apparent failure to take care of that responsibility. Periodically, some of the resellers KF deals with have encountered financial problems and have strung out their payments, which often caused a mad scramble for cash at KF. And if Owen decides to sell, he knows that he is likely to be involved in some stressful negotiations surrounding the company's value. Though he would hire a consultant to aid him in any negotiations, he decides it is a good idea to educate himself about KF's financials.

Another reason that Owen is interested in the firm's financials is so he can better judge Tessa's managerial competence. When KF was first starting, Owen thought Tessa did a fine job, but now he wonders whether she is capable of operating the firm. Actually, if Owen were convinced that Tessa is a competent manager, he would not consider selling out since he genuinely enjoys being an owner of a creative software developer. But he thinks the industry will face even tougher times in the next few years, and wonders whether Tessa is talented enough to successfully meet these challenges.

 ## BORROWING ISSUES

Tessa's personality compels her to make virtually all major operating decisions. Owen is concerned that firms the size of KF have had difficulty maintaining a stable bank relationship. Due to increasingly strict federal regulations, some lenders have called in loans, and most are scrutinizing new business loans very carefully. Consequently, Tessa views bank debt financing as unreliable, a potential problem should business become slow, and thinks that loan officers are capable of wasting her time.

Owen isn't sure what to make of these arguments, but he is concerned that avoiding debt has significantly reduced KF's financial flexibility because it means that all projects will have to be equity financed. In fact, over the past five years there have been no dividends because all earnings have been reinvested. And three years ago each of the partners had to contribute $20,000 of capital in order to meet the company's needs.

Another infusion of capital may be necessary since the firm's present cash position is low by historical standards. More important, however, Owen feels that the company is not benefiting from the leverage effect of debt financing, and that this hurts the profitability of the firm to the two owners.

 ## WORKING CAPITAL

Owen suspects that KF's inventory is excessive. He stated, "Capital is unnecessarily tied up in inventory." Tessa's position is that a large inventory is necessary to provide speedy delivery to customers. She replied, "Our customers expect quick service when a game is in demand, and a large inventory helps us to provide it." Owen is skeptical of this argument and wonders if there isn't a more efficient way of providing good service.

He also questions Tessa's credit standards and collection procedures, and believes that Tessa has been quite generous in granting payment extensions to customers. At one point, nearly 45 percent of the company's receivables were more than 90 days overdue. Furthermore, Tessa would continue to accept and ship orders to these resellers even when it was clear that their ability to pay was marginal. Tessa's position is that she doesn't want to lose sales and that the difficult times are only temporary.

Owen wonders about the wisdom of passing up trade discounts. Vendors frequently offer KF terms of 1½/10, net 30. That is, KF receives a 1½ percent discount if a bill is paid in 10 days and in any event full payment is expected within 30 days. Tessa rarely takes these discounts because she "wants to hold onto our cash as long as possible." She also notes that "the discount isn't especially generous and 98½ percent of the bill must still be paid."

 ## FINAL THOUGHTS

Despite all of Owen's concerns, however, the relationship between the two partners has been relatively smooth over the years. And he admits that he may be unduly critical of Tessa's management decisions. "After all," he concedes, "she seems to have reasons for what she does, and we have never lost money since we started, which is an impressive record, really, for a firm in our business."

Owen has discussed with two advisors the possibility of selling his half of the firm. Since KF is not publicly traded, the market value of the company's stock must be estimated. The consultants believe that KF is worth between $35 and $40 per share, figures that appear reasonable to Owen.

 ## QUESTIONS

1. Using the data in Exhibits C2.1 and C2.2, calculate and analyze the firm's 2012 and 2013 ratios.
2. Part of Owen's evaluation will consist of comparing the firm's ratios to the industry as shown in Exhibit C3.3. Discuss the limitations of such a comparative financial analysis. In view of these limitations, why are such industry comparisons so frequently made? (Note: Sales are forecast to be $8.25 million in 2014.)
3. Owen thinks that the profitability of the firm has been hurt by Tessa's reluctance to use much interest-bearing debt. Is this a reasonable position? Explain.

4. The case mentions that Tessa rarely takes trade discounts, which are typically 1½/10, net 30. Does this seem like a wise financial move? Explain.
5. Is the estimate of $35 to $40 for Owen's shares a fair evaluation?
6. What do you recommend that Owen and Tessa do to improve their company?

**EXHIBIT C2.1**   KF Income Statements: 2012–2013

|  | 2012 | 2013 |
|---|---|---|
| Sales | $6,572,800 | $7,811,500 |
| Cost of goods sold | 4,896,700 | 5,866,200 |
| Gross margin | $ 1,676,100 | $1,945,300 |
| Administrative | 1,281,700 | 1,492,200 |
| Depreciation | 72,000 | 86,000 |
| Earnings before interest and taxes | $ 322,400 | $ 367,100 |
| Interest | 37,900 | 31,600 |
| Earnings before taxes | $ 284,500 | $ 335,500 |
| Taxes (at 40%) | 113,800 | 134,200 |
| Net income | $ 170,700 | $ 201,300 |

**EXHIBIT C2.2**   KF Balance Sheets: 2012–2013

|  | 2012 | 2013 |
|---|---|---|
| **Assets** | | |
| Cash | $ 300,000 | $ 244,000 |
| Accounts receivable | $ 915,000 | $1,106,600 |
| Inventory | $ 700,000 | $1,222,300 |
| Other current | $ 36,200 | $ 46,800 |
| Current assets | $ 1,951,200 | $ 2,619,700 |
| Gross fixed assets | $ 340,000 | $ 493,600 |
| Accumulated depreciation | ($ 135,000) | ($ 233,800) |
| Net fixed assets | $ 205,000 | $ 259,800 |
| Total assets | $ 2,361,200 | $2,879,500 |
| **Liabilities and Net Worth** | | |
| Accounts payable | $ 345,700 | $ 544,800 |
| Notes payable | $ 63,200 | $ 63,200 |
| Accruals | $ 164,300 | $ 156,100 |
| Current liabilities | $ 573,200 | $ 764,100 |
| Long-term debt | $ 316,000 | $ 252,800 |
| Common stock (62,000 shares outstanding) | $ 948,000 | $ 1,137,600 |
| Retained earnings | $ 524,000 | $ 725,000 |
| Total liabilities and net worth | $ 2,361,200 | $2,879,500 |

**EXHIBIT C2.3**   Financial Ratios for the Electronic Arts Industry

|  | Industry Averages* |
|---|---|
| Current (times) | 2.6/<u>1.7</u>/1.3 |
| Quick (times) | 1.6/<u>0.8</u>/0.6 |
| Debt % | 41/<u>57</u>/71 |
| Times interest earned (times) | 7.4/<u>3.9</u>/1.3 |
| Inventory turnover (times) | 8.1/<u>6.0</u>/3.5 |
| Total asset turnover (times) | 3.5/<u>2.8</u>/2.0 |
| Average collection period (days) | 41/<u>50</u>/68 |
| Return on equity % | 27.3/<u>19.5</u>/7.8 |

* Third quartile, <u>median</u>, and first quartile results

# Miller Building Supplies

NNE ARUNDEL COUNTY IS LOCATED south of Baltimore, MD, and is the home of Annapolis, MD, the location of the U.S. Naval Academy. Annapolis and the surrounding area has become a popular recreational and retirement community due to its access to the Chesapeake Bay, historic areas, and decent medical care. Furthermore, a major airport (BWI Thurgood Marshall Airport) is less than one hour away, and Washington, DC, is approximately the same distance.

The potential growth of the county has attracted numerous businesses, with more expected to follow. The economy is diverse. Roughly 75 percent of employment is in service, education, and government; retail; financial; and the hospitality industry. Many Maryland state offices are in the area of Annapolis, and the county has such institutions of higher learning as St. John's College and Anne Arundel Community College, in addition to the Naval Academy.

##  JOSEPH MILLER STARTS MBS

Joseph Miller founded his building supply company after returning from the Korean War. He saw the migration of economic activity in the county from agriculture to a diversified mix of businesses, and located Miller Building Supplies (MBS) in the town of Glen Burnie in 1953. His choice of Glen Burnie was motivated by access to the major highways in that part of the state and the recent opening of the Chesapeake Bay Bridge to access the Eastern Shore of Maryland.

The firm began as a wholesale distributor of various building supplies like paint, lumber, flooring, drywall, fencing, and cleaning supplies. As Miller developed his customer base, he came to realize that construction companies needed a full range of electrical, plumbing, and heating/air conditioning supplies and equipment in addition to basic building materials.

MBS has been run by Joseph Miller's children and now his grandchildren. As of 2010, Joseph III is the president, although he has been considering retiring. Joseph III's cousins are the chief financial officer (CFO), the marketing vice president, and the chief purchasing officer. The family has been quite successful in managing the business, and MBS is continuously profitable despite the fact that sales are sensitive to the economy of Anne Arundel County, of southern Maryland, and the Eastern Shore counties.

##  VARIATIONS IN WORKING CAPITAL REQUIREMENTS

The company's sales are seasonal, and during the colder months building activities slows down. If the winter is mild, some building projects continue, but large new projects are not usually started until the spring. The low point of the year is January, and from that time on, sales build. MBS has a small year-round labor force and employs seasonal workers during peak business periods.

Management is quite aware of the seasonal variation in the working capital position of the company. Historically, MBS has maintained large cash positions, and when receivables and inventory have increased, it has primarily financed them by drawing down cash. However, the company is taking a critical look at this strategy. The CFO realizes that further expansion of MBS may be difficult using internally generated funds. The cash philosophy may be unnecessarily tying up capital, and it may be appropriate to use short-term financing for seasonal working capital needs.

The president thinks that the CFO's suggestion is worth pursuing, particularly as it would free up long-term capital for expansion. The marketing vice president is not convinced and thinks that the company's financing methods continue to be appropriate. In addition, he is opposed to additional interest expense and having to deal with a bank. His cousin, the sales manager, is not opposed to using debt to finance working capital and argues that receivables and inventory should be supported with short-term debt.

 ## A BANKER'S ASSISTANCE

The Bank of Maryland (the "Bank") has dealt with MBS for four decades. The company has never established much of a relationship with the Bank except for an occasional term loan, depository and disbursement services, and a few other services. As noted, long-term capital has generally been internally generated. The Bank has tried to develop a stronger relationship as it considers MBS to be a stable, well-run company. When Sara Williams, the Bank's calling officer for MBS, received a phone call from Joseph Miller III, she was more than willing to meet him. The CFO asked for help in analyzing MBS's working capital needs to do the following:

- Estimate MBS's working capital needs.
- Determine if the Bank is willing to extend MBS a line of credit sufficient to finance the company's working capital.

 ## QUESTIONS

1. Using the data in Exhibit C3.1, estimate the amount of working capital that is required during each quarter of the year. Does MBS have excess working capital during these periods? If so, what do you suggest?
2. Are there specific working capital management suggestions that you can make to the company?
3. If a line of credit is requested from the Bank, should it be offered? At what interest rate? Specify terms that the Bank can reasonably require. You should refer to Exhibits C3.2 through C3.4 in your analysis.
4. Would a monthly cash budget improve forecasting and support for a line of credit? If so, provide a cash budget (to the best of your ability based on the data in the case). Assume that the contractors who purchase from MBS pay when they are paid by their residential and commercial customers, which is one-half in the second month and one-half in the third month following sales. Assume also that MBS must pay one-half of its payables in the month the expense is incurred, and one-half in the following month.

**EXHIBIT C3.1**   Recent MBS Quarterly Financial Statement Results (in $000)

1st Quarter: Sales, $11,191; Net income, ($83)
2nd Quarter: Sales, $25,309; Net income, $1,247
3rd Quarter: Sales, $27,877; Net income, $1,554
4th Quarter: Sales, $15,439; Net income, ($21)
1st Quarter: Beginning cash, $12,102; Total current assets (TCA), $38,708; Current liabilities (CL), $7,579
2nd Quarter: Beginning cash: $6,768; TCA, $43,454; CL, $11,101
3rd Quarter: Beginning cash, $1,484; TCA, $40,773; CL, $6,809
4th Quarter: Beginning cash, $8,392; TCA, $39,456; CL, $5,121

**EXHIBIT C3.2**   Selected Industry Ratios

Current ratio: 1.8 times
Quick ratio: 0.9 times
Total debt ratio: 55.4%
Average collection period: 45 days
Asset turnover: 2.5 times

**EXHIBIT C3.3**   MBS Income Statements, 2008–2010 (year ending January 31) (in $000)

|  | 2008 | 2009 | 2010 |
| --- | --- | --- | --- |
| Sales | $57,496.3 | $69,619.2 | $79,816.1 |
| Cost of goods sold | 40,990.5 | 51,352.6 | 58,505.7 |
| Gross profit | 16,505.8 | 18,266.6 | 21,310.4 |
| Sales and administrative costs | 12,164.7 | 13,397.2 | 14,810.2 |
| Depreciation | 1,265.0 | 1,532.8 | 1,756.3 |
| Earnings before interest and taxes | 3,076.1 | 3,336.6 | 4,743.9 |
| Interest expense | 159.6 | 104.9 | 171.0 |
| Earnings before taxes | 2,916.5 | 3,231.7 | 4,572.9 |
| Taxes | 1,168.6 | 1,293.1 | 1,826.9 |
| Net income | $ 1,747.9 | $ 1,938.6 | $ 2,746.0 |

**EXHIBIT C3.4** MBS Balance Sheets, 2008–2010 (year ending January 31) (in $000)

|                                      | 2008       | 2009       | 2010       |
|--------------------------------------|-----------|-----------|-----------|
| **Assets**                           |           |           |           |
| Cash                                 | $ 9,262.1 | $10,651.6 | $12,568.9 |
| Accounts receivable                  | 10,821.3  | 12,838.9  | 13,388.6  |
| Inventory                            | 11,499.4  | 12,563.4  | 13,021.2  |
| Other current                        | 344.6     | 418.9     | 479.0     |
| Current assets                       | 31,927.4  | 36,472.8  | 39,457.7  |
| Gross fixed assets                   | 19,312.7  | 19,734.5  | 20,853.8  |
| Accumulated depreciation             | −10,948.2 | −12,480.1 | −14,236.5 |
| Net fixed assets                     | 8,364.5   | 7,254.4   | 6,617.3   |
| Total assets                         | $40,291.9 | $43,727.2 | $46,075.0 |
| **Liabilities and Owners' Equity**   |           |           |           |
| Accounts payable                     | $2,568.6  | $3,063.7  | $3,044.7  |
| Accruals                             | 917.3     | 1,247.8   | 1,577.6   |
| Current portion of debt due          | 500.0     | 500.0     | 500.0     |
| Current liabilities                  | 3,985.9   | 4,811.5   | 5,122.3   |
| Long-term debt                       | 1,542.4   | 2,221.5   | 1,510.3   |
| Common stock                         | 10,000.0  | 10,000.0  | 10,000.0  |
| Retained earnings                    | 24,763.6  | 26,704.2  | 29,442.4  |
| Total liabilities and owners' equity | $40,291.9 | $43,737.2 | $46,075.0 |

# Office Smart

O FFICE SMART SELLS AND SERVICES office and telecommunications equipment to businesses in the New Haven, CT, area, which includes Hartford, Wallingford, Waterbury, and Milford. The company has a market reach into western Massachusetts, most of Connecticut (except for the southern part of Connecticut near Stamford), and Rhode Island. The CEO of the company is Eric Farland, who has been dealing with the local bank, Equitable Bank of New Haven (assume $250 million in assets).

The bank is small in size and had a firm house limit to any one borrower of $200,000. However, Office Smart is growing and in need of short-term working capital financing in excess of $200,000; in fact, a $400,000 line of credit is being requested. You are a loan officer with the Connecticut Merchants Bank of Hartford, CT (assume $15 billion in assets). Office Smart went looking for a larger bank in its market area, and found some interest at your bank.

This case presents the typical concerns as a small business transitions from a friendly, local bank to a more formal regional bank located nearby. These issues include requirements for the transfer of bank activity to the new lender, agreement on loan covenants and other restrictions, protection for the bank from the possible loss of the company's leader, potential changes in the outside auditors, and other considerations.

 ## THE BUSINESS OF OFFICE SMART

Office Smart has been enjoying increased market share on a consistent basis since the first decade of the 2000s. It aggressively doted on area businesses, offering excellent service at reasonable prices. The company was founded in 1975 and had survived a few recessions, and through its marketing efforts grew sales from a minuscule $300,000 in 1986 to an anticipated $6 million for fiscal year 2008. The fiscal year ends on December 31. See the accompanying exhibits for financial statements and significant ratios.

The company began by selling office supplies and furniture, and became aware of the rapidly changing needs of businesses for communications support including landlines, wireless telephones, mobile telecommuting, computer systems, fax machines, and various other services. The large communications companies are certainly willing to provide the comprehensive service packages but do not have the capacity to fully wire businesses and train employees on their various telecommunications and computer requirements.

Office Smart has developed a reputation for quick responses to the inevitable problems that can occur in businesses, including service, repair, backup systems, and even the outsourced operations of call centers. The company has also been working with area universities (Yale; the universities of Connecticut, New Haven, Hartford, and Massachusetts; and various colleges) and the State of Connecticut government. Because of the growing size of the business, management has been able to buy equipment and transportation vehicles in sufficiently large volumes to offer attractive prices to area businesses.

The CEO of the company is a gregarious, friendly executive, Eric Farland, who inherited the business from his father, Ed Farland, a cautious, careful businessman who passed away in 1982. Using his charm and attractive pricing, Eric convinced many of his customers that not only was the company competitive in its offerings but also it could deliver products on time or would provide a substantial discount for failure to do so.

Eric had something of a just-in-time philosophy on behalf of his customers, maintaining extra inventory so that a systems problem could be diagnosed and resolved. Area businesses have become increasingly confident that Office Smart will be able to service their requirements literally overnight. In fact, it was a key to the company's marketing strategy. Sales are invoiced on a net 30-day basis.

In considering any new credit arrangement with a financial institution, Eric would prefer to sign a simple promissory note and not have any loan covenants, consistent with his prior arrangement with the New Haven bank. You have listened to his request but think loan covenants must be part of any lending arrangement. Your assignment includes the preparation of such covenants that should be included in the loan agreement. Additionally, you need to consider whether the working capital loan will require an annual cleanup (i.e., repayment in full for, say, 30 days), or if it will be a term loan, and if it is a term loan, for how long and with what, if any, amortization.

You have already talked to a few of the company's customers to verify the story presented by Farland. To summarize their report: "Office Smart delivers, pure and simple. We don't get the runaround about slow deliveries, poor installation or repair work, or inept service people. I don't think Eric has ever failed to deliver on time to our locations. And he is a funny, delightful guy with whom we like to have drinks and laughs."

 ## FINANCIAL ISSUES

In your discussions with Eric, he has stressed that sales in 2008 will in all likelihood be a record year, reflecting a tremendous growth in market share and expectations of record numbers of systems installations and upgrades. Although the borrowings from his prior bank never quite reached $200,000, Eric is certain with these expanded sales forecasts that he will need a $400,000 working capital line of credit.

In talking to Eric you were emphatic that it was critical to keep borrowings within the $400,000 limit, as your management was quite conservative and was not willing to see borrowers exceed their credit limits under any conditions. Pricing is open, but you—as the account officer—believe the prime rate plus 2 percent is appropriate. The company will provide you with unaudited quarterly financials, and year-end financials will be audited by a local New Haven accounting firm.

In assessing loan covenants that you would require, it may be quite helpful to project the revenues for fiscal 2008. You should consider what might be receivable and inventory levels, and the resulting borrowings. In talking to your credit department, one analyst noted concerns over the future value of inventory, noting that certain Office Smart technology could become obsolete and not salable at market rates due to new developments in computers and telecommunications.

There are several questions that should be considered in the Office Smart case as you decide on the best approaches to doing business with Eric Farland. In developing your responses, use the data in Exhibits C4.1 and C4.2.

**QUESTIONS**

1. Given Eric's philosophy of just-in-time in meeting customer requirements, is he too accommodating in his inventory policies, and could this potentially lead to a cash-flow problem? Do you have any specific suggestions or recommendations, such as a loan covenant limiting inventory to a certain percentage of sales?

2. What is your assessment for receivables in terms of credit quality? In other words, how did Office Smart increase its market share—possibly by lowering credit standards? Would it be prudent to ask for detailed data on receivables for at least for the top 10 customers?

3. What documentation will you require? Customary documentation includes monthly income statements, statements of cash flows, and balance sheets. In addition, you may wish to see data on forecast economic activity in the Connecticut–Massachusetts–Rhode Island area, student enrollment projections at area universities, tax returns for each year, and other information that supports the loan.

4. Which firm would be acceptable as an outside auditor? Is your bank going to be satisfied with a local accounting firm that may have Office Smart as an important client? Recall that Arthur Andersen was deferential to Enron on its audit due to substantial consulting fees and the fear of losing that company as a client.

5. Can Office Smart do an annual cleanup? If not, if you price the credit as a working capital loan, do you underprice the loan? If the loan is not seasonal, what is it?

6. Do you want key man life insurance for Eric? In what amount? Key man insurance is a life insurance policy purchased by a business to compensate for financial losses that would arise from the death or extended incapacity of an important member of the business, in this case, Eric Farland.

7. Should you require all operating accounts to be with your bank, and if so, what advantages does this bring to the bank?

8. Do you want a personal guarantee from Eric Farland? Your bank could require his agreement to be liable for the debts of Office Smart. A personal guarantee signifies that the lender (obligee) can lay claim to the guarantor's assets in case of the borrower's (obligor) default.

9. What do you believe the outcome will be to this loan request?

**EXHIBIT C4.1**   Office Smart and Industry Significant Ratios

|  | Office Smart (for 2007) | Industry |
|---|---|---|
| Current ratio | 1.52 | 2.1 |
| Quick ratio | 0.61 | 1.8 |
| Debt ratio (%) | 65.5 | 65.9 |
| Inventory turnover (times) | 2.3 | 37.3* |
| Receivables turnover (times)** | 8.3 | 7.4 |
| Asset turnover (times) | 2.5 | 3.2 |
| Return on equity (%) | 92.1 | 78.0 |
| Return on sales (%) | 12.7 | 8.4 |

*Results in published sources show significant variation; the reported result is the mean of three asset-size categories.
** Equivalent to 44 days in accounts receivable.

**EXHIBIT C4.2**   Financial Statements, Fiscal Years 2006 and 2007 ($000s)

|  | 2006 | 2007 |
|---|---|---|
| **Income Statements** |  |  |
| Net sales | $4,725 | $ 5,075 |
| Cost of goods sold |  |  |
|    Beginning inventory | 700 | 788 |
|    Purchases | 2,538 | 2,713 |
|    Ending inventory | 875 | 1,050 |
| Net cost of goods sold | 2,363 | 2,450 |
| Gross profit | $2,363 | $ 2,625 |
| Operating expense | $1,400 | $ 1,444 |
| Interest expense | 88 | 105 |
| Net income before taxes | $ 875 | $ 1,076 |
| Income taxes | 350 | 431 |
| Net income | $ 525 | $ 645 |
| **Balance Sheets** |  |  |
| Cash | $ 88 | $ 88 |
| Accounts receivable, net | 525 | 612 |
| Inventory | 875 | 1,050 |
| Current assets | 1,488 | 1,750 |
| Property, net | 262 | 280 |
| Total assets | $1,750 | $ 2,030 |

(continued)

**EXHIBIT C4.2** *(Continued)*

|  | 2006 | 2007 |
|---|---|---|
| **Balance Sheets (cont.)** | | |
| Notes payable, bank | $ 0 | $ 420 |
| Accounts payable | 525 | 298 |
| Accrued expenses | 350 | 437 |
| Current liabilities | 875 | $ 1,155 |
| Long-term debt | 175 | 175 |
| Total liabilities | $ 1,750 | $ 1,330 |
| Net worth | 700 | 700 |
| Total liabilities and net worth | $ 1,750 | $ 2,030 |

CASE FIVE

# Quacker Cracker

Q UINCY CYNSKY began the Quacker Cracker Company (QC) in St. Louis, MO, 65 years ago after he came home from World War II. He created a tasty, fancy cracker aimed at a party and restaurant audience who liked to entertain, and right from the outset paid special attention to quality.

"We only make crackers and fancy breads, but we make them in various flavors with the finest flour and other ingredients," Quincy was fond of saying. Because fancy foods were in scarce supply during the war and military personnel received most of the available U.S. production, the company was an immediate success with civilians and with former military.

Specialty food is among the fastest-growing industries in the United States, with sales increasing by 22.1 percent between 2010 and 2012. The industry's revenue grew 14.3 percent in 2012, with total specialty food sales topping $85.87 billion. Much of the industry operates through such small companies as Annie's (Annie's Homegrown), a publicly traded company with $185 million in sales, and MOM Brands ($500 million in sales and privately owned). Large food companies contain specialty food segments, including Ralcorp ($4 billion in sales), a subsidiary of ConAgra Foods, and Smucker's, with sales of $6 billion.

 ## THE ATTITUDE TOWARD DEBT

QC expects strong growth this year (assume that it is now January 2012) and Dianne McCabe, the chief financial officer (CFO), hopes she can make a case for borrowing to finance the company's expansion. She realizes, however, that she is likely to face stiff opposition from Quincy's family.

Quincy detested borrowing money, and his motto was, "Never go into debt and hang onto cash as long as possible—because you never know . . ." In fact, his family and employees called him chintzy Quincy.

For the first half of the company's existence, the Cynsky family owned all the company's stock. Due to the need to finance expansion, shares have been sold during the last 30 years to individuals outside the family. By 2007, the Cynsky family's ownership share had declined to half of all shares, and although the family has not been active in running the firm in recent years, it does insist on keeping the family traditions: avoiding debt and keeping high cash balances.

To this day, QC has never owed anything beyond its accounts payable and accruals. (Accrued expenses are liabilities that have been incurred but not yet invoiced.) CFO McCabe believes that the "no debt" and "high cash" policies have hurt the owners' profits. At each annual meeting, she has tried unsuccessfully to convince the Cynsky family to consider more aggressive financial management. She is becoming concerned that her objective financial advice is irritating the family.

 ## FINANCIAL PLANNING

McCabe decides to estimate the amount of funds QC will have to obtain in 2012. She knows that 2012 is expected to be a big year for the company, particularly as the weak economy increases the sales of fancy foods for entertaining at home. As a result, sales are predicted to increase by 25 percent, to $230 million.

Due to the strong demand, the marketing vice president feels any cost increases can easily be passed on, and McCabe estimates that the cost of goods sold (mostly food ingredients) will be $180 million. Cost of goods sold does not include depreciation (estimated at $5 million), and administrative and selling expenses ($15 million). The corporate tax rate is 35 percent.

Fixed assets are likely to increase sharply in the coming year. Currently, QC is operating near capacity, demand is expected to remain high, and new plant and equipment will be needed. In addition, some major improvements to existing facilities will have to be made in order for the company to remain competitive. The planning for these changes has been occurring for some time, and though all of these changes do not have to be made in 2012, it is clear that the company cannot continue to grow without them. The total cost of these capital improvements is $30 million. See Exhibits C5.1 and C5.2.

**EXHIBIT C5.1** Ratios for the Fancy Foods Industry

| | |
|---|---|
| Price–earnings ratio (times) | 16.0 |
| Current ratio (times) | 1.8 |
| Quick ratio (times) | 0.6 |
| Total debt ratio (%) | 53.0 |
| Total asset turnover ratio (times) | 1.5 |
| Return on equity (%) | 8.0 |
| Return on sales (%) | 2.5 |
| Average collection period (days) | 27.0 |

**EXHIBIT C5.2** Quacker Cracker Balance Sheet for 2012 ($000s) (prepared before any financing decisions have been made)

| Assets | | Liabilities and Equity | |
|---|---|---|---|
| Cash and marketable securities | $16,000 | Notes payable | $ 0 |
| Accounts receivable | 16,000 | Accounts payable | 19,500 |
| Inventory | 23,000 | Accrued expenses | 6,000 |
| Current assets | 55,000 | Current liabilities | 25,500 |
| Gross fixed assets | 52,000 | Long-term debt | 0 |
| Accumulated depreciation | –12,000 | Common stock ($10 par)* | 40,000 |
| Net fixed assets | 40,000 | Retained earnings | 29,500 |
| Total assets | $95,000 | Total liabilities and equity | $95,000 |

* Not publicly traded; the last private sale was at $50 a share.

## QUESTIONS

1. Using the data in Exhibits C5.1 and C5.2, discuss how QC's results compare to its industry. You will need to prepare a 2012 pro forma income statement before proceeding. Discuss specific metrics that can be used to analyze working capital performance.
2. Show changes to the 2012 pro forma balance sheet assuming the company borrows the necessary funds for the capital improvements at an interest rate of 7 percent. Ignore depreciation on the new equipment. Does this cause any significant change in the financials?
3. Play the role of a financial analyst and explain your recommended course of action.
4. The Cynsky family controls the company through its ownership of one-half of the outstanding stock, with outsiders owning the balance. Should this influence McCabe's presentation of her recommendations? What arguments can you make in support of *and* against McCabe's position?
5. Why was information provided in the second paragraph about competitive companies in the fancy food industry?

# Young Brands

Y OUNG BRANDS (YB) is a manufacturer of sports clothing and team uniforms. Its industry is quite competitive, so the management team has attempted to operate a modern operation with state-of-the-art production facilities. Careful cost management has been an important factor in attaining profits. YB is considered a leader for its fashion sense, pricing, marketing, and product quality.

Professional and university-team uniforms and affiliated products are sold by company salesmen to teams and to retail stores throughout North America. YB currently uses a network of manufacturers' representatives to reach retailers in Europe, Latin America, and Asia. (A manufacturer's representative [MR] is an independent individual, sales agency, or company that sells a manufacturer's products to wholesale and retail customers in foreign countries.)

There is a large demand for licensed (approved) clothing with team logos and colors, and premium prices can be charged to retail customers who buy for themselves as fans, for friends and relatives as gifts, or simply to affiliate with a local (hopefully winning) team. The licensed clothing line includes sweatshirts;

caps; jogging suits; baseball, football, and hockey shirts; and various accessories (such as tote bags, scarves, and towels).

 ## CHANGES IN YB'S GLOBAL MARKETING STRATEGY

About a year ago, the senior managers concluded that YB products in global markets were "underappreciated" and that "sales could—and should—be substantially higher." See Exhibit C6.1 for recent global sales results. They reasoned that trade shows in the major international markets are a relatively inexpensive way to display the company's products and provide an opportunity to meet major corporate buyers face to face.

That is precisely what happened. The firm's exhibits were impressive, former athletes were used as spokespersons, and the company made important contacts with Asian and European buyers. The long-term plan is to eliminate the use of MRs and to sell directly to major retail chains. This will improve market saturation in metropolitan areas and end the commissions paid to the MR network (currently about 6 percent of revenue on average).

As a result of this, YB's sales growth is expected to increase sharply in the next three years, and revenues are estimated to more than double by the end of 2018. The marketing vice president forecasts worldwide sales of $160 million in 2016, $200 million in 2017, and $250 million in 2018. Management is pleased with the forecast because it is evidence of what they have long believed: that the company manufactures quality products with global appeal at a reasonable price. The downside is that such growth will undoubtedly require external financing and could cause administrative and operational difficulties.

Although YB will explore a number of financing alternatives, it is recognized that the first step is to estimate the external funds needed for the period ahead. After all, before a financing option is explored, a reasonable projection

**EXHIBIT C6.1**   Recent Financial Results

|  | Sales ($ millions) | Price–Earnings Ratio (times) |
| --- | --- | --- |
| 2015 | $123.2 | 11.4 |
| 2014 | $ 111.3 | 13.5 |
| 2013 | $104.6 | 14.0 |
| 2012 | $101.0 | 14.2 |
| 2011 | $ 96.4 | 14.0 |

must be made of what needs to be raised. And it is even possible that a portion of the expected growth can be internally financed.

## FORECASTING CONSIDERATIONS

In order to develop the forecast, the president, Henry Gilmore, called a group meeting of his senior managers. All agree that the sales projections are "quite reasonable" in view of the activity resulting from the trade shows and the global obsession with sports teams and competitions, and may even be a bit low. They also decide to concentrate on the 2016 forecast at their initial meeting.

A few months ago, YB began implementing a number of cost-cutting measures that are expected to generate a 32 percent gross margin each year of the forecast. Due to economies of scale, operating expenses are expected to increase less than proportionately with sales, and the manager group agrees to a 20 percent increase in 2016. The relevant tax rate is 40 percent.

The purchasing vice president noted that the financial forecast needs to consider the tighter credit terms offered by many of the firm's suppliers. Company records show that two years ago, about 70 percent of YB's purchases were on terms of 2/10, net 30. That is, most suppliers offered a 2 percent discount to customers who paid within 10 days, with full payment expected by day 30. "We always took the discount when it was offered."

Company records show that during the past year, about half of the suppliers offered the 2/10, net 30, discount. Fewer vendors are likely to offer cash discounts in the future, which will impact the firm's gross margin due to slightly higher prices paid for materials. Therefore, he recommends that the gross margin estimate be reduced to 31 percent, which the group accepts.

## WORKING CAPITAL ISSUES

The discussion then turned to working capital management. Inventory control has been a problem for YB at times. Some in the group believe that inventory turnover can be increased to eight times mainly by using suppliers with shorter delivery times. Others are skeptical, believing that it is unrealistic to think that inventory management can be improved unless there is specific evidence to support this conclusion. The group finally concurs that an estimate based on historical inventory patterns is appropriate.

Given the new global customer base, it is clear that the firm's historical experience with its accounts receivable will be of little help in predicting future receivables. For the purpose of this forecast, the group decides to assume that they will offer credit terms of net 30 and that 50 percent of customers will pay on time and all other receivables will be received in 50 days. YB expects that this experience will improve in future years.

The marketing vice president is tasked with the responsibility of making payment terms clear to the new foreign buyers, and to working with YB's banks to establish letter of credit facilities. (A letter of credit is a document issued by a bank ensuring payment to a seller of goods, provided certain documents have been presented to the bank. These are documents that prove that the seller has performed the duties under an underlying sales contract and the goods have been supplied as agreed.)

The group expects that nearly all sales will be collected, and it estimates that bad debt expense will be "insignificant" and can be ignored. The group also thinks that cash should be 4 percent of sales. The firm's predicted 2016 spending on fixed assets is $35 million. These expenditures partly reflect the replacement of existing equipment but mainly result from the new facilities necessary to accommodate the growth in sales.

The note payable will require a 20 percent payoff in 2016. Other current liabilities will increase at the same rate as sales. Existing bond debt and bank loans will require an average payoff of 15 percent of the principal amount.

## FINANCIAL ISSUES

YB will pay $1 million in dividends during 2016, the same amount as in 2015. Although this might appear stingy, the group believes that most profits should be reinvested in the aggressive plans for global growth. Ignore any interest expense for the purpose of calculating the 2016 financial statements. The group realizes that it is likely that most of any new required funds will be borrowed. The finance vice president says he has enough information to develop an estimate for 2016.

## QUESTIONS

1. Using Exhibits C6.1 and C6.2, develop a pro forma income statement for 2016. Assume that depreciation equals the 2015 amount plus one-sixth of 2016 capital spending. The relevant tax rate is 40 percent.
2. (a) What will be YB's 2016 average collection period?
   (b) Predict the 2016 level of receivables. Assume that there are no cash sales.

3. Using the 2015 results, calculate the inventory for 2016.
4. Calculate accounts payable, assuming that the amount will increase at the same rate as sales.
5. Develop the 2016 pro forma balance sheet.
6. How much funding will be required in 2016? How much must be raised from external sources? Refer to Exhibit C6.3 for data on the industry.
7. When offered terms of 2/10, net 30, YB has always taken the discount. Does this make financial sense?

**EXHIBIT C6.2**  Financial Statements ($ millions)

| Income Statement 2015 | | Other Financial Data 2015 | |
|---|---|---|---|
| Sales | $123.2 | Beta | 1.20 |
| Cost of goods sold | 91.2 | Risk-free return | 1.0% |
| Gross margin | 32.0 | Market return required | 8.0% |
| Operating expenses | 14.0 | Dividend yield | 1.0% |
| Earnings before | 18.0 | Growth in stock price over | 8.0% |
| taxes | | previous 3 years | |
| Taxes (40%) | 7.2 | Earnings per share | $10.80 |
| Net income | $ 10.8 | Dividends per share | $ 1.00 |

| Balance Sheet 2015 | | | |
|---|---|---|---|
| **Assets** | | **Liabilities** | |
| Cash and short-term | $ 2.6 | Accounts payable | $ 7.1 |
| investments | | | |
| Accounts receivable | 13.0 | Notes payable | 2.4 |
| Inventory | 13.0 | Other current liabilities | 3.7 |
| Current assets | $ 28.6 | Current liabilities | $ 13.2 |
| Gross fixed assets | $ 55.0 | Bonds and bank debt | 21.0 |
| Net fixed assets* | 39.8 | Owners' equity | $ 34.2 |
| Total assets | $ 68.4 | Total liabilities and owners' equity | $ 68.4 |

\* After accumulated depreciation.

**EXHIBIT C6.3**  Selected Industry Ratios and Other Financial Data

| | |
|---|---|
| Current ratio | 3.1 times |
| Quick ratio | 1.5 times |
| Debt ratio | 46.8% |
| Times interest earned | 10.6 times |

Major competitors with sales greater than $1 billion:
    Cintas
- Sales: $3.8 billion
- Beta: 0.92
- Price–earnings ratio: 15.8 times
- Dividend yield: 1.8%
- Debt/asset ratio: 47%

    PVH Corp.
- Sales: $4.6 billion
- Beta: 1.91
- Price–earnings ratio: 11.6 times
- Dividend yield: 0.3%
- Debt/asset ratio: 64%

Competitor with sales below $1 billion (beta about 1.50)
    Fossil Inc. (debt/asset ratio: 28%)

# Basic Financial Concepts

T HE THREE FINANCIAL REPORTS OR statements required under accounting rules are the balance sheet, the income statement, and the statement of cash flows. These rules are established by the Financial Accounting Standards Board (FASB), a self-regulating organization managed by the accounting profession, with oversight by the Public Company Accounting Oversight Board (PCAOB) for companies traded on stock exchanges ("public companies"). FASB oversees GAAP (generally accepted accounting principles), which provides accounting standards that are considered as the foundation of financial reporting.

Public companies are required to publish annual reports containing an explanation of the past year's activities, nonconfidential plans for the future, and financial reports including an opinion letter by external auditors as to their accuracy. In addition, they must file detailed financial analyses with the primary regulatory agency, the Securities and Exchange Commission (SEC). The annual version of this report is called a 10-K; quarterly reports are known as 10-Qs. Most public companies provide them on their websites.

## ■ GENERAL BALANCE SHEET ISSUES

Several issues relate to the entire balance sheet:

- **Date.** The balance sheet in Exhibit 1.1 is as of December 31 for two recent years. All balance sheets are as of a particular date and are valid only for that date. This particular business uses a calendar year reporting period. However, any date can be used to show financial results, and the period that is used is referred to as the **fiscal year.** As an example, retailers often close the accounting (fiscal) year before or after the Christmas selling season; Best Buy closes its year at the beginning of March.
- **Asset/liability life.** By convention, the lives of current assets are presumed to be less than one year, while fixed assets are expected to be used by a company and reported on the balance sheet for greater than one year. These assumptions can change and are simply what is expected or known on the balance sheet date, and are limited by tax regulation.
- **Listing order.** Assets and liabilities are presented in the order they are likely to be turned into cash, with cash and near-cash items listed first and other items listed later. This characteristic is known as liquidity and is used throughout finance in evaluating investment decisions and calculating capital requirements.
- **Valuation.** All balance sheet items are valued at the lower of cost or market value; cost means the full acquisition cost including freight and installation. Market is used when an asset has permanently lost value due to deterioration, changes in style or other obsolescence, or the loss of a customer for whom inventory was acquired. This convention is particularly important when a business has owned an asset that has greatly increased in value, such as real estate in New York City, which must be carried at cost and not the current market.
- **Balance.** The left side of the balance sheet—total assets—must equal the right side of the balance—the total of liabilities and net worth. This is accomplished by the procedure of double-entry accounting, with a left-side entry (a **debit**) equaled by a right-side entry (a **credit**) as entries are made to reflect transactions that occur.
- **Notes to financial statements.** The notes that accompany the financial statements may significantly affect the meaning of the data. For example, long-term contractual obligations (such as an operating lease) may be

reported only in the notes; yet few investors, lenders, or others who rely on these reports bother to examine the notes.

## ASSETS AND LIABILITIES

As we discussed in Chapter 1, working capital involves current assets and current liabilities. In this section we define noncurrent entries on the balance sheet. The **fixed asset** that is presented in Exhibit 1.1 (i.e., assets with lives of more than one year) is plant and equipment, calculated at cost less depreciation. The concept of "net" refers to the accounting convention of writing off a portion of the cost of a fixed asset over the estimated life of the asset. In making this calculation, various methods are permitted as selected by management.

These methods are collectively known as **depreciation**, and the choice is usually made for tax reasons. The total original cost of the plant and equipment was $85 million. If the life of these assets was estimated to be five years, the company would be allowed to expense $17 million each year ($85 million divided by 5 years). Accelerated depreciation methods are also permitted.

There are various conventions used to write down the value of fixed assets. If a company acquires such intangible property as patents, copyrights, or licenses, these assets are subject to **amortization**, which is treated in the same way as depreciated property. If it owns natural assets such as oil or gas reserves, coal, or other minerals, this property would be subject to a similar treatment known as **depletion.** Land is presumed to exist forever and is not depreciated or depleted.

The two long-term liabilities will be due in periods beyond one year, and include bonds payable and mortgage payable. **Bonds payable** is debt held by outside investors; **mortgage payable** is a loan taken to acquire real property (land and buildings).

## NET WORTH

**Net worth** is what the company is worth after liabilities are subtracted from assets. The two accounts in net worth are defined as follows:

1. **Common stock**. This account represents the total of all monies paid for stock, including various stock offerings as new stock is sold to investors.
2. **Retained earnings**. All of the income (after taxes) remaining (i.e., not paid as dividends) is included in retained earnings.

**COST OF CAPITAL**

**Cost of capital** is the calculation of the cost to finance a business based on several factors:

- The interest yield on debt
- The corporate tax rate (as interest is a deductible expense in computing taxable income)
- The dividend yield on equity shares
- The expected growth in the price of equity shares
- The weighting of debt and equity on a company's balance sheet

Exhibit A.1 shows a company that has a 10 percent cost of capital. This is the assumption used throughout this book. However, each business would have to do this calculation based on its own unique situation.

Any investment above this cost should be considered, assuming it is consistent with the company's long-term strategy. Any investment returning less than this cost should be rejected as it would negatively affect owners' equity and impair shareholder value. Calculations of returns are a concern of **capital budgeting,** which includes such techniques as net present value (NPV) and internal rate of return (IRR).

An alternative method for the cost of equity capital is the **capital asset pricing model** (CAPM). The idea of the CAPM is that the relationship between the expected return and beta can be quantified. In this method, the risk-free return (the rate on U.S. Treasury Bills) is added to the beta ($\beta_e$) for the company multiplied by the risk premium required by the market for that class of securities.

**EXHIBIT A.1**  Calculating the Cost of Capital

| | Percentage of Balance Sheet | Pre-Tax Cost | After-Tax Cost | Weighted Cost |
|---|---|---|---|---|
| Debt | 40% | 7½% interest yield | 5%* | .02 |
| Equity | 60% | 4% dividend yield + 9½% growth yield | 13½% | .08 |
| Total Financial Structure | 100% | | | .10 or 10.0% |

*Calculated as 7½% times (1 – corporate tax rate)
= 7½% times the assumed tax rate of 34% = 5%

The concepts of beta and risk premium effectively require that the equity be a publicly traded security. The equation that determines this result is as follows:

Expected return of a stock (based on CAPM) = Risk-free return + β of the stock × Market's expected return – Risk-free return (on a short-term U.S. Treasury security)

*or*

$$R_e = R_f + [\beta_e \times (R_m - R_f)]$$

CAPM shows that the expected return of a stock (or other asset) depends on the risk-free return that is available to investors, the reward for bearing systematic risk, and the amount of systematic risk.

For a discussion of these concepts, the interested reader should consult any standard finance text.

# Websites of Working Capital Organizations*

| | June 2013 Assets ($ millions) | Websites |
|---|---|---|
| | **Commercial Banks** | |
| JPMorgan Chase & Co. | $1,947,794 | www.jpmorganchase.com |
| Bank of America Corp. | 1,429,737 | www.bankofamerica.com |
| Citigroup | 1,319,359 | www.citigroup.com |
| Wells Fargo | 1,284,538 | www.wellsfargo.com |
| U.S. Bancorp | 349,333 | www.usbank.com |
| PNC Financial Services Group | 294,526 | www.pnc.com |
| Bank of New York Mellon | 281,339 | www.bnymellon.com |
| Capital One Financial | 235,243 | www.capitalone.com |
| State Street Corp. | 223,225 | www.statestreet.com |
| TD Bank | 212,167 | www.tdbank.com |
| HSBC Bank USA | 182,541 | www.us.hsbc.com |
| BB&T Corp. | 177,895 | www.bbt.com |

*(continued)*

*(Continued)*

| | Websites |
|---|---|
| **Finance Companies** | |
| GE Commercial Finance | www.gecapital.com |
| Ally Financial | www.ally.com |
| 1st Commercial Credit | www.1stcommercialcredit.com |
| ORIX USA | www.orix.com |
| CIT Group | www.cit.com |
| Textron Financial | www.textronfinancial.com |
| **Other Vendors\*** | |
| ADP | www.adp.com |
| Insperity | www.insperity.com |
| Paychex | www.paychex.com |
| TriNet Group | www.trinet.com |
| Troy Group (printing systems) | www.troygroup.com |
| **Information Providers** | |
| *Barron's* | www.barrons.com |
| *Business Finance* | www.businessfinance.com |
| Business Monitor International | www.businessmonitor.com |
| *Bloomberg Businessweek* | www.businessweek.com |
| Dun and Bradstreet | www.dnb.com |
| *The Economist* | www.economist.com |
| Equifax | www.equifax.com |
| *Euromoney* | www.euromoney.com |
| Experian | www.experian.com |
| *Forbes* | www.forbes.com |
| *Fortune* | money.cnn.com/magazines/fortune |
| *Handbook of Finance*, 3 volumes, John Wiley & Sons (F. Fabozzi, editor) | No website; library resource |
| Hoover's | www.hoovers.com |
| Moody's | www.moodys.com |
| *New York Times* | www.nytimes.com |
| *QFinance* | www.qfinance.com |
| RMA | No website; library resource |
| Standard and Poor's | www.standardandpoors.com |
| *Treasury and Risk Management* | www.treasuryandrisk.com |

| | **Websites** |
|---|---|
| Leo Troy's *Almanac of Business and Industrial Financial Ratios* | No website; library resource |
| *Wall Street Journal* | www.wsj.com |
| **Government** | |
| Federal Deposit Insurance Corporation | www.fdic.gov |
| Federal Reserve System | www.federalreserve.gov |
| Office of the Comptroller of the Currency | www.occ.treas.gov |
| Securities and Exchange Commission | www.sec.gov |
| **Organizations** | |
| American Institute of Certified Public Accountants | www.aicpa.com |
| American Bankers Association | www.aba.com |
| Association of Financial Professionals | www.afponline.org |
| Financial Executives International | www.fei.com |
| Treasury Resources @ Phoenix Hecht | www.phoenixhecht.com/ treasuryresources/index.aspx |

*Selected banks and providers. Other companies and associations are noted throughout the text. For example, SCM vendors are listed in Exhibit 7.4.

# Glossary

N OTE: THE TERMS EXPLAINED IN this glossary are integral to the management of working capital. Acronyms and full-word descriptions are included and are listed in order of general use (i.e., EOQ is listed first before economic order quantity, while application service provider is first listed before the acronym ASP). Other major terms are noted, but no attempt has been made to include every possible financial concept. Two excellent references on finance are *QFinance* and *The Wiley Handbook of Finance*, listed in Appendix II.

**ACH (Automated Clearinghouse):** The electronic payment mechanism offered by regional organizations that performs interbank clearing of entries for participating financial institutions. ACHs are governed by operating rules and procedures developed by their participating financial institutions. ACHs make it possible for participating financial institutions to offer bill payment, direct payroll deposit, and other services. ACH payments generally move on a next-day basis.

**Account analysis:** A commercial bank's invoice for services provided to corporate customers. These statements are produced monthly and contain such details as average daily book balance, average daily float, average available balances, itemized activity charges, earning credit rate (ECR), balances required to compensate for services, and balances available to support credit arrangements and other bank services.

**Account maintenance:** A basic charge for a bank account, to cover the overhead costs associated with the various services provided by the bank. Even if an account is idle, a maintenance charge is assessed. Typical charges are about $25 a month for middle market banks.

**Account reconciliation:** A bank service used to reconcile corporate bank accounts, providing a serial number listing of items paid (called partial reconciliation), or by matching a list of items issued (from a positive pay transmission) to the actual items paid, producing full reconcilement including outstanding items, balance by date, exceptions, and numerous optional reports.

**Accounts payable:** A current liability that involves money owed to creditors representing obligations to pay for goods and services that have been purchased or acquired on credit terms.

**Accounts receivable:** A current asset that represents amounts owed or the balance due to a vendor from a company for the goods sold or services rendered but not yet paid for.

**Accrual accounting:** A method of keeping accounting records that attempts to match revenues and the accompanying costs incurred. A convention used in accrual accounting is depreciation, which expenses a capital good over its useful life.

**Accrued expenses:** Costs that have been incurred as of the date of a balance sheet but not paid.

**Activity utilization:** Ratios that indicate how efficiently the business is using its assets. Important working capital utilization ratios are receivables turnover (and its complement, average collection period) and inventory turnover (and its complement, inventory turnover days).

**Aging schedule:** An organization of accounts receivable classified by time intervals based on days due or past due; used to identify delinquency patterns.

**Amortization:** A convention used in accounting to write down the value of intangible property such as patents, copyrights, and licenses.

**Application service provider (ASP):** A business that sells access to software applications through central servers over a communications network; this effectively outsources these information technology activities.

**Array:** A listing of the members of a group in either ascending or descending order.

**Asset-based financing (asset-based lending):** A method of financing (lending) for rapidly growing and cash-strapped companies to meet their short-term cash needs; current assets (accounts receivable or inventory) are pledged as collateral.

**Asset:** Any tangible or intangible valuable resource that a business entity owns, benefits from, or has use of in generating income and that could be converted to cash.

**Available balances:**   Those collected balances in an account that can be invested, disbursed, or wired out. Available balances are defined as book balances less float.

**Availability:**   The number of days that elapse between the deposit of checks and their accessibility for disbursement. An "availability schedule" lists drawee points or locations, specifying availability granted in business days. Availability is based on a bank's recent experience in clearing deposited checks.

**Bank information (treasury) technology:**   Internet-based systems that allow companies to electronically access a full range of financial services and to execute many transactions; contains various modules accessible through a common interface.

**Balance reporting:**   Systems using a communications network to consolidate daily balance and activity information from one or more banks for the accounts of a specific user corporation. These systems consolidate information prior to opening of business and for report to the customer.

**Bank relationship management:**   The process of managing the relationships between banks and companies in a comprehensive approach involving the credit and noncredit services offered by a bank and used by a company.

**Bank statement:**   A periodic statement of a customer's account detailing credits and debits posted to the account during the period and book balance as of the statement cutoff date.

**Banker's acceptance:**   Endorsement of a draft or bill of exchange by the buyer's bank where the bank is obliged to pay the buyer's bill from a specified creditor when it is due on assurance of the buyer's financial strength and stability, and on payment of acceptance fee; primarily issued to finance international trade.

**Basis point (bp):**   Market abbreviation for 1/100th of 1 percent, usually used in conjunction with comparisons of interest rates.

**Basel 2/3:**   A set of standards and regulations recommended by the Basel Committee on Bank Supervision that regulates banking and financing activities internationally; determines specific amounts of capital that financial institutions must hold to reduce the risks associated with lending and investing practices.

**Benchmarking:**   Compares the processes of a business and selected performance metrics to industry best practices or those from other industries.

**Beta:**   Often denoted using the Greek letter $\beta$. The amount of systematic risk present in a particular asset relative to an average, usually defined as the Standard & Poor 500 stock index. Systematic risk is a risk that affects a large number of assets (such as the financial system credit crisis of 2008–2009).

**Bill of lading:**   A document issued by a carrier to a shipping company that specified goods have been received on board as cargo for transporting to a named place to a recipient (usually the purchaser).

**Book balance:**   The balance in a bank account that represents the net of debits and credits and before any consideration for availability, reserve requirements or other deductions.

**Capital Asset Pricing Model (CAPM):**   A securities evaluation model that establishes the fair value of an investment by relating risk and expected return to the market as a whole; based on the theory that markets are efficient and prices of securities represent all known information about the security.

**Capital budgeting:**   Refers to the analytical process of making long-term planning decisions by comparing the expected discounted cash flows with the internal rates of return (IRR) to determine the return from a capital investment; an alternative capital budgeting technique is net present value (NPV).

**Cash accounting:**   In contrast to accrual accounting, cash accounting is a method where revenues are recorded when they are received and expenses when they are actually paid; no attempt is made to match revenues and costs incurred as in accrual accounting.

**Cash budget:**   An estimate of cash receipts and disbursements for a future period, usually calculated daily by large companies and semi-weekly or weekly by middle market companies.

**Cash conversion cycle:**   The number of days between disbursing cash and collecting cash in connection with undertaking a discrete unit of operations.

**Cash discount:**   A reduction in the base price for the buyer by the seller where the buyer agrees to pay immediately or in a period shorter than the conventional period as set by the credit terms of sale; an example is 2/10, net 30, where the cash discount is 2 percent if the invoice is paid within 10 days of receipt, with payment due in full within 30 days.

**Cash letter:**   A batch of checks, accompanied by a letter detailing transit routings, amounts and totals, sent directly to a bank or to another check clearing site, containing items drawn on that bank.

**Category killer:**   Megastores with the size and general appearance of warehouses; they dominate their industry.

**Check:**   A negotiable instrument or a written order instructing a bank to pay or draw against deposited funds for a specific amount of money to a designated person on a demand by the person who draws the instrument.

**Clearing (of checks):**   A period of time between the deposit of a check by a payee to the receipt of the check by the drawee bank. Checks are cleared through the Federal Reserve System, Clearinghouses, and bank Direct Send Programs following presentation at the drawee bank.

**Clearinghouse:**   A location where banks exchange and settle paper and electronic checks (e.g., ACHs) and where mutual claims are settled between the accounts of member depository institutions.

**Commercial paper:**   A negotiable discount note issued by investment-grade issuers on an unsecured basis for up to a nine-month maturity. The yield on commercial paper normally exceeds the yield on U.S. Treasury Bills by 30–50 basis points given the additional risk of default.

**Commodities futures:**   A contract to buy or sell a commodity at a specific price on or before a certain date. Futures contracts are traded on organized exchanges (e.g., the Chicago Board of Trade) for a wide variety of agricultural, energy, foreign exchange, precious metal, interest rate, and other assets.

**Common stock:**   A security that provides an investor with ownership and voting rights with limited liability; the owner is entitled to dividends (if declared) to share in a company's profits after taxes; these securities are often traded on organized stock exchanges (e.g., the New York Stock Exchange).

**Comprehensive payables (or receivables):**   The outsourcing of all or a major portion of a disbursement or collection activity. Comprehensive payables usually involves the company resolving all payment decisions and sending a transmission to a bank or vendor that processes the payment, including issuing checks or electronic payments and remittances advice, mailing payments, and reconciling clearing checks. Comprehensive receivables usually involve a bank or vendor receiving all remittances, depositing the items, and accounts receivable updating.

**Concentration bank:**   A term that is no longer in general use. Such banks are referred to in the text as "principal banks," serving as the central point for all incoming or outgoing movement of funds from other corporate accounts. Generally this account is funded by deposits of incoming wire transfers, collection account transfers, and branch deposit concentrations. The account furnishes funds for outgoing wire transfers, disbursing account transfers, and charges for ACH.

**Controlled disbursement:**  A checking account service capable of providing a total of the checks that will be charged to the customer's account(s) early each business day.

**Corporate governance:**  Administration of a business through rules, processes, or laws regarding responsible behavior as referenced by the ownership, management, employees, customers, and other stakeholders; required of public companies operating in the United States as mandated in the Sarbanes–Oxley Act of 2002.

**Cost of capital (weighted average cost of capital [WACC]):**  The weighted average of a firm's cost of debt (after tax) and cost of equity (common stock and retained earnings). The WACC is expressed as a percentage.

**Cost of goods sold:**  An income statement account that includes all the expenses associated with the manufacturing costs of a company's products including its raw materials, work-in-process, finished goods, and shipping expenses.

**Credit reporting:**  Procedures that review the credit history of a company or a person using detailed information on credit accounts and loans, payment history, and other recent financial data.

**Counterparty:**  An entity with whom one negotiates for a particular transaction, with the counterparty on the opposite side of the transaction.

**Country risk assessment (CRA):**  The quantification of the possibility that transactions with international counterparties may be interrupted by the interference of the foreign government or due to local conditions; measured through the analysis of political and economic risks.

**Current assets:**  The total of cash and other assets that are readily converted to cash within one year, helping to satisfy liquidity needs for daily operations. Assets with a life of greater than one year are fixed assets.

**Current liabilities:**  The funds owed by a company that are to be settled or paid off within a year.

**Current ratio:**  A financial ratio that measures the capability of the firm to pay its debt over the next year; defined as current assets divided by current liabilities.

**Days' sales outstanding (DSO):**  A company's average collection period in days. The calculation is 360 days divided by receivables turnover. Receivables turnover is credit sales divided by accounts receivable.

**Debt collection agency:**  An independent business that pursues payments on unpaid debts owed by individuals or businesses, usually for balances older than 90 days past due.

**Debit:** An accounting entry on the left side in a double-entry accounting system. The parallel right-side entry is called a "credit."

**Demand deposit account (DDA):** Deposited funds that are available to the customer at any time during regular business hours, and that require no advance notice of withdrawal. They are usually accessed by writing a check. Checking accounts are the most common form of demand deposit. The required reserve against time deposits is 10 percent.

**Deposit reporting service (DRS):** A service that mobilizes funds in local depository accounts to the concentration account.

**Depreciation:** A convention used in accrual accounting that attempts to match the expense of a fixed asset for a specific reporting period with the revenue it produces.

**Deregulation, financial:** The elimination of restrictions on interstate banking and lines of business in financial services in the 1990s, allowing U.S. financial institutions to enter any activity in finance in any geographic location.

**Direct deposit:** An ACH service that permits a company to pay its employees without writing checks. The company generates credit entries representing deposits and delivers them to its financial institution before each payday, which posts them to employee bank accounts on payday.

**Discount rate:** The rate of interest charged by the Federal Reserve on loans it makes to member banks. This rate influences the rates banks then charge their customers.

**Distribution method:** A forecasting technique that estimates the distribution of cash flow by day of the week and day of the month.

**Dividend yield:** A percentage indicating the amount a company pays out as a dividend each year; measured by dividing the annual dividend payment by the stock price.

**Drawee bank:** The bank on which an item is drawn and to which it must be presented to collect cash.

**Dynamic discounting:** The situation when vendors offer prorated cash discounts based on days paid prior to the due date.

**Earnings credit rate (ECR):** A rate used by a bank to determine the earnings allowance associated with a customer's demand deposit balances. Depending upon the bank, the rate may be arbitrarily set or tied to some market rate, such as federal funds.

**Electronic commerce (or e-commerce):**  The exchange of business information in an electronic format in an agreed-upon standard.

**Encoding:**  An amount that is MICR (magnetic ink character recognition) encoded in the lower right corner with the check amount, using special MICR printing equipment.

**Enterprise resource planning system (ERP):**  An integrated system that manages internal and external company resources including tangible assets, financial resources, and materials purchasing. ERP systems are based on a centralized computing platform, consolidating all significant business operations into a uniform environment.

**EOQ (economic order quantity):**  The optimal quantity to order from a supplier that minimizes the total costs of processing orders and the cost of holding inventory.

**Equity:**  A stock or any security that represents ownership interest in a corporation.

**Factoring:**  The sale or transfer of title to accounts receivable to a third party, the factor.

**Fed funds (Federal funds):**  Reserves traded among banks for overnight investment and to fund a bank's deficit position with the Federal Reserve System. Most U.S. interest rate transactions (such as bank credit arrangements) are quoted as an increment from federal funds.

**Fedwire (Federal wire transfer):**  The Federal Reserve System's electronic communications network used in transferring member bank reserve account balances and government securities as well as other related information. This network interconnects the Federal Reserve offices, the Treasury, various government agencies, and the member banks.

**Financial leverage:**  The degree to which borrowed money is utilized to increase volume in production, sales, and earnings; generally, the higher the amount of debt, the greater the financial leverage.

**Fiscal year:**  The accounting period chosen by a company for its reporting period. Any year-end may be chosen by management, although companies usually choose a quiet period when sales activity is at a seasonal low.

**Fixed assets:**  Long-term assets with lives greater than one year that cannot be easily converted into cash, including manufacturing equipment, furniture, office equipment, or any other tangible assets held for business use; contrast fixed assets to current assets.

**Float:**  Refers to the status of funds in the process of collection or disbursement. Float has the dimensions of money and interest and thus is computed as the product of funds being collected or disbursed and the applicable interest rate. This product is expressed in dollars (or other currency).

**Foreign exchange (FX):**  The buying and selling of currencies worldwide, which consists of the currencies themselves, the transfer mechanisms, and the information needed to make sound multicurrency decisions. FX services are needed when more than one currency is involved in an international business transaction. Most of the European Union transacts its business in the euro (€), which replaced national currencies (except for the British pound [£], the Danish krone, and the Swedish krona).

**Forward foreign exchange rates:**  Hedging the delivery of a foreign currency on a specified later date by arranging with a bank to "lock in" a guaranteed rate when it is likely that an international transaction will settle at a future time.

**Freight payments:**  The auditing and payment of bills from transportation carriers. Freight invoices are reviewed for excessive charges such as misclassifications, incorrect discount levels, incorrect mileage calculations, extension mistakes, and other errors.

**Funds (cash) mobilization:**  Where multiple collection and disbursement accounts exist, cash needs to be mobilized into and funded from a principal bank relationship. This process is known as funds or cash mobilization.

**Full reconciliation:**  A bank product that takes the issued and cleared item files and matches them monthly.

**Futures contracts:**  Hedging vehicles based on standard-sized contracts available through U.S. commodities exchanges. Futures are similar to forwards in that the FX is for delivery at a later date.

**Gross profit (or gross margin):**  The income statement account that is calculated by subtracting cost of goods sold from sales (revenues).

**Growth yield (capital gain):**  The component of a business's cost of equity capital that calculates investor expectations for an increase in the stock price, usually measured for the period of one year. The other component of the cost of equity capital is the dividend yield.

**Hedge (hedging):**  A transaction that mitigates exposure to a risk by taking a position opposite to the initial position; hedging instruments include forwards, options, swaps, and futures contracts.

**Imaging:**   The capture of an electronic picture of the check and/or the remittance document received, which can be archived, retrieved, and transmitted to the company.

**Interest yield:**   The expected return on a debt security measured by dividing the interest paid for one year by the price of the debt security. Except for tax-free municipal bonds, the final cost to a business is then reduced by the appropriate tax deduction (calculated as 1 less the tax rate).

**Interquartile range:**   The area in an array of results from the 25th to the 75th percentiles (or the first to the third quartiles).

**IRR (internal rate of return):**   A capital budgeting procedure; it is the discount rate that forces the net present value of a proposed capital investment equal to zero.

**Intrabank transfer:**   A transfer of funds within a bank between accounts; an example is the funding of a bank's controlled disbursement account from a concentration account in that bank.

**Inventory financing:**   Asset-based financing used to gain working capital, with a company's inventory functioning as the collateral for the loan.

**Inventory turnover:**   A ratio calculated as cost of goods sold divided by inventory, showing the utilization of that asset as compared to a peer group of companies.

**Just-in-time (JIT):**   A method of managing inventory levels to minimize working capital. Successful implementation depends on strict production planning/control techniques and integrated communications with suppliers and customers.

**Letter of credit (LC):**   An instrument primarily used in international business transactions; issued by a bank to an individual or corporation that allows the bank to substitute its own credit for that of the individual or corporation.

**Liabilities:**   A major portion of a balance sheet showing amounts owed to vendors and lenders. The current portion shows amount due to be paid within one year; the long-term portion shows the amounts due beyond one year.

**LIBOR:**   The London Interbank Offering Rate on funds traded between banks. Some interest rate transactions (such as bank credit arrangements) are quoted as an increment from LIBOR, although most transactions in the United States are based on federal funds.

**Lien:**   A legal claim that attaches to property owned by a debtor. A creditor who holds a lien often can have property sold to satisfy the lien.

**Line of credit (credit line):**   A prearranged amount of credit a lender will extend to a company over a specified period of time, usually one year.

**Liquidity:**   The cash used in a normal business environment, including operating cash flow and short-term investments and credit sources.

**Loan covenants:**   Restrictions established by lenders on borrowers that apply to lines of credit and other types of credit agreements, requiring a certain level of performance.

**Lockboxing:**   A collection mechanism in which mail containing payments bypasses corporate offices, going directly to a post office box maintained by the bank of deposit, thereby reducing collection float. After deposit of the check, remittance advices, photocopies of the check, and other supporting material are forwarded to the corporate credit department. Wholesale processing provides check copies and original remittance documents to the client; retail processing captures encoded MICR and/or OCR information on the bottom of the check and/or remittance documents and transmits it to the client in a data file.

**Long-term liabilities:**   See "liabilities"; includes loans (e.g., mortgages payable) and bonds payable.

**Mean:**   The arithmetic average of the total of all items divided by the number of items.

**Median:**   The middle item in an array is the median (the 50th percentile).

**MICR (also OCR):**   Acronyms for magnetic ink character recognition and optical character recognition; a set of unique characters printed on a check or remittance advice that is scannable by reader-sorter equipment.

**Money market mutual funds (MMMFs):**   Pools of various types of short-term investments that offer shares to corporate (and individual) investors through the format of mutual funds.

**Mortgage payable:**   A loan taken to acquire real property (land and buildings).

**Multicurrency account:**   A single international bank account with the capability to receive deposits and withdrawals of major currencies; used to simplify the management of foreign exchange.

**Munis (municipal securities):**   State and local government municipal securities that have their interest payment exempt from federal taxes; yields are less than those of other investment instruments.

**NACHA:**   The electronic payments association that establishes rules for ACH transactions.

**NAICS:** The North American Industry Classification System, used to classify business establishments according to type of economic activity (process of production). The Department of Commerce and the Office of Management and Budget (OMB) are the principal sponsoring federal agencies.

**Netting:** A system used to reduce the number of counterparty payments by summing debits and credits and transferring the resulting balance. Netting systems are used in cross-border payments and in industries where there are many individual transactions, such as in broker-dealer activities.

**Net worth:** The accounting determination of a company's value based on its total assets less total liabilities.

**NPV (net present value):** A capital budgeting technique that calculates the difference between the cost of an investment and the present value of all predictable future cash inflows. Also, see IRR.

**NSF (not sufficient funds):** The situation when a check is presented for clearing and sufficient funds are not in the maker's bank account. The bank may reject (bounce) the check unless the maker has arranged overdraft protection.

**Outsourcing:** Bank or vendor processing of a business activity not considered as core or critical to profitability. Examples include cash handling activities, certain information processing, and other functions.

**Owners' equity:** A balance sheet account that shows the amount of a business that has been paid in by the shareholders for their stock; the other major category in net worth is retained earnings.

**Partial reconciliation:** A list of paid or cleared items, including check numbers and dollar amounts that the company must then reconcile against its own ledgers.

**Payback method:** A capital budgeting procedure that calculates the time required by an investment to generate sufficient cash flows to recover the initial cost.

**Paycard:** ATM cards specifically issued for payroll. An employee receiving a paycard need not have an account at the payroll bank. Instead, the card is issued along with a PIN number, allowing access through any ATM machine or at merchants that accept the card family (e.g., Visa or MasterCard).

**Payment stream matrix:** A road map that lists working capital flows by name, dollar volume, and manager.

**PO (purchase order):** A commercial document indicating types, quantities, and prices for products or services the seller will provide to the buyer. Sending a PO to a supplier constitutes a legal offer to buy products or services. Acceptance of a PO by a seller usually forms a contract between the buyer and seller.

**Pooling:** A product offered by international financial institutions that aggregates the debit and credit balances of a company's separate bank accounts to calculate a net balance, with interest paid or charged on the net debit or credit.

**Positive pay:** A bank service used to reduce disbursement fraud, with the issuer sending an issued file to its bank of serial numbers and check amounts. Only those checks that match this listing are paid.

**Prepaid expenses:** Assets paid in advance of expenses as incurred; an example is insurance paid in advance of the incurrence of the expense.

**Presort (for postage discount):** A discount to regular first class postage provided by the USPS based on a minimum quantity of letters presorted by zip code.

**Preferred stock:** Ownership shares in a business with dividend priority over common stock, normally with a fixed dividend rate, sometimes without voting rights.

**Presentment:** The actual delivery of a negotiable instrument by a holder to the drawee bank for payment or acceptance.

**Prime rate:** A benchmark rate used by banks to determine loan pricing for their best small- and middle-market corporate customers.

**Processing expenses (costs):** Each transaction along a working capital timeline has a cost that directly impacts profitability. These costs may be internal and/or paid to a bank or vendor.

**Procurement (purchasing) cards:** A payment mechanism involving the use of credit cards by authorized company employees for routine purchases.

**Profitability:** A measure of a business's net income after taxes, either as a sheer calculation or compared to owners' equity or sales.

**Pro forma statement:** A financial statement prepared on the basis of assumptions of future events that affect the expected condition of the company as a result of those events or actions. For example, assumptions as to future sales levels generally enable a company to project anticipated income.

**Quick ratio:** A liquidity ratio with current assets less inventory in the numerator and current liabilities in the denominator.

**Ratio analysis:** A financial technique that allows the examination of a company's financial statements. It compares a numerator and a denominator to changes over time and/or against its competitors.

**Receivables turnover:**   A calculation of receivables efficiency, calculated as credit sales divided by accounts receivable.

**Reinvoicing center:**   A central financial subsidiary used by a multinational company to reduce transaction exposure by billing all home-country exports in the home currency and reinvoicing to each operating affiliate in that affiliate's local currency.

**Remittance advice:**   Information on a document attached to the check (such as an invoice) by the drawer, which tells the payee why a payment is being made.

**Repo (repurchase agreement):**   A holder of securities sells securities (usually U.S. Treasuries) to an investor with an agreement to repurchase them at a fixed price on a fixed date, usually overnight. The security "buyer" effectively lends the "seller" money for the period of the agreement.

**Reserve requirement:**   A portion of financial institution deposits that must be kept on deposit by member banks at the Federal Reserve.

**Retail lockbox:**   A lockbox based on automated processing of scanlines (known as magnetic character ink recognition or MICR-lines) of documents; used primarily for consumer payments.

**Retained earnings:**   The accumulation on a company's balance sheet of net profits after taxes not paid out in dividends.

**Revolving term loan:**   Loans for periods longer than one year (sometimes called "revolvers") and lasting for up to five years.

**RFP (request for proposal):**   A formal document soliciting responses to specific questions in several areas. The typical RFP begins with a description of the organization, including its locations, the number of transactions, banks and vendors currently used, and other pertinent data. A statement is provided regarding the specific requirements to be addressed by the proposal, including the timing of the selection process and of implementation.

**Risk:** The possibility of loss or injury. The measurement of risk has traditionally been through the frequency of human or property loss in specific categories, such as death or disability by age, sex, and occupation or the frequency of fire damage to specific types of construction at various locations. Newer techniques have been used to manage business risk.

**Risk-free return:**   The return from an investment without risk, usually defined as the rate on U.S. Treasury bills. This rate reflects the absence of default risk and inflation risk.

**Risk management:**   The attempt to identify, prioritize, and quantify the risks from sources that threaten the working capital and strategic objectives of the corporation. This effort can be directed to individual risks or to risks that transcend company operations.

**Risk premium:**   The excess return required from an investment in a risky asset over that required from a risk-free investment. Used in the calculation of the CAPM.

**Sales financing:**   Lending money for the purpose of selling capital goods through a contractual installment sales agreement. Companies provide loans to businesses where the collateral of the loan is the goods purchased.

**SCM (supply chain management):**   An integrated system to optimize all of the components of a manufacturing process, including purchasing, inventory management, and transportation-logistics. Two key concepts in SCM are EOQ and JIT.

**Securitization:**   A financing technique in which a company issues securities backed by packages of assets with regular income flows, such as mortgages or car payments.

**Spot foreign exchange rates:**   The standard format for commercial foreign exchange transactions, with delivery in two business days.

**Statement of cash flows:**   A required financial statement for public companies that uses balance sheet accounts and income that affects cash and cash equivalents, and analyzes operating, investing, and financing activities.

**Sweep:**   A bank account from which all the funds above a specified figure are automatically transferred out of the account for investment overnight, and then returned to the bank account next day.

**Tax-advantaged centers:**   A service offered in several countries offering low corporate taxes and other benefits to attract multinational companies; the host country anticipates that corporations will establish offices for the management of their various business functions. In return, the local economy receives economic activity and employment.

**Term loan:**   Loans for periods of greater than one year, known as revolving term loans (sometimes called "revolvers") for periods of up to five years. These types of loans are not appropriate for working capital; instead, they are used for capital budgeting needs.

**Terms of sale:**   The length of time allowed before payment on a commercial invoice is expected. Terms are stated as "net" and the number of days, usually beginning on the date of the receipt of the invoice or statement, as in "net 30" or "n30."

**Time deposit:**   An interest-bearing deposit at a banking institution, either with a specified maturity (a "certificate of deposit" or CD) or open-ended (a "savings account"). Time deposits by regulation require notification to the institution for redemption, although in practice they will honor requests for savings accounts distributions on demand.

**Time value of money:**   The calculation of the present value of a future sum, or the future value of a present sum.

**Times interest earned:**   A ratio that measures the amount of interest paid against earnings before interest and taxes, or EBIT divided by interest expense.

**Transaction exposure:**   A risk that results from the movement in foreign exchange rates between the time a transaction is booked and the time it settles.

**Transit routing number (TRN or ABA [American Banking Association] number):**   A series of machine-readable digits on a check that facilitate the routing for collection of funds from the drawee bank by the Federal Reserve. The TRN appears in the MICR line at the bottom of the instrument as well as in the fraction in the upper-right-hand corner. The number represents the Federal Reserve District of the drawee bank, the Federal Reserve Bank head office, or branch through which the item should be cleared, and the bank-specific address. A ninth digit may be present, which is a verification of the logic of the TRN.

**Translation exposure**:   The balance sheet exposure that results when a company consolidates its financial statements and is required to report the change in the net value of its foreign currency assets. The exposure results from fluctuations in FX, which change the rate at which the net assets are valued.

**Transparency:**   The concepts of ethical behavior and enhanced financial disclosure, mandated in law and regulation because of situations arising from Enron, WorldCom, and other incidents of corporate corruption and malfeasance.

**Uniform Commercial Code (UCC):**   A set of regulations covering commercial transactions adopted by the individual states. The UCC defines the rights and duties of the parties in commercial transactions and provides a statutory definition of commonly used business practices.

**Value-at-risk (VaR):**   An approach to determining the risk exposure in a portfolio of assets. Although certain risks (e.g., financial instruments, credit, commodity prices) can be forced into the VaR model, it is a process that is heavily dependent on historical patterns.

**Value dating:**   The determination of a future date on which payment will be credited in a bank; used in some countries instead of availability (but not in the United States).

**Wholesale lockbox**: The original form of lockbox services, established to handle low-volume, high-dollar checks.

**WIP (work-in-process):** A category of inventory that represents materials that are in the process of being manufactured into salable finished goods.

**Working capital:** The difference between a firm's current assets and current liabilities, measured in dollars or another currency. Working capital is also the amount of money available for use in operating the business.

**Working capital flow:** An activity of the organization that generates a cash inflow or outflow.

##  U.S. LEGISLATION SIGNIFICANT TO WORKING CAPITAL MANAGEMENT

**Check Clearing for the 21st Century Act of 2004 (Check 21):** Allows the electronic delivery of check images, significantly speeding the processing, and allows the recipient of an original check to create a digital version, which eliminates the need for further handling of the physical document.

**Federal Reserve Act of 1913**: Widespread bank failures and panics continued from the end of the Civil War until the Panic of 1907. As a result, Congress adopted the Federal Reserve Act in 1913. The Act established the Federal Reserve System as the central bank of the United States. The purpose was to provide a stable currency, to improve supervision of banking, and to stabilize interest rates and the money supply.

**Glass-Steagall Act of 1933:** This legislation separated commercial and investment banking activities, forcing such firms as J.P. Morgan to separate into Morgan Guaranty Bank and Morgan Stanley. Congress believed that such a separation was necessary to prevent the types of transactions that may have caused the stock market crash in October 1929.

**Gramm-Leach-Bliley Act of 1999:** This law creates the concept of the financial holding company, authorizing these organizations to engage in underwriting and selling insurance and securities; conduct both commercial and merchant banking; and invest in and develop real estate and other activities. The act repealed the Glass-Steagall Act (see previous entry).

**McFadden Act of 1927**: Restricted commercial banks to doing business within the state in which they were chartered (with certain exceptions).

**Riegle-Neal Act of 1994**: This legislation deregulated banks permitting mergers across state lines provided they were adequately capitalized and managed. Prior to Riegle-Neal, banks were limited to doing business within the states in which they were chartered as mandated by the McFadden Act of 1927.

**Sarbanes-Oxley Act of 2002:** Enacted as a reaction to a number of major corporate and accounting scandals. These losses cost investors billions of dollars when the share prices of affected companies collapsed, shaking public confidence in the securities markets. Two important sections of Sarbanes-Oxley deal with corporate responsibility and enhanced financial disclosures.

# About the Author

D R. JAMES S. SAGNER has taught MBA-level courses in finance and international business at the School of Business of the University of Bridgeport (Connecticut), and is senior principal of Sagner/Marks. He has managed over 250 large-scale studies for global organizations and is recognized as an expert in financial management and economic analysis. His clients have included financial service and manufacturing companies. Previously, he was with the First National Bank of Chicago (now JPMorgan Chase) and A. T. Kearney, financial and economic consultants; and served as chief economist of the Maryland Department of Transportation.

He is the author of 9 books and over 60 papers and articles that have appeared in various publications. His most recent book is *Handbook of Corporate Lending* (with Herbert Jacobs), with a revised edition published in 2014. In addition, he has taught in the executive education program at the University of North Carolina. Dr. Sagner received his BS from Washington and Lee University, his MBA from the Wharton School of the University of Pennsylvania, and his PhD in business and economics from The American University. Dr. Sagner, who was honored as a Rockefeller Fellow, is a CCM and a CMC, and was selected for Beta Gamma Sigma.

# Index

Page numbers with an "n" indicate a note.

Electronic payments, 43–45
  ACHs (automatic clearinghouse transactions), 44
    advantages and disadvantages, 44–45
    cost, 45
  Fedwires (Federal Reserve wire transfers), 43–44
    advantages and disadvantages, 44
    cost, 44
  terminal-based electronic payments, 44, 163–164
Enterprise resource planning (ERP). See Information technology
Enterprise risk management (ERM), 179–180. See also Risk
  concept, 179
  prioritizing, 180
process, 180
  Value-at-Risk (VaR), 179–180

**F**
FASB (Financial Accounting Standards Board), 251
Factoring. See Asset-based financing
FDIC (Federal Deposit Insurance Corporation), 64n9
Federal Reserve Board regulations
  Regulation Q, 59
  Regulation Y, 176n4
Fed wire transfer. See Electronic payments
Finance. See Banking; Working capital
Financial deregulation, 66–67
Float, 10–12, 46–49. See also Accounts payable management; Accounts receivable management; Lockboxing
  base case, 46–47
  improvements, 48–49
Forecasting, short-term, 52–53
  distribution method, 52–53
Foreign exchange (FX), 145–151
  cross-border clearing and settlement, 153–154
  documentation flow, 146
  electronic payments, progress toward, 150–151

  Single Euro Payments Area, 151
  factors influencing rates, 149–150
  summary of economic factors, 150
  transaction mechanisms, 147–150
  continuous link settlement, 148–149
  forward rates, 147
  futures (commodities) contracts, 147
  multicurrency accounts, 150
  recent rates, 148
  spot rates, 147
  structures to manage, 152–154
  reinvoicing centers, 153
  status of European centers, 153
  tax advantaged centers, 152
Fraud, 40–46
Freight and logistics services, 134
  transaction flow, 134
Funds mobilization. See Banking

**G**
GAAP (Generally Accepted Accounting Principles), 251
Global capitalism, advantages, 142
  financial risk, 144
Glossary of terms, 261–278

**H**
Harmonization, tax, 153
Hedge (hedging), 123n1, 147

**I**
Information technology, 160–169
  application service providers (ASPs), 160
  bank systems, 161–169
    advanced service modules, 164–165
    standard service modules, 162–164
    original development of, 162
    payment modules, 163–164
  cost of, 161, 166, 171
  Internet technology, 165–167
    benefits, 166–167
    disadvantages, 167
    features, 165
    support for organizational decision making, 166

Printed in the USA/Agawam, MA
November 30, 2021

785439.001